W9-BWI-561

Becoming Bamboo

Becoming Bamboo

Western and Eastern Explorations of the Meaning of Life

ROBERT E. CARTER

McGill-Queen's University Press
Montreal & Kingston • London • Buffalo

© McGill-Queen's University Press 1992
ISBN 0-7735-0884-8

Legal deposit second quarter 1992
Bibliothèque nationale du Québec

Printed in Canada on acid-free paper

This book has been published with the help of a grant
from the Canadian Federation for the Humanities,
using funds provided by the Social Sciences and
Humanities Research Council of Canada. Publication
has also been supported by Trent University through
the Presidential Discretionary Fund.

Canadian Cataloguing in Publication Data

Carter, Robert Edgar, 1937–
  Becoming Bamboo
  Includes bibliographical references and index.
  ISBN 0-7735-0884-8
  1. Philosophy, Japanese. 2. Philosophy. 3. Values.
  4. Philosophy, Comparative. I. Title.

B799.C37 1992   181'.12   C92-090095-X

Typeset in Palatino 10/12 by
Caractéra production graphique inc., Quebec City

To my wife
Marjorie J. Haugan
who has learned to treasure the
magic of the everyday
while continuing to deconstruct

Contents

Foreword

Robert Carter's *Becoming Bamboo* is a creative piece of philosophizing in a new key. Let me try to place his work in a wider perspective. For the fact is that such cross-cultural essays are vital in the development of a global civilization, which is not only desirable from a human perspective but is necessary to the survival of us all. The planet is evidently one, but for the first time we humans have the possibility of wrecking it. To avoid that, we need both co-operation and sensitivity. Both are pointed to in this book.

It is an irony that in these latter days, when the stock exchanges form a single network and when aeroplanes provide magic carpets, whisking people from civilization to civilization, Western philosophy remains particularly tribal in its interests. Whether we look to the prevailing analytic philosophy of North America or the more exotic themes of French and German philosophy, there is generally among professional philosophers a neglect of, and often a disdain for, ideas that flow from Asian culture, the Islamic world, and the South. Admittedly, some of what goes on in the Indian and Chinese traditions, for example, does not correspond to Western philosophy as it is understood today. But it is worth noting that much of previous Western philosophy does not so correspond either. The speculations and analyses of Buddhist philosophy, for instance, are not so distant from the themes and style of some notable Westerners, such as Pyrrho, Spinoza, Schopenhauer, and Heidegger. The nature of philosophy, because it so often contends against orthodoxy, is essentially debatable. So it is unwise to neglect alternatives and alternative traditions. Consequently, philosophy should include philosophies – that is, it should be cross-cultural in its scope. This lesson is too often ignored today.

Apart from this, philosophy often plays an ideological or religious role. It helps to form world-views. Notably in the West, Hegel managed to provide a framework out of which grew, among other world-views, that of Marxism, until recently so influential a system of ideas. Analytic philosophy tends to promote scientific humanism as a world-view. Because reflection shapes values and is in turn shaped by them, it is important for each culture to come to terms with its philosophical tradition. But now we are no longer living in discrete cultures. The differing civilizations of the world are merging into each other as we move finally towards a world civilization. Philosophy has a role here in articulating the contributions of different traditions.

This means that we all have each others' intellectual and heroic ancestors. The Westerner has Confucius and Shankara as his forebears, as the Easterner has Plato and Locke. She has the Mughals and Tokugawas as the Japanese has the Caesars and Napoleons. Hiroshige and Cézanne are equally forebears. In this commonalty of ancestors there is recognition of other values, and helping to relate these in the contemporary world is an important function of philosophical reflection.

Now though all this is a strong argument for the vital need for comparative or cross-cultural philosophy, this latter enterprise contains an ambiguity. One sort of comparative philosophy may be called descriptive, and another sort may be called constructive. By descriptive comparative philosophy I mean that enterprise that seeks descriptively to analyse the similarities between ideas, arguments, and themes in differing cultures. For instance, one might wish to see the overlaps between the respective arguments of Hume and Ramanuja against the validity of versions of the teleological proof of God's existence. Such a comparison can be interesting and suggestive: the remarkable anticipations of a number of Hume's arguments in Ramanuja's commentary on the *Brahmasūtra* tend to reinforce them, while Ramanuja's additional arguments have a good effect on Western imaginations. But descriptive comparisons represent only one level of cross-cultural philosophy. They are essentially the work of historians and analysts.

The other level is constructive work at the cross-cultural interface. This involves the creative synthesis of ideas out of two or more traditions and the development of ideas out of such synthesis. It involves reflecting from within two or more cultures. It is of course hard to do: we can never immerse ourselves in two cultures completely. But because the aim is to create new ideas and new perspectives, this imperfect immersion does not matter too much: what matters is the illuminating character or otherwise of what emerges.

Sometimes academia blocks such creativity. You often hear it said that it is necessary to know with absolute command two or more languages to undertake such an enterprise. Acquiring such a command will take so many years that it may stultify philosophical reflection. Or it may be said that cross-cultural philosophy is not a recognized discipline. Yet disciplines themselves are often arbitrary in their history and scope. So in order to involve yourself with constructive cross-cultural philosophy you have to be bold, and launch into it.

Robert Carter's *Becoming Bamboo* essentially belongs in this category of constructive cross-cultural philosophy. I think he very well articulates a novel synthesis of Eastern and Western ideas, notably in taking up themes from modern Japanese philosophy as well as from the Zen tradition. The path he has followed was in part prepared by the Japanese themselves, since in their remarkable cultural experiment, dating from the Meiji restoration or even before, in which they modernized, to protect themselves, and then, after the disaster of the Second World War, fashioned a remarkable synthesis between traditional Japanese, modern technological, and American and other Western values, they also created new forms of philosophy. In these new syntheses of ideas they anticipated further developments in which Westerners might use Eastern ideas in delineating a worldview that might have global outreach.

In the context of such a global philosophy Professor Carter's instincts are sound, since both the cultures created essentially by Buddhist and Christian values must play a central role. There are three great missionary faiths – Christianity, Buddhism, and Islam. All three eventually must contribute heavily, though not exclusively, to the formation of a world culture. But the times are not ready for this. I shall come to the reason why shortly. Meanwhile let us note that there are other vital faiths, not primarily missionary, that also have something important to say: Judaism and Hinduism, the sisters, so to say, of Christianity and Buddhism respectively, not to mention the religions of all the smaller peoples not struggling for self-expression desperately in wider seas of Western post-colonial strength – native Americans, the people of Papua-New Guinea, Australian aborigines, Maoris, Siberian groups, the heirs to classical African traditions, and so on. Such smaller-scale religions have much to teach the world. Then there are new religions both at the interface of such groups and modern societies and within these societies. There are various other religions also of noble heritage, such as those of the Sikhs, Parsees, Mormons, Baha'is, and so on. All these cultural manifestations have a contribution to make to our global awareness and philosophy.

But we cannot assume the compatibility of these diverse faiths. Far from it: there are serious rifts of assumption among them. This is all the more obvious once we set other world-views alongside, such as scientific humanism and Marxism, not to mention the multiple values of nationalism, of such power today. We cannot see a global world-view emerging as something that at the ground level will unify all world-views and philosophies. But we can hope (and I have argued this in *Beyond Ideology* and in my forthcoming *Buddhism and Christianity: Rivals and Allies*) that the various traditions can be friendly critics of one another, to keep each other honest. They can complement one another. This thesis of cultural and spiritual complementarity can accommodate both diversity and a kind of harmony. It will do the human race no good if the religions and ideologies continue to struggle against each other in a hostile way. They can debate with each other in a peaceful way, and so strive to promote their values within a broadly pluralistic framework.

This general position, which could be described as liberal or modernist, has its enemies. It is because, for understandable reasons, revivalist Christianity and Islam (to go no further cross-culturally) have not fully reached a modernist outlook, and still repudiate it, that we are not at all ready for an easy synthesis of values, even at the higher-order level of the complementarity thesis. However, the necessities of living in a plural world – where many adherents of each faith must live in a minority and where at the macroscopic level every religious or ideological tradition is in a world minority – and the softening effects of living beside others who have diverse cultural values will eventually cause all traditions by and large to enter the liberal or modernist fold. There they can maintain their values, together with a toleration of others' values, by accepting some version of the complementarity thesis. Within that framework, moreover, syntheses will occur. Already Westerners have embraced aspects of yoga and Zen, while Easterners and Southerners have absorbed some Western values alongside modern techniques and attitudes. So within a framework of complementarity, closer unities of value can be forged by creative synthesis.

It is within this perspective, I believe, that we can view the achievements of what I have called constructive cross-cultural philosophy. Here Robert Carter proves himself a pioneer in this mode at presenting a view of life, drawing on East Asian and Western themes in a synthesis that will have a practical as well as a theoretical outreach.

Becoming Bamboo taps Zen values and through them Taoist ones in a way that resonates with Western ecological concerns: but it does much more than this in giving an intellectual understanding of a newly conceived way of life. I would hope therefore that the book will gain a wide readership. It represents a direction in which the blend of Western and Buddhist culture can go. It is therefore part of that Pacific dialogue that is creating a vital new centre of human activity at the vast blue crossroads between North America and East Asia. It may be that the world will form itself into differing areas of ideas. It is clear that *Becoming Bamboo* does not form a synthesis that echoes some of the more conservative theistic notions such as dominate parts of the West and the Islamic crescent that runs from West and North Africa round to Indonesia. But it does express with poetry and good sense a way in which Eastern and Western philosophy can grow together. Moreover, it takes us beyond a shallow individualism and humanism that can so easily in our day substitute for the deeper meanings of individual and human life.

Acknowledgments

To the students and colleagues who are not cited here but who have helped me to shape my horizon of perception and understanding both in and out of the classroom, I offer my thanks. To Ninian Smart, of the University of Lancaster, England, and the University of California at Santa Barbara, who read and introduced this book, I extend my heartfelt appreciation. Professor Smart's encouragement of this and other projects of mine has been steadfast, and of the utmost importance to me. His special blend of academic rigour and achievement and down-to-earth availability for assisting others is to be treasured.

My wife, Marjorie Haugan, who talked with me for hours on end about how I might shape this study, also helped mightily with the editing of the manuscript in its various stages. Her encouragement was unflagging and her insights were predictably on target. I am grateful both for these offerings and for the dialogue that continues.

Many have read various portions of the manuscript at stages of its development: Professor Alan R. Drengson of the University of Victoria, and Professors Sean Kane, Constantine V. Boundas, Stephen Regoczei, Marlene Castellano, Don McCaskill, and Peter Kulchyski, all of Trent University, have provided invaluable assistance. Charles Bawden, Peter Van Wyck, Oliver Antkowiak, and Roy Wright have also helped to make the manuscript a better one. Jerry Larock, Brendan Driscoll, and Oliver Antkowiak worked long and hard in assisting me with the index. Of course, none of those named is to be blamed for whatever deficiencies still exist.

A special thank you is due to Toshiba Computers for their generous support of my comparative study by making available a portable computer during the research and writing stages of this book.

Chapter 2 appeared in an abbreviated form in the *Journal of Moral Education* as "Beyond Justice" (16, no. 2 [May 1987]: 83–98). A shorter and quite different version of chapter 3 appeared as "Die Notwendigkeit von Freiheit" in a volume honouring Viktor Frankl on his eightieth birthday, *Wege Zum Sinn: Logotherapie als Orientierungshilfe, für Viktor E. Frankl*, ed. Alfried Langle (Munchen: R. Piper GmbH & Co. KG 1985), 71–81. My thanks to the editors and the publishers for allowing me to use material from these publications.

I am also grateful to the Canadian Federation for the Humanities and its reviewers, both for being constructively critical of this manuscript and for underwriting some of the costs of publication.

Finally, I am grateful to Peter Blaney, editor of McGill-Queen's University Press, who shepherded *Becoming Bamboo* through the review and publication process with unusual sensitivity.

Becoming Bamboo

The joy and meaning of life is enhanced through increased self-realization, through the fulfillment of each being's potential. Whatever the differences between beings, increased self-realization implies broadening and deepening of the self ...

As I see it we need the immense variety of sources of joy opened through increased sensitivity toward the richness and diversity of life, through the profound cherishing of free natural landscapes ... Part of the joy stems from the consciousness of our intimate relation to something bigger than our own ego, something which has endured for millions of years and is worth continued life for millions of years. The requisite care flows naturally if the self is widened and deepened so that protection of free nature is felt and conceived of as protection of our very selves.

Arne Naess
from *Thinking Like a Mountain: Towards a Council of All Beings*, ed. John Seed et al.

Introduction

What is a value? This question has daunted, excited, and plagued thinkers from the beginnings of history. There are many divergent opinions, each technically adept and partly convincing, but as with other great questions of humankind, the question has to be asked again in each age and tradition and answered in a way that attends to the specific issues and concerns of the time. Here I want only to sketch out an approach to value and valuation that will serve to make sense of the distinctions that will arise in later chapters of this exploration. It is not the only way to go, but I think it will prove to be both helpful and reasonable.

The Scottish philosopher John Laird maintains that a value is whatever matters to someone. Whatever matters to someone positively is a value to that person, and whatever matters negatively is a *disvalue* – that is, a negative value. Something is merely a matter of indifference only if it matters to no one. Laird adds that "since everything matters to itself, self-maintenance is a value to every existent," including inanimate as well as animate entities. Accordingly, "everything is valuable to itself" and, for Laird, "elects" or is impelled to continue to exist, rather than to perish.[1] For the moment we do not need to raise the issue of the obviously metaphorical claim that a rock or, to use Laird's example, an iron filing "elects" to continue to exist, except to report that he argues that it is difficult to draw a line between the animate and the inanimate, particularly with respect to persistence and self-maintenance. It follows from this that whatever "helps or hinders" a thing to do or be something is a value (positive or negative) to it. Daring to follow the implications of this insight as far as it leads, Laird concludes that "the universe must be said to be valuable to itself." Lest you think that the universe itself is in the valuation business, deciding which parts of itself are valuable and which disvaluable, Laird warns that "the universe, however, does not pick and choose within itself; for everything within it contributes to its characteristic being."[2] But for us as individuals within the universe, whatever weakens us or even closes us to growth and strengthening is a disvalue, while whatever opens us to growth or strengthens us is a value.

Yet there is more to the picture than this, for some attempt will have to be made to say whether what matters to you is what *ought* to matter to you, and furthermore whether what matters is what is *best for you, for your significant others, and perhaps even for some portion of the universe itself beyond the human.* The ethical dimension leads us not only to considerations of what is best for others, however widely or narrowly we decide to define "others," but also to considerations of what is best or better for non-human living things, for non-living things, and for the greater environment in which we find ourselves, at least as we understand it. Values are relative to the elective agent and do not exist apart from mattering to someone, somewhere, at some time. Something is a value only from someone's point of view. Still, while some points of view are limited to what matters to the individual, or to a slightly wider circle of inclusions only, others are expansive even to the point of taking what is a cosmic perspective. And just as in ethics there are good reasons for demanding that what is right for the individual ought to be generalized – even universalized, to apply to all others in similar circumstances (and with other things being more or less equal) – so it might be argued that you ought also to generalize your concern for others and for things until it is the cosmos that, in all of its known complexity, *matters*. Thus, it will matter dearly to many whether species survive, whether beauty is destroyed, whether pain is inflicted on animals or people, whether lakes are polluted, trees logged, the wilderness lost, and whether silence becomes as impossible to experience as a night sky without reflected human-made light.

THE LENSES OF TRADITION

However, while a value pure and simple is whatever matters to you, however limited the perspective that generates it, it is also possible to *choose* from among perspectives – that is, to be able to hold that one perspective is better for you than another, or at least that *in certain respects* one perspective is superior, even if not in other respects. It may be ultimately impossible to compare perspectives in a wholesale way and yet be quite possible to compare perspectives on specific issues of importance. In the final analysis a perspective, or way of seeing-in-general, is foundational simply because it is the pair of lenses through which you come to "see" whatever you see.

In making this analogy of the "lenses" work, however, it is important to note that these are the lenses that are not removable but are standard human equipment, as though the outer surface of the eyes were malleable. Thus, to some extent we all look at the world through the lenses of our tradition. We rest content with the lenses that we have, for as long as we do, for pragmatic reasons: the perspective afforded by means of the lenses offers us various instrumental values in the living of our lives. From their use we gain security, comfort, and surprisingly clear vision, for the purposes we have decided upon, of the things and aspects of our environment that we elect to look at, or merely look at out of reflex habit.

Yet such perceptual lenses of perspective can be polished, and ground finer to take in yet more detail or an even wider peripheral vision of things, and even made bi- and tri-focal through critical reflection and cross-cultural comparison. The image I have in mind here is that of the adding of various lenses to the ones already worn, as at the optometrist's office, when the target-chart is made clearer or blurred, blacker or faded, single or double, depending on the lenses added to the ones currently worn. The lenses can be significantly altered without swapping them for a different set altogether. Thus, someone might be unable to decide whether Plato's philosophy is better than Aristotle's and yet still learn a great deal about both, others whether Christianity is superior to Buddhism as a guide to the living of a life. Indeed, you might be selective, opting for Buddhism's emphasis on inborn human goodness, which only becomes corrupted by individual and social delusion, over Christianity's conception of a human being as fallen and prone to error. Similarly, Aristotle's analysis of change as generally lawful might be chosen over Plato's apparent inability to deal with change because of his emphasis on permanence and stability.

Yet what makes such specific comparisons possible is a wider context or perspective that each of us at least implies when deciding that one view makes more sense than another. It will do so because of the broad context of the way or schema within which you understand. In the case of inborn human goodness over fallenness, you have to consider first the broader "story" or context of cosmic beginnings, the status and importance of this life now being lived, the nature of ethical living, and so on. Each of us is, at least unconsciously, in the process of developing a philosophy of life, a context for understanding, an explanatory account of how, in some general sense, things are, and we look through this philosophy-in-the-making, this broad understanding in *process*, in deciding whether one specific claim is preferable to another.

If you are more empirically minded you will look for the tangible evidence, or require an experiential ground, or test the claim from within the body of scientific knowledge. If you are rationalist in stance, you may assess the claim in the light of its coherence with the rest of your understanding about the nature of things. Among those who are religious, some may consult scripture, others seek direct revelation, and yet others find guidance through prayer. A "postmodernist," by contrast, may seek to upset such habits of understanding to unmask their unspoken assumptions and strip naked their claims to power and authority, letting things afterwards take their own course in clarifying where things stand in the wake of this defrocking.

Whatever stance you take, you read the evidence in the light of your general stance until you can question the adequacy of the stance or its completeness. Then you begin the process of re-grinding your lenses. This may happen slowly, over years of gradual refinement, or quickly, as you now look at the world differently and have come to see, or need to see, what heretofore was not seen at all, or at least not clearly. A *shift in seeing has occurred*, and you may or may not realize that your lenses have been re-ground already. Of course, what is not included in this metaphor of lenses is the mental horizon-of-understanding, which interprets what we see and which "powers" the actual *seeing* through the lenses in much the same way that a video camera is unable to operate without the mass of solid-state circuitry that predetermines how the information received through the optical lenses of the camera is to be processed. The circuitry, too, may be changed, and black and white may give way to colour, two dimensions to three, and so on. The metaphor needed must refer to the entire complex of seeing-processing-interpreting-relating-systematizing, and the playing back of the whole for further reconsideration.

WIDER-ANGLE LENSES

A central thesis of what follows is that this shift to new, heretofore untried, and wider-angle lenses arises in part as a direct result of the attempt to comprehend by constructing the widest possible context of understanding. Not only is such construction worthwhile in itself as an activity, but it is through this search for a wider and more adequate context of understanding that you come to comprehend yourself as inextricably linked with others: with the world, both culturally and physically, and with the cosmos, as widely conceived as we can imagine. What follows here, then, is *one* journey, *one* way of exploring the interconnectedness of people, nature, and the cosmos, both as it is imagined and as our further understanding of it unfolds before us. It is *a* way, *a* path to meaning, to the enhancement of the value-experiences of living a life and to more genuine encounters with others, as well as with nature. It is not, of course, the *only* way, and that, too, is part of the journey that this book occasions.

There is no such thing as a definitive journey, or a definitive account. There are only journeys that prove to be worth taking and accounts that are worth reading or listening to. They all appear to be so close to the beginning of the trip, as though we have all just begun. The Zen Buddhist priest and scholar of American literature Shigematsu Sōiku expresses this well:

Zen followers have always embraced the ecological point of view. They see all in each and each in all, macrocosm in microcosm and microcosm in macrocosm: all nature in one great harmony. They live in the love of nature, and always see themselves as a part of all – despite the humbling awareness that as human beings we are newcomers to the history of life (3,000,000,000 years old) on this earth (4,500,000,000 years old) in this universe (12,000,000,000 years old). Compare the history of the earth to a calendar year: ego-centred modern man showed up only a few seconds before the very end of the last day of the year, December 31.[3]

In what follows I will use Zen Buddhism and Japanese culture as the focus of the cross-cultural comparisons that I make. There are other cultures to which I might have turned, and indeed I might well have attended to strictly Western sources. Much of what I want to explore and say is brought into sharper focus through cross-cultural comparison, and Japan is the "other" culture that I know best. Not only will I compare Western tendencies with contrasting Japanese attitudes and assumptions, but I will also alter my presentational style by including the occasional reminiscence of my several stays among the Japanese people as illustrations of my general thesis.

One final "instruction for the reader" concerns the intensity of some of my appreciative comments about Japanese culture on the one hand and critical remarks about our own modern or (postmodern) Western cultural climate. My aim is not to recommend Japanese culture as superior, for I do not think it either possible, or fruitful, to compare whole perspectives, as I have said. My aim rather is to infuse our own cultural understanding with heavy doses of cross-cultural insight, in order to assist in the sort of critical reassessment that I think we desperately need. Moreover, cross-cultural investigations ought to cut sharply in both directions, and they usually do.

Our technological perspective has already radically affected the Far Eastern cultures, and especially the Japanese: that is not news. It is my hope that together with them we will have the good sense to weigh the values (and the disvalues) that our way of life and its attendant outlook provide, and that we will have the heart and the intelligence to drink deeply of their cultural successes and failures in order to shape our own valuational destiny better. It is not to be expected that we will each borrow wholesale from the other and give up crucial dimensions of our own cultural traditions. Instead, if we learn from each other, Japan will become stronger and more vital because of its own critical reassessment in the light of its encounter with the technological West, and the West will do the same because of its encounter with what is ancient and mysterious in the East. The result will be a different Japanese culture, as we already can observe, and an increasingly altered cluster of Western traditions due to the intensity of the Japanese "invasion," both cultural and economic. But the stamp of Western culture will only be modified, not eradicated, and Japanese culture will undergo still further changes because of its continued success in competing with Western peoples on their own terms. The two will not become one (nor shall we wish it so), for it is the diversity-in-mutual-influence that will continue to present us with differences to explore and to learn from.

My stance is not intended to be either Eastern or Western, but rather a gathering of wisdom from both traditions in so far as they contribute to a whole-universe perspective rather than an anthropocentric individual perspective, an ethnocentric cultural perspective, or even an ecological world-perspective. The perspective that I shall focus upon *is* ecological in its concern for the environment, but it urges us to think beyond the limits even of the living environment of the Earth. It is the sense of connection with the cosmos that has enthralled me in the writing of this book. I hope that it calls, even if only as a faint whisper, to you as well.

COMPARATIVE VALUE THEORY

■■■■ My research into Japanese philosophy and culture would take me back to Japan several times. My interest was in learning something about the Japanese sensitivity to the beautiful and to human and spiritual values at first hand. All of my reading had prepared me for an encounter with a culture that was rich in the capacity to value intrinsically: from the love of

nature to the delight taken in the perfection of a single blossom, or in the sound of a cricket chirping, or a cicada buzz-
ing in warm summertime, or water gurgling in a tiny pool. I
encountered an instance of this attention to the details of the
beautiful in one of the formal gardens of Japan. A tiny rivulet
was diverted down a trough leading to a concrete cauldron
about the size of a basketball cut in half. The water swirled
in, was caught for a moment or two as it circled the edges of
the hollow, and then continued on its way, exiting at the far
side. As I watched and listened, the swirling motion caused a
handful of pebbles, just the right size to be agitated by this
subtle motion, to tumble over and over again at the bottom of
this four-inch-deep kettle. The result was a sound, amplified
by the hollow construction that served as the sound-box for
this instrument of nature, resulting in a faithful imitation of a
rushing mountain stream.

It was sensitivity such as this to the details of beauty, and
the acceptance of the phenomenal world as a major source of
meaning in life, that led me to inquire into the Japanese life-
experience in the first place. While every culture, including
the Japanese, evidences human injustice and environmental
carelessness and exploitation, few possess robust traditions of
human sensitivity, environmental concern, and aesthetic and
valuational prescriptions and practices that distinctly enhance
the quality of life of their people. While the Japanese are to be
condemned for their lack of respect for dolphins and other
forms of sea life, and for environmental pollution generally,
the Zen Buddhist and Shintō perspectives appear to be unusually rich in prescriptions and practices of remarkable value.
Sensitive cultural awareness is rarely more than a thin veneer
at the best of times, and must be celebrated and reinforced,
notwithstanding numerous cultural shortcomings in other
respects. I wanted to explore these affirmative cultural
strands, to experience their effect at first hand. Perhaps we in
the West could learn from them how to gain joy in the simple
sounds and sights of nature, and to feel more at home in the
world than we do now.

I expressed this to a colleague who taught philosophy and
aesthetics at a university in Tokyo. I added that it seemed to
me that the Japanese were more sensitive to intrinsic valuation
than were we in North America. My hunch was that my culture was extrinsically oriented – that is, was adept at utilizing
nature for our own life-purposes rather than at opening to

nature's delights and gaining value-experience by sitting in the midst of it, responding to it rather than controlling it. I emphasized the intrinsic/extrinsic value distinction (the valuable for its own sake, just for what it is, as opposed to the valuable as that which is not valuable for its own sake but because it leads to something else that we value for its own sake), assuming it to be common currency everywhere in the academic world.

My colleague looked at me in surprise and then responded, "What an interesting distinction! Intrinsic values are those given in immediate experience, and are valuable in themselves, whereas extrinsic values are those which are valuable because of the intrinsic value-experiences to which they lead. What an interesting way to divide the world of values." He shook his head in philosophic delight, and then continued, "But we make no such distinctions in Japanese philosophy, or in Japan generally. Rather, we focus on values, and on what enhances our value-experience. Our aim is to become sensitive to the values of living, especially to the appreciation of nature. We find ways to teach others to respond to the values inherent in everyday living. But what an interesting distinction you make! I have never before thought of values in accordance with your classificatory scheme."

It was clear to me that my approach to the Japanese sensitivity to "intrinsic valuation" was not going to be as straightforward as I had anticipated. My schema was an artificial imposition on the data found, and my unanticipated task would now be to try to ensure that the resultant distortion was as slight as possible. Could I be sure that it was the direct experience of values that I was engaged in rather than the collecting of a knapsack full of value-instances that merely fit my own categories of thought? Could I even *begin* to *become* Japanese in my sensitivity to values, or was that an arrogance to be abandoned at the outset?

CHAPTER ONE

Values and Valuation

W.T. Stace remarked that one of the benefits of "a God in the sky" was the sense that "the universe, created and governed by a fatherly God, was a friendly habitation for man."[1] Yet it is not the case that *only* a belief in a parentally concerned God can provide a sense of being-at-home in a friendly world. Stace also observed that the modern world appears to be "nothing but an immense spiritual emptiness. It is a dead universe."[2] Most of us no longer see ourselves as an integral part of the universe, dwelling in the midst of nature as beings at home, but as a species alienated from it and even in mortal combat with it. Such a view is not solely the result of our loss of religious awe. We have also adopted a stance-in-the-world that has transformed the realm of nature into an array of materials for our use, usually economic; astonishingly, to some extent we have extended this "usable-goods" metaphor for the world to human beings as well. We have systematically reduced our world and ourselves to considerations of profit and loss, gain and material impoverishment. We have become *homo economicus* and have reduced those who do not succeed in the game of wealth to the status of "resources," cheap labour, and the "underdeveloped." It is as though we can only be underdeveloped or developed *economically*, and not aesthetically, spiritually, or morally, or in terms of our sense of community or chosen lifestyle. The field of human action is less that of self-development and more that of economic and resource development.

Whether or not God is dead, as Nietzsche announced, is of but incidental concern to this inquiry. Either way, it remains a fact of our times that both religious and non-religious people have come to adopt the economic stance: trees, bacteria in the laboratory, homeless children and/or wombs for rent, human kidneys, the oldest remaining trees in the few remaining forests, elephants for ivory, and dolphins that may get caught in fishing nets are but *commodities-at-hand*, possessing no inherent or intrinsic value[3] in themselves, only economic significance. Perhaps we have further "evolved" since Stace wrote and, rather than seeing the world as spiritually empty and dead, now view it as one grand economic resource, an all-too-limited reservoir of timber, minerals, oil, animal and vegetable food, and genetically transformable cells. Our postmodern world is valuable as an economic resource, and we too, as sources of labour and even as "spare parts," are valued economically rather than for our own sakes and for our inherent richness.

This book means to explore is what has been lost by the commodification of existence, and what might be done either to recover or to reinvent a sense of the worth of the world in which we live, and of ourselves. Otherwise we, like the other inhabitants and things of the world, both living and inanimate, will be valued only for the economic contributions we make, and/or for the uses to which we might be put. The change in organizational nomenclature from "Personnel Department" to "Department of Human Resources" betrays a managerial change of attitude towards employees. From being persons who contribute, workers have become a resource to be used, and possibly to be used up.

This view of men and women as commodities was actually put into practice in this century. The state of mind described by commodification did in fact release evil. Nazi abuses required that soldiers and officials come to think of their victims as things-for-use, or as economically and socially worthless or harmful. It is revealing that one of the techniques used to render soldiers unfeeling with respect to their victims was to have them gouge the eyes out of live and unanaesthetized cats held in their laps. In order to be able to think of Jews as sides of beef, or logs, one had to quell previously existing feelings towards them. They must be thought of as non-human, as thoroughly unrelated to the genuine and superior human being. The cats too had to be experienced as fodder for experimentation, or as mere training instruments.

Notice that the transformations of language required are all technological. The language of technology is the language of *materials-at-hand*, and so we must recognize the link between economic and technological perspectives. All too often technology is the instrumentation of economic objectives. To cite a current example, the Indians along the Brazilian Amazon must be moved if not eliminated if the mineral and timber resources of the region are to be realized efficiently and in order to transform the region into pasture-land for beef production, primarily for North American use. These rare tribal human beings, and the magnificent rain forests themselves, are but impediments to resource harvesting and instances of it, respectively. But the economic-technological perspective is an impoverishment of the *value* of human beings, of trees, and of the cosmos in which we live. The analysis of value and valuation that I offer attempts to make clear why this is so, and what might be done to improve our capacity for fuller and more appropriate evaluation.

An enrichment in our capacity to value may also yield an increase in our sense of the meaning and worth of our lives, and a key result might be that we will adjust our lenses to a vision of what it means to *dwell* in a world from which we are no longer alienated, and in which we recognize ourselves and others as far more than economic resources. Technology will be driven and shaped by whichever outlook on the world dominates. It is imperative that we adopt a perspective that is humane and environmentally aware if we are to improve the quality of life, or even to survive.

INTRINSIC VALUE AND MEANING

The link between intrinsic valuation and meaning in life needs to be explicated. A recent analysis has been provided by James O. Bennett, who writes that "whether or not 'life has meaning' is to an important extent determined by the quality of one's experience." He elaborates further:

I take it that "the meaning of life" cannot be considered apart from the experience of meaningfulness at a personal level. Meaningfulness, then, appears to be the more appropriate category, and rather than asking, "what is the meaning of life?" it seems more helpful to ask, "under what conditions can life be experienced as meaningful?" ... Rather than taking meaningfulness as a primitive, indefinable term, *I assume that talk about meaningfulness can be translated into talk about intrinsic value without loss of content.*[4]

It will not be enough to note that some experiences of intrinsic value are richer than others, for it may be that whole populations appear to have lost the value sensitivity needed even to detect these values, let alone the capacity to compare value experiences. James Bennett, too, emphasizes this point, for he stresses that we must find ways to assist in the development of *"the kind of person for whom the potential for meaningful experience inherent in some kinds of situations can be realized."* In order to be able to experience this richer field of values, it is not enough to learn that they exist, however, for the transformation required is not merely an intellectual one. Instead, "it involves making oneself into a certain kind of person."[5] What, in addition to the intellectual, is in need of cultivation? In answering this question we must take a closer look at the nature of valuation and its several dimensions.

AN ANALYSIS OF VALUES

Values do not exist apart from our experience of them. This is not to say that the conditions that normally or regularly trigger an experience of value do not exist apart from us, for they assuredly do. A giant redwood has value for many, even (perhaps especially) apart from its potential economic value, but we do not need to think that the value that we perceive exists within the tree, like its growth rings. Rather, it is we who have experiences of value, and it is the tree that has what C.I. Lewis terms "inherent value." He suggests that *the goodness of good objects consists in the possibility of their leading to some realization of directly experienced goodness.*[6] Inherent value is one of the *extrinsic* values in Lewis's account, and it and all other extrinsic values are values only "because the end, by relation to which alone anything is ultimately to be judged genuinely valuable, is some possible realization of goodness in direct experience."[7] What is not an experience cannot be of *intrinsic* value since it can have, at best, only the potential of leading to realization of directly experienced goodness, but it cannot itself *be* a direct and immediate experience. The term "intrinsic value" always implies experience of immediate value. Only experiences are immediate and direct, and it is these that may be of intrinsic value. All other attributions of value are termed "valuable" for the direct experiences of value to which they lead, or may lead.

Intrinsic value or, as Lewis sometimes calls it, immediate goodness, is a whole gamut of experience for which no simple description is adequate to cover its richness. Lewis writes:

It must cover the active and self-forgetting satisfactions as well as the passive and self-conscious ones; the sense of integrity in firmly fronting the "unpleasant" as well as "pleasure"; the gratification in having one's own way, and also the benediction which may come to the defeated in having finished the faith. It must cover innocent satisfactions as well as those of cultivation; that which is found in consistency and also that of perversity and caprice; the enjoyment of sheer good fortune, and that which adds itself to dogged achievement. All this in addition to the whole range of the sensuously pleasing and emotionally gratifying. And the immediately disvaluable has its equal and corresponding variety.[8]

Goodness or value that is immediately found and unmistakable when disclosed is termed "intrinsic" because it is value that is good in itself, or valuable for its own sake alone. But both of these phrases – "in itself," and "for its own sake" – are subject to an interpretation that Lewis wishes to reject. Both may be taken to apply to things in themselves apart from subjects or consciousness of any kind, and not only to the experiences *of* subjects, as Lewis intends. Lewis applies the term "valuable" to things *only* with the meaning "[capable of contributing] to a life ... found good in the living of it."[9] A further ambiguity is to be found in the "in itself" formulation. The phrase "in itself" implies a distinction between those values that are part of the intrinsic nature of some object and those that are not. For Lewis an *immediate given* is what is given, and it makes no claim on us about any objective reality beyond itself. No judgment is made concerning whether what is given is *objectively* grounded in the experience and its causes: "There can be no illusion of present enjoyment or present pain"[10] or of anything else directly given. It is precisely as it is perceived, for that is what "immediate" means.

In grappling with the rock-bottom or foundational issue of how valuing gets started, Lewis suggests provocatively and honestly that

The sense of good and bad ... is primordial to conscious life at large. Indeed it would be plausible that mere feeling of euphoria or dysphoria is the most ancient form of consciousness. Though what is humanly experienced with these qualities has become complex, as the human mentality in general has become complex, still the distinction itself remains basically the same; and the sense of good and bad is something which man brings forward from his prehuman ancestry.[11]

Lewis breaks with those who speak of intrinsic value as somehow objective, or "absolute" and unchanging, or to be discovered rather than made. Rather, in so far as he makes intrinsic values the foundational values for all other values, they are simply to be accepted as we experience them. The result is that intrinsic values – or immediate values, as Lewis prefers to call them – are subjective, or dependent on the state of mind of the beholder. It is not that no values are objective, for Lewis provides a convincing account that they are, but only that immediate values, as the bedrock of valuation, are to be accepted for what they are: immediately good or bad. He writes:

The problem of characterizing the immediately good is a baffling one; an irritating one even; because, in the first place, everybody knows what it is; and if anyone should not, we could hardly tell him. We here arrive at a point where we realize that between words and what they signify there is a gap; and more words will not build a bridge across it. So we are likely to say that such a quality as immediate goodness is ineffable; or that it is a simple quality, like the redness of a red rose, and being unanalyzable, is indefinable. It has not parts or distinct ingredients, by reference to which and their relations we can convey what is intended. And it stands in no invariant text and has no stable correlations, by reference to which we might locate it map-wise through its external relationships.[12]

The immediately given in experience cannot be known in its fullness through words alone. To use Lewis's example, one could not convey to the blind Helen Keller what one had experienced in the seeing of a rose, at least not completely, although one could define and even describe the experience of a colour sensation to her. We may well err in our definition or description or in both, for we do often mislead. Yet we cannot be mistaken about the content of our experience. It is what it is, and *as* we experience it. Indeed, this is because the apprehension of an experiential content is both immediate or direct and non-judgmental.

BACKGROUND TO VALUATION

For Lewis, judgments of value are a type of empirical cognition.[13] His value theory is built on his theory of knowledge, in which he defends a three-fold classification of empirical statements: formulations of what is presently given in experience; terminating judgments and statements of them; and non-terminating judgments that assert some objective reality. As to the first, without the certainty of the *given* in experience there would be no possibility of empirical knowledge whatever, since knowledge of objective empirical facts is expressed in the form of non-terminating judgments that are "translatable into some set of predictive statements each of which formulates some possible confirmation in direct experience"[14] – that is, into terminating judgments that refer to the given for their confirmation or verification. All empirical statements attempt to describe the content of the given in experience and are, for Lewis, formulated in what he terms *expressive* language. Expressive language *"neither asserts any objective reality of what appears nor denies any."*[15] It is the language of appearance just as it appears – that is, as it is given to us in direct and immediate experience.

Expressive language merely attempts to describe the *content* of direct experience precisely as it appears to us. Rather than making any logical or empirical claims about what the facts of the situation are objectively, expressive language is replete with such locutions or safeguards as "'looks like', 'feels like'; thus restricting it to what would fall completely within the passage of experience in question." Lewis's example is "I see what *looks like* granite steps before me,"[16] which makes amply clear that nothing is being claimed about whether there are stairs before him, or whether they are made of granite, or even that he is awake and not dreaming, or pretending, or writing a novel about seeing a set of granite stairs. Expressive language restricts itself to what is given in immediate experience, and is indubitable in itself. How could one doubt whether one was actually seeing what one was seeing? One might doubt its objectivity, or explain it away as the result of drug use, or a hallucination, but the seeing would still be valid as that which one actually saw. The content is as given, whatever one might say about its validity, causes, implications, or significance.

Before going on to discuss the second class of empirical statements, it is perhaps best to weave in the import of this account of expressive statements for valuation, which, after all, is our prime focus. Recalling that Lewis maintains that valuations are a type of empirical cognition, then the bedrock of valuation (as with the given as the "hard kernel" in perception generally) is value as immediately given and indubitable, which Lewis chooses to call *"intrinsic value."* It is the basis of all verification or confirmation, and nothing is to be judged valuable without reference to it. Otherwise, value judgments would be non-empirical in kind.

While it is the case, for Lewis, that the concern for "objectivity" in value judgments will find expression in his analysis of *"extrinsic value,"* intrinsic values themselves do not refer to objective reality. Intrinsic (immediate) values are to be taken as found, and are necessarily spoken of in expressive language. Whether it turns out, upon further reflection, to be empirical sense qualities or empirical value qualities of which we are aware, no judgment is made in the experiencing of them about what might follow from this awareness, or about whether the perceived qualities are subjective or objective, real or imaginary. It is simply the awareness that is of concern; about that no judgment is made, and hence no truth or falsity is possible. Expressive statements are not judgments at all; they merely express what is experienced more or less as it is experienced. Error is possible only in our choice of expressive language used to describe the content of the value given. If one sees a ghost, then it is a ghost-like form that one has seen, whatever its actual cause or ontological status.

While no claim is made about the objectivity of the immediately valuable, the matter is not as simple as Lewis thought. It is less than clear that we actually do have an experience of the "given," that is, of something immediately apparent *yet* unencumbered by any subtle and even involuntarily added ingredients of interpretation and organization. Surely what is immediately apprehended is seldom, if ever, apparent and transparent. Whether through anticipation, expectation, prejudice, or mere intellectual and linguistic structuring, in order to apprehend, and even in the very act of simply remaining aware, we have likely added something to what is given (granted that there is even a way to determine what is given in the first place), and sometimes we have so added long after the moment of apprehension is past, in recollection. Further, in finding expressive language that is adequate to our experience, we may add to, subtract from, or interpret what was "given." This is not merely to say that it is not easy to find language that clearly expresses what we have experienced, or that we may use misleading or inappropriate words to express it, but that the very attempt to express in language may require that we abstract from, add to, or distort the original experience in order to get it in mind clearly enough to formulate it in language. Indeed, as post-structuralists would remark, the allegedly given may *always already* have been in language, such that whatever the given may mean, it must be a fact of language, for there is no such thing as a fact before language, and hence the experience always already displays the contours and restrictions of a given language and its cultural and structural assumptions and requirements.

Lewis's second class of empirical statements, *terminating judgments*, are actual predictions of some further possible experience. They are either completely confirmed or completely disconfirmed by reference to the occurrence or non-occurrence of that possible experience. Terminating judgments take the form of a hypothesis: if x, then y. As with the first class of empirical statements, terminating judgments are also formed in expressive language. Hence, they too are "confined to description of the content of presentation itself,"[17] and make no claim about objective properties possessed by the states of affairs described, only about their appearance. For this reason judgments of this kind are generally expressed in language that restricts our attention to what occurs in experience itself, such as "looks like" or "feels like." Examples of terminating judgments are "If I taste what is [appears to be] before me, I shall enjoy it," "If I touch this [which appears to be] red-glowing metal, I shall feel pain."[18]

But expressions of this type are genuine judgments, and while they do not make claims about objective reality, they do make claims about the real world of everyday experience. "If you put your hand on the glowing stove burner-ring, you will experience extreme pain" is a claim that can be tested in experience, and once and for all. You will be in no doubt about whether the prediction was true or false. Such judgments are not said to be "objective" because they make no such claim to objectivity in fact. They do not pretend to attend to the properties of the object, only to the properties of the experiences of the subject in question. The burner-ring *appears* to be glowing, and you will actually experience pain if you place your bare hand upon it. The pain is a response of the subject and in this sense is again "subjective." It is solid enough as a predictable response that we will now act on the evidence, and will act with extreme care around glowing burners. But the claim that a glowing burner is always dangerously hot, or that non-glowing burners are not also hot, is an objective claim that requires us to investigate the *objective* properties of burnerrings, the varieties of heat, the relation between the properties of "glowing" and "heat," etc.

Non-terminating judgments are the third class of empirical statements, and they do *assert* objective reality. They can never be completely verified, but yield only judgments of probability. In order to determine that something objectively possesses a certain property, some confirmation or verification must be sought. In so far as confirmation or verification can never be attained with complete certainty, but only with a high degree of probability, *it always remains possible that the original judgment will be upset by new facts*. Some small amount of doubt is always justified, always remains. Each confirmation adds to the probability that the judgment is correct, but the number of instances of confirmation is without termination – hence the name "non-terminating" judgments.

In all three kinds of value judgment, then, the ground of judgment is value that is immediately given and indubitable, i.e. intrinsic value. Extrinsic values are values attributed to objects in so far as these objects are conducive to intrinsic value experiences. Evaluations differ from other forms of empirical knowledge only in the type of immediate data relevant to their confirmation. For evaluations, the relevant datum is immediately found value – i.e. intrinsic value; for other empirical judgments, sense data provide the required immediate content. Terminating judgments are completely determinable, for they predict *only* what will happen next: "If you touch the granite, it will feel cold." And they do so in strictly expressive language. Non-terminating judgments, by contrast, do make claims about the objective properties of things, and are not merely expressive in formulation: the stairs *are* actually made of granite; they do not merely look as though they were made of granite. Formally speaking, no number of confirmations will guarantee that the next viewing of what looks like the same granite stairs will yield the anticipated results. Unlikely though it may be, an accident may have necessitated the replacing of the original stairs with a faithful reproduction of synthetic material. Or what used to provide you with pleasure may no longer do so, or may not appeal to someone else. "Try it, you'll like it!" may reveal differences in subjective opinion, or objective change in your physical body or psyche over the years. It may reveal change in you due to maturation, or personal misfortune, or physical incapacity.

THREE KINDS OF EXTRINSIC VALUE

Values attributed to objects are always extrinsic values, while intrinsic value "attaches exclusively to realizations of some possible value-quality in experience itself."[19] Extrinsic value includes *inherent* value, value ascribed to objects in so far as they tend to produce experiences of immediate value upon presentation to someone, and *instrumental* values, which are not themselves immediate values but lead to immediate values. A beautiful mountain stream might be said to be of inherent value even though no one had ever seen it before. Its value is potential value, and this potential is inherent in the properties of the stream and its environment such that, were someone to encounter it now or in the future, and were that person "normal" in her or his sense of appreciation, she or he would gain one or more experiences of intrinsic value as a direct result of exposure to the specific properties possessed by it.

Instrumental values yield no immediate intrinsic value upon presentation but are only useful in bringing about that which by itself, or in addition to something else, can yield such value experiences: "A, which is said to have extrinsic value, may be instrumental to B, and B to C, and so on for any number of steps; but intrinsic worth is something, Z, to which A is directly or indirectly instrumental, is commonly implied."[20] Lewis maintains that nothing is to be called extrinsically valuable unless it is thought to be conducive to an intrinsic-value experience. Something that is useful or instrumental towards something else that is not specifiably of intrinsic value is said to have *utility*, but not to have extrinsic or any other kind of value.[21]

The third kind of extrinsic value is *contributory value*. Contributory values are values that, while they themselves are not intrinsic, nevertheless contribute to experiences that are of intrinsic value. They are components in intrinsic-value experiences rather than instrumental to same. To use Lewis's example, the fact that a child is working to earn ticket money to attend a circus enhances both the immediate value quality found in the work itself, through anticipation, and no doubt the actual circus experience later on, out of pride of accomplishment.[22]

INTRINSIC VALUES AS BASIC

The complexity of the classification of values is evident, but it need not detain us further. However, it may prove useful to extract a specific *trace* of meaning apparent in "intrinsic value" that will be of importance to the later discussion. The immediacy of intrinsic value, its alleged "givenness" and status as a datum of experience, points to its rock-bottom quality. Intrinsic values are values on which all other value claims and distinctions are based. In this sense they are basic, or fundamental. Why do we prefer satisfaction over dissatisfaction, all other things being equal? Why do we prefer pleasure over pain? The only possible response to such questions is that we do. We are at the end of the valuational line, or better, at the beginning. One way of writing of meaning in life is to ask what sorts of experiences, generally, yield higher or greater satisfactions. A life is meaningful to the extent that it consists of experiences of intrinsic value, and meaningless if it produces few or none, or if the balance of intrinsic disvalue over intrinsic value is overwhelming. Life is then out of skew.

In the chapters that follow, claims of the intrinsic value of something are meant to be taken as shorthand for "something is valuable in so far as it does, or might lead to someone's having experiences of intrinsic value (immediate value) upon presentation of it to someone." Nature is, on this account, inherently valuable, in that "sensitive" people will likely continue to find it an incredibly rich (re)source for intrinsic-value experiences. Whether only humans can have such experiences is not an issue to be resolved here. It is enough to recognize that for many – for the Japanese, for example – rocks are held to be of inherent value because they yield such a high intensity and frequency of intrinsic-value experiences for the people who have come to admire and cherish them, and therefore they are considered to be nearly priceless treasures.

VALUES AND VALUATION

Values are the products of valuers who evaluate, and valuation is an inextricable aspect of human consciousness itself.[23] Stace and Lewis are agreed that values are to be found in consciousness as specific sorts of experiences, and are as immediately discoverable as is any sense datum. All experiences are *immediate* apprehensions, and Stace urges that an analysis of experience will reveal that it implies consciousness. His summary account is worth quoting in full:

All consciousness includes valuation. This does not mean that we have two things, consciousness and valuation, always accompanying one another. It means that we have two inseparable aspects of one and the same process. We may for certain purposes separate out the cognitive side, but then it is an abstraction.

Every act of consciousness as such values or disvalues its data. Thus *what* is valued is always data. And what values is always consciousness. Data are the *objects* of valuation. We suppose that we value a thing or a person. But things are only complexes of data. And we value the red hue of the rose, the taste of the food, and so on. And in a person we value his gestures, his words, his smile, his voice, his actions. In what is called "instrumental" value we value something because it will lead to certain data beyond itself. It is these ulterior data that are in the end valued. And this value is intrinsic.[24]

Stace then adds, without a flinch, that "valuation is the same thing as feeling." He distinguishes between "feeling" and "emotion," for the latter class of responses includes such emotions as fear, jealousy, anger, etc. It does not normally include *feelings* such as "the dislike of pepper and the desire for drink," nor the *passion* of the scientist to observe, to study, and to experiment. This same scientist does not ordinarily wish to be "emotional," however, for an angry scientist or a sobbing scientist might lose some of the sought-for impartiality that we rightly associate with the scientific method. But she or he had better not lose interest in what she or he is doing, nor is it encouraged that the passion of the beginner disappear altogether. It is in this broader sense of taking an interest in a task, of wishing to understand more about oneself and/or the external world, or of becoming increasingly competent in one's use of a second language, in teaching well, in having accounted for the alleged "facts" of the situation, that Stace affirms that "there cannot be bare cognition of a datum. For without feeling of some kind that datum collapses and disappears. And if the datum collapses, the consciousness collapses."[25] John Laird would say much the same by pointing out that whatever is engaged in, or attended to, or sought out – in short, whatever "matters" to someone, in whatever way – is a value for that person. Lewis would be less likely to extend the claim quite so far, although he would accept the above analysis, I think, so far as valuation extends. Knowing and valuing, however, he would distinguish by separating the function of knowing generally from the function of valuing specifically. Yet I think he would be hard pressed to deny that his or anyone else's *interest* in knowing (in epistemology generally) was not an instance of valuation. To know is to care about knowing, even if one does not care very much.

A recent writer has elaborated this point further. Richard Peters, in his book *Reason and Compassion*, attacks the common assumption that "the use of reason is a passionless business, the prerogative perhaps of the unfeeling or the middle-aged."[26] He rejects the common assumption of the antithesis between reason and passion. Rather, what should be emphasized is that certain passions are inappropriate when one is engaged in reasoning. For example, one ought not to be so self-interested when discussing an ethical matter that one is unable even to listen to, let alone understand, the points of view of the others affected. One regularly attempts to extend one's context beyond the petty interests of one's own narrow concerns and beyond the concerns of the moment as well. Peters writes of the "rational passions," such as the love of clarity and the hatred of confusion, "without which words could not be held to relatively constant meanings and testable rules and generalizations."[27] And subsequent *motives* to action are both cognitively and valuationally drenched, as a result.

A further refinement of the relationship of reason to feeling (or emotion) is to be found in John Macmurray's *Reason and Emotion*. Rather than Peter's "rational passions," Macmurray writes of "emotional reason." He, too, rejects the seeming opposition between reason and emotion, noting that the assumption that the emotions are "irrational" is symptomatic of this dichotomous conception. Reason, by contrast, is a state of mind "which is cold, detached and unemotional."[28] To be emotional is to be unreasonable, and to be reasonable is to be unemotional.

An even more pernicious view of feelings and emotions is that they represent the beast in us. Feelings are animalistic, and reason is divine. This view can be found in Plato,[29] but it is endemic in the Judaeo-Christian tradition. Sensuality has long been suppressed because it is directly associated with our *fallenness*. Adam and Eve, upon eating the forbidden fruit in the garden of Eden, became aware of their nakedness, and generations of us have been denying our physical nakedness, our drives, emotions, feelings, and the temptations of the flesh ever since. There have been times when within the Judaeo-Christian tradition we have been warned against too much thinking as well, and have been instructed to depend upon authority of some sort, or revelation, instead. But throughout, the warnings against the biddings of the flesh, and against the feelings and emotions associated with the flesh rather than with the mind, have been constant. Puritanism is perhaps the ultimate flowering of such anti-flesh, anti-feeling teachings. It is true, of course, that we can be swept away by our emotions, and that we can be excessively determined in this way by the generally negative emotions of anger, or hatred, or even by love. But in so far as all reasoning rests, at least ideally, upon the *desire* to know things in their own natures or as they are, or in so far as reasoning is deliberation about and the selecting of activities and behaviour, it is inescapably drenched in feeling and valuation.

Furthermore, both reasons and feelings can be rational and irrational. An irrational reason is one that does not refer properly to reality, or leads to fallacious conclusions, or to bad or unexpected consequences. An unjustified feeling is one that does not conform to the facts of the case, or leads to bad or unexpected consequences. What is irrational about reasons and feelings is that they do not correctly refer to the facts of the actual circumstances, and so they do not bring us what we expect when we act in accordance with them. Rational reasons and feelings do. Macmurray reverses the usual order of primacy of reason and emotion, suggesting that "reason is primarily an affair of emotion, and ... the rationality of thought is the derivative and secondary one. For if reason is the capacity to *act* in terms of the nature of the object, it is emotion which stands directly behind activity determining its substance and direction, while thought is related to action indirectly and through emotion, determining only its form, and that only partially."[30]

Reasoning is a special form of emotion or feeling: it is, as Peters argued, the methodological, logical, and careful application of consciousness that defines reason, broadly speaking. One has to decide that these qualities matter, and become passionate in one's defence of them. We can educate people to reason "correctly," to come to learn about and to care about correct argument, logical form, and defended content. We bring them to have an interest in such things. Perhaps it is too much to claim that reason is actually a species of feeling, and enough to note that one has to care about being rational before one can begin to exercise one's capacity for logical and rational thinking. I prefer to leave aside the question of priority and to emphasize instead the necessity that reasoning must include some feeling component or association, and that feeling must include some reasoning component, however slight. The problem is that we spend enormous amounts of time improving our reasoning and intellectual skills and virtually none improving our feeling capacity, or honing our ability to select from among our feelings those that are more worthy of refinement and sensitization. And John Macmurray has done as much as anyone to suggest just how this might be done.

EDUCATING THE EMOTIONS

Macmurray echoes Peters in diagnosing "the real problem of the development of emotional reason" as being the need "to shift the centre of feeling from the self to the world outside."[31] This point will occupy centre stage in later chapters, in which the developmental thesis of the late Lawrence Kohlberg's seven stages of moral development will be discussed, as well as our relationship to other people and to the environment. Macmurray's language is even developmentally psychological: he adds that "we can only begin to grow up into rationality when we begin to see our own emotional life not as the centre of things but as part of the development of humanity."[32] Our connection with "humanity" and with the cosmos will also form part of the focus of later chapters. For now, however, I will follow Macmurray in his articulation of a theory of emotional education.

MACMURRAY'S THEORY

Emotional reason expresses itself most directly and fully in the field of art, where the artist strives to give expression to his/her own emotional reaction to some fact of or situation in the world, including him/herself as a part of the world. The resulting art must move us in such a way that we are transformed. We must gain a new perspective, a new feeling of and into some aspect of the world of which we either knew nothing before or which we knew not nearly so well nor felt as deeply towards. The artist must not simply take us on her or his personal trip but must take us along by finding expression that involves and includes us in the journey of insight and feeling.

Emotional reason "is not a mere reaction to a stimulus. It is an immediate appreciation of the value and significance of real things."[33] Macmurray terms this *objective* valuation, but I am not willing to make such a claim without considerable qualification. Suffice it to say that emphasis on a community of reaction is at least part of what determines whether or not an artist has "said something" significant. An artist who speaks only to herself or himself and whose work never speaks to others, even to the end of time, cannot be said to have expressed something of significance, for it has not been of significance to anyone else. When we appeal to others by means of an artistic creation/expression, we ask them only secondarily or incidentally to "think about" what we have done, and primarily to "react" to it emotionally, or in feeling: "There is one crucial thing that thinking cannot do at all. It cannot decide whether the thing it reveals is good or bad, beautiful or ugly, to be shunned or to be sought. For the determination of values we are dependent on our emotions – or on those of someone else."[34] Even so-called rational or expert judgments of aesthetic worth and taste are themselves ultimately based on previous emotions, often stretching back into the dim recesses of human history. Macmurray's "rule," as I will term it, is that "a judgment of value can never be intellectual in its origin." And just as we must learn to think for ourselves, so we must also learn to feel for ourselves, and to form our own valuational standards by means of which we can judge what is worthy and what is not. The way we learn to do this is "primarily an education of our sensibility ... the training of our sensuality."[35]

SENSUALITY

Training in sensuality is one direct path to the education of the emotions, to the realization of our potential for feeling. In many ways, this is the actual theme of this entire book. To enhance one's capacity to feel, and particularly to be able to identify the valuationally superior or preferable, is to enrich the nature and the extent of meaning in one's life by making possible a perception of the relatedness of life within a living cosmos. The enrichment of meaning is the enrichment of feeling, and the genuine enrichment of feeling capacity is both quantitative and qualitative. We must enhance our emotional life quantitatively *and* qualitatively. Yet our Graeco-Judaeo-Christian cultural traditions have more often than not discouraged the intensifying of human emotions. In Macmurray's words,

there lies behind us a long tradition which would persuade us that this capacity is undesirable, and should be eliminated altogether. It will have it that we ought to get rid of the desire to satisfy our senses, that we should be trained to suppress our sensuality, and to prevent it from issuing in action. As a result of that tradition, the word has come to have a shameful meaning, and has acquired the power to shock us when we hear it used. It has come to be associated in our minds with the lack of self-control and with an immoderate and vulgar indulgence in bodily pleasures.[36]

Macmurray refers to the senses as the "gateways" of our awareness, and he associates richness of sense experience with the development of sensuality, feeling capacity, and eventually of valuational sensitivity and discrimination. "If we are to be full of life and fully alive, it is the increase in our capacity to be aware of the world through our senses which has first to be achieved." He warns that we can use our senses more narrowly and restrictedly as guides to what is available for practical gain, and in order to avoid harm: "If the interest is narrowly practical, what we perceive in the world will be a narrow range of utilizable facts."[37] The full use of our sense capacity is less strictly "pragmatic," but rather "contemplative."[38] Martin Heidegger makes a similar distinction when he writes of "meditative" as distinct from "calculative" thinking.[39] More on Heidegger shortly.

To contemplate the world through our senses is to *enjoy* the world of sensation for its own sake, as a source of intrinsic-value experiences and not merely instrumentally because of the practical additional results it may afford. This has long been a capacity of people of Far Eastern religious and philosophical traditions, who have learned to dwell in the world, open to its incredibly rich satisfactions, and open in subtle ways to the possibility of sensual *joy*. In a later chapter I will describe the Japanese love of nature as a prime example of this, and the contrast will be between those who have only learned to *use* the world for their own purposes as against those who have learned to sink into the world sensually and have come to *identify* with it – a key emotional capacity. In any case, one who can listen for the sake of listening, who takes joy in the sound of the cicada or the crow, in the feeling of wet moss underfoot, in the warmth of rock in sun on a cold wintry day, and in the whiteness of the first spring flower, is not only likely to find the world valuationally richer; s/he will also find it more meaningful.

A reading of the present chapter has told us that meaning means intrinsic valuation, and that an increase in the ability to apprehend intrinsic values will be to increase the quantity and quality of meaning in our lives. "We touch things because we want to feel them," Macmurray tells us, and he speaks our language by adding that "sensitive awareness becomes then a life in itself with an intrinsic value of its own which we maintain and develop for its own sake, because it is a way of living, perhaps the very essence of all living."[40] Life lived in this way is "glad awareness," joyful, overflowing with value, meaning, and significance. Putting all of this in more philosophical terms, he suggests that such awareness is knowledge, but knowledge not of the intellect but of the senses:

You don't want merely to know about the object; often you don't want to know about it at all. What you do want is to know *it*. Intellectual knowledge tells us about the world. It gives us knowledge *about* things, not knowledge *of* them. It does not reveal the world as it is. Only emotional knowledge can do that ... The wider use of the senses for the joy of living in them, is knowing the world itself in and through emotion, not by means of the intellect. This is not to disparage intellectual knowledge but only to insist that it is meaningless and without significance, apart from the direct sensual knowledge which gives it reality. One cannot really know about anything unless one first knows it. Intellectual awareness is egocentric. It uses the senses as its instrument. But the direct sensual awareness has its centre in the world outside, in the thing that is sensed and loved for its own sake.[41]

This departure from egocentric knowing to the submersion of oneself in the immediate and living particulars of life is part of the training in selflessness, or the "forgetting of the self," that is such a central feature of training in sensual sensitivity in the Far East. One learns to paint the bamboo by becoming the bamboo, not by thinking about it or reading about it but simply by reaching out to it until one feels what one can of bamboo-ness itself.

Macmurray concludes that this training in the capacity to live in the senses for the intrinsic value experiences they yield is also the route to coming to know the world not for what it can provide us economically, or technologically, or instrumentally in some other way, but because it is rich in value for us simply as contemplated, as drunk in sensually, and as a home that we have learned to come home to, a homecoming whereby we now know how to dwell meditatively and joyfully in the very midst of our living. Such awareness of the world around us "is a good half of the meaning of life."[42] The other half is our relationship with other people as members and creators of community, for we dwell not only in the world but in the world with others, in community, as families, as lovers, as friends.

If we persist in encouraging and educating only the intellect in our schools, we will "inevitably create an instrumental conception of life, in which all human activity will be valued as a means to an end, never for itself."[43] Our living will be instrumental living, with intrinsic worth pushed to the far-off future that never arrives, or even to an afterlife. Additionally, in so far as the intellect analyses, dissects, and examines life piecemeal and not as a wholeness, the result will continue to be specialization without comprehension of how this specialization fits into the whole of life and reflects the whole personality of its practitioners. Instead, we come to accept the expansion of particular aspects of human activity into complete conceptions of life, the substitution of the part for the whole.

It is in this way that the sense of the whole of things, the creation of a philosophy or way of life, a metaphysical vision, a religious path, is a key ingredient in the development of meaning in life, for a sense of the whole modifies the hold that any specialization has on us. As well, the holistic stance is not only an intellectual apprehension of the wider sense of things but is also holistic in demanding involvement through the three capacities of human consciousness: knowing, feeling, and willing, or intellect, feeling, and evaluation, which is the exercise of the will to carry out what we value and to act in accordance with what matters to us. In this sense the intellect is divisive, for it prefers to work alone, whereas the emotional side of us is unificatory and enabling, for we do analyse what we value, ask how to achieve what is worthwhile, and then steel ourselves to carry out whatever it is that the intellect and feeling indicate we ought to do to gain what matters, ideally with all of our capacities and energies focused. W.T. Stace makes this same point when he contends that "all movement and behaviours of men and animals is the product of valuation. If I make even the slightest movement, if I raise my hand, if I flicker an eyelid, it is valuation which produces the movement."[44]

SPECIALIZATION
AND SYNTHESIS

Human beings are capable of specialization, but also of synthesis. It is the synthetic capacity that must evaluate a specialized part, or skill, by assessing how it does or does not contribute to the living of life as a whole, both for oneself and for others likely affected. This assessment includes questions about whether or not attending to this part or using this skill will or will not be likely to do harm to the broader environment in which one lives. In deciding what to do, one must not only consult one's rules of specialization but the ethical, social, environmental, aesthetic, religious, and exceedingly long-term implications of an action as well. To be responsible is to be as aware as one can be of the context in which one lives and acts and of the results of one's own actions upon this broad sweep of concern. One is responsible for one's actions to the extent that one is able to foresee the likely results stemming from them, and one is responsible for using the means available in deciding what these results will be.

It is a moral requirement that one extend one's horizon of vision to include the broadest and most far-reaching results of one's way of living. Specialization is important, but it is only the beginning, not the end of the evaluative process. Specialization must itself be evaluated in terms of the broadest context of understanding and feeling of which one is capable. And while the establishment of the "widest" and most "far-reaching" context is never complete, nor is it unchanging, this flux is not to be taken as an excuse for attending to what is known with greater certainty. Being human requires making the best of what one has, without recourse to additional guarantees or promises of unchanging stability. To be human is to develop a tolerance for ambiguity, because of which one is able to act *now* on the basis of the best information available. One's information, one's outlook, and one's sense of the context of things is, for each of us, the best-up-until-now summary of things that we have. It is then up to us to reach beyond the present limits to a perspective more adequate still, based on a search for the wisdom of others, the constant critical reassessment of our present position, and an openness to new information, different ways of life, and the possibility of revision in our capacity to feel, to care, and to value generally.

OFF THE BEATEN PATH

It was my first journey to Japan, and each and every encounter with the strangeness of the language underscored the fact that I was undergoing culture-shock of the most intense kind. I had somehow made it known in the Nagoya train station that I was looking for the train to Takayama (Hida), itself one of the most traditional villages in all Japan and home of a village restoration from times considerably past. The little train was akin to the Budd Liners of North America. Two motorized passenger cars, crammed with Japanese heading to the mountains and the other scenic splendours of the area, slowed down shortly after departure. I was the only Westerner – *gaijin*, or foreigner – on board, and was left with a double seat all to myself.

Suddenly there was commotion in every direction, and as I glanced around the car, it was evident that all eyes were on me. The stares were good-natured, as the slight smiles and mischievous eyes made evident. Everyone else knew how to swing his or her seat around, and was busily at it. It sounded like a machine shop in full production.

I stood up, ducking to avoid the low ceiling overhead, and searched for the lever that would unlock my seat. I could not find it anywhere. I glanced around to see if others were still completing their change, a glance that I would come to use often in Japan to enable me to appear experienced when trying to behave more or less as the Japanese do. Do I eat the leaf that the beans are cooked on, however aesthetically beautiful it might be, or do I simply scrape the beans off and leave the crispy leaf as mere garnish? This time my glance around the car netted me no last-minute instruction about how the Japanese unlocked their seats. Instead, my glance revealed that every pair of eyes on board now showed intense merriment. It was a delicious moment when my confusion at why we were doing all this was met by their recognition of my inability to decipher either the need or the remedy.

In the briefest of instants, thirty passengers came rushing towards me to help me unlatch and then turn my seat. They did so with remarkable good humour, and apparent friendliness. Everyone wanted to help, to break the tension that had afforded a moment of shared delight, and when I laughed back so as to indicate that I shared in the humour of the awkward situation, a bond of some sort was created. The ice had melted, and in a limited way, to be sure, I was now a friend.

The train stopped, then began retracing its steps, and at a switch veered sharply to the right. We had reversed direction at the "Y"; and now we were on our way to Takayama, and rather than facing backwards we were once again facing fowards. Next occurred a remarkable series of events. A few minutes along our journey we passed by the usual rice paddies and charming farmhouses. In near unison the passengers intoned an appreciative "ahhhhhhh," and two Japanese rushed to my side to explain – in Japanese – that the cloth fish-kites on the flag-poles of each farm home indicated the number of boys in the family. Children's Day, a holiday taken very seriously in Japan, was but a few calendar days away. On the particular flag-pole that was being pointed out to me, *eight* kites were flying. It was evidently fertile soil, and my hosts were keen that I should share in the remarkable fact of a modern family with eight boys, and who knows how many girls. I will only note here that girls and women are not afforded the same grounds for celebration in Japan as are boys and men, and while this is one of my greatest regrets about Japanese culture, it remains a fact that is only ever so slowly changing. This was "boy's day," and while there is a "girl's day," there is little of the pomp, celebration, and expensive gift-buying that is accorded boys. Fish-kites fly for male children, but rarely if ever for girls.

Given my limited Japanese, it may well be asked how I was able to learn all this when I could only recognize a few words and was able to speak even fewer. One of Japan's greatest surprises and delights is that people are more often than not willing to take the time to try to communicate with others, and succeed in doing so by means of a series of gestures, pantomimes verging on charades, and the occasional recognizable word or phrase, in your language or theirs. This communication by gesture and facial expression was continued later that day when I arrived at a Japanese inn where absolutely no English was spoken. My maid-hostess sat me down on the tatami mats opposite her, and she giggled at the Japanese-English dictionary I held in my hands. She reached out, gently pushed my hands and book closed with her hands, and continued holding my hands in hers for a few seconds while somehow reassuring me that we would learn to speak with each other without the need of a dictionary. Then she withdrew her hands, and we laughed heartily at this remarkable situation. How funny it was that we were together, and that she would have to determine my needs while I was in her care. A bath? At what time? Dinner? What time? Was I able to eat Japanese food? What did I like? Would I be reading tonight? If so, she would fold out my futon and make certain that my lamp was on the floor by my head. The same routine had to be discussed for breakfast the next morning. The entire transaction still sticks in my mind as one of the true human treasures of my now several visits to Japan. We laughed at our situation, struggled with the language, gestured, laughed again, then tried once more. Rather than being an ordeal, it became a great event, and has remained a vital memory for me, and, I suspect, for her. We were creating a language of our own, and enjoying every moment of the search.

Meanwhile, the train sped along, and again without warning everyone was up and out of the seats, peering out of the windows opposite me. Someone tugged at my shoulder, and I was whisked to the closest window opposite. My guide pointed a finger as we passed by the most beautiful rapids and waterfall, which had carved a small but impressive gorge. Again the chorus of "ahhhhhs," except this time I joined in. This rushing from window-side to window-side of the coach continued over several hours, all the way to Takayama. We *appreciated* the natural beauty of rock formations, old forests, rivers and streams, and even individual trees gnarled with age. Several seasoned travellers along this route were able to give enough advance warning that a "natural treasure" was soon to be in view to allow all of us to rush to the correct

side, express our emotions, glance at one another with appreciative shared delight in our eyes, only to await the next treasure along the way.

HEIDEGGER ON DWELLING

I have already used the verb "to dwell" on several occasions, and it
is the work of Martin Heidegger that sharpens the meaning of this
term in surprising and rewarding ways. Heidegger is a controversial
figure in the history of modern thought at the best of times.[45] He is
also among the most obscure and complex. I intend, however, to take
from him specifically what relates to the process of sensitization that
I am attempting to depict, and thereby to expand the possibilities of
meaning-in-life that such enhanced valuational capacity provides.
Heidegger attempts a rethinking of the history of thought in the West
such that what is recovered is a renewed sense of the worth and
meaning of the world, and of our place in it, which can arise only if
we free ourselves and our world from the tyranny of technology.[46]
The more detailed way of going about this philosophically is to
attempt to reconstruct Heidegger's distinction between Being and
beings, but that would be an arduous journey. Instead, I will explore
Heidegger's reconstruction of language, at least to some small extent,
in order to indicate what it is to dwell rather than merely to live or
exist in the world.

BUILDING DWELLING
THINKING

In the remarkable, unusual, and insightful essay "Building Dwelling
Thinking" Heidegger attempts to recover the original – or more original – meaning of "to build" and "to dwell." His etymologies are
always idiosyncratic, hotly disputed, and in doubt, but the sense that
he wishes to take from them is usually both clear and important. I
choose to look through the etymologies and focus on the revision as
what is important. His struggle is with language itself, for he drains
words of their ordinary signification in order to discover a "trace"
from out of the past of the history of the word, a trace that has been
all but forgotten but might have been a major meaning or use at one
time. He muffles the overwhelming noise of the ordinary meaning
in order to free a background whisper. The whisper increases in his
hands to a roar and becomes *the* meaning of choice. Yet it may be
that the whisper was always a whisper and that it is Heidegger's
"roar" we are listening to, for his vision often overpowers both noise

and sound, foregrounding his own "melody" as the refined result of the allegedly historical search. His melody is overpowering, yet somehow one that we have heard before, a homely melody, a welcome tune.

We build dwellings, and we construct buildings. We do not dwell in our public buildings, in our "bridges and hangers, stadiums and power stations ... railway stations and highways, dams and market halls," but all of these do exist within the "domain" of our dwelling. They are a part of where we live and how we live. Indeed, we make use of them as part of our daily lives, and we often sleep within sight of them, in our dwellings. We often apply a homey phrase to describe our being comfortable in our work, or place of occupation. Thus we may say that even "the truck driver is at home on the highway, but he does not have his shelter there." At the same time, there is no guarantee that we actually dwell – are comfortably and rewardingly at home – in our dwellings. One can live in a dwelling without dwelling there. But both dwellings and constructions in which we do not dwell *ought* to be built with human dwelling in mind. They should all contribute to our sense of dwelling, to our neighbourhood and to our world. Indeed, to build appropriately is necessarily to build for dwelling. In this sense building ought not simply to contribute to dwelling; the building and the buildings ought themselves to *be* dwelling. To build properly *is* to dwell.[47]

The German word for "to build" is *bauen*, and its original meaning is, according to Heidegger, "to dwell." A trace of the word appears in the High German word for neighbour, as one who dwells nearby, the "near-dweller." A further trace of *bauen* is also found in the verb "to be." Hence, as we build, or dwell at home, or make our way to our place of work, or till the soil, we *are* dwelling: "The way in which you are and I am, the manner in which we humans *are* on the earth, is *buan*, dwelling," or rather, it ought to be the way we are in the world, and with each other. And "to dwell" has now swelled in signification, for Heidegger, to include "to cherish and protect, to preserve and care for, specifically to till the soil, and to cultivate the vine. Such building takes care – it tends the growth that ripens into its fruit of its own accord. Building in the sense of preserving and nurturing is not making anything."[48] The contrast drawn is between building and cultivating, except that the contrast is emphasized only to be removed, for both building and cultivating are to be thought of as acts of nurturing, preserving, cherishing, protecting, and caring for. All building is dwelling in this sense. Yet we have not yet fully defined "to dwell."

The Old Saxon *wuon* and the Gothic *wunian*, relatives of the German *bauen*, mean, as does *bauen*, "to remain, to stay in a place," but *wunian* also means "to be at peace, to be brought to peace, to remain in peace." And the Gothic word for peace, *friede*, means "to be free," and even "to be free from harm and danger," to be safeguarded, protected, and to be spared from any attack on one's way of being as well as on one's person. Thus, *"the fundamental character of dwelling is this sparing and preserving."*[49]

THE FOURFOLD

As though he had not yet done enough to fix the meanings of build and dwell by significantly altering their modern meanings, Heidegger next embarks upon a poetic, mythic description of what this dwelling upon the earth implies. It implies that we dwell (1) on the earth – the earth as the "serving bearer." And to dwell on the earth is to dwell (2) under the sky – the sky as the vast expanse and openness of those possibilities that exceed what is underfoot and what is imaginable. Earth and sky require (3) the "divinities" – the divinities as "the beckoning messengers of the godhead." The divinities both represent one's sense of the sacred and imply that what we know also *conceals* what is beyond our knowing. Knowing is always concealing, and truth – *alētheia* (the Greek term that Heidegger he adopts to mean "truth" as "clearing") – is itself revelatory of this fact, for *lēthē*, in Greek, means "concealing," while *alētheia* means "un-concealing." Therefore, the root component of "revealing" is "concealing," and in saying "reveal" one is thereby automatically saying or implying "concealment" as well. Our awareness of the gods and of truth is at once an approaching and a withdrawing, a revealing and a concealing, an understanding and a lack of comprehension, yielding recognition of that which is caught *and* that which has escaped the net of language and of thought altogether. To understand, even to understand "fully," as we say, is at the same time to come up empty-handed.

The fourth component (implied by the other three elements, as each of the three implies the others) is identified as (4) we "mortals" – mortals as human beings who exist on earth, under the sky, before the divinities, open to the awesome sacredness of things, knowing that what is revealed in the "clearing of understanding" is at the same time a concealing of the not-known. The result is a *fourfold*, the awareness of which is implied when one comprehends what Heidegger means by "to dwell." We dwell in the world, a

world that is a "serving bearer," that lets us be in such a way that
we can be ourselves, can find out who we are and what it means
to be ourselves, that allows us to decide who we shall be and how
and with whom we shall dwell. In return we must dwell on the
earth in such a way that we leave the world as it is, at least to the
greatest extent possible. We dwell in such a way that we "save" the
world, and "to save really means to set something free into its own
presencing."

To save the earth means neither to exploit it, nor even to wear it
out. In saving the earth one does not seek to master the earth or to
subjugate it. The implication of expressions such as "to master" and
"to subjugate" is still to *spoil* what is there, to alter it for one's own
purposes or in accordance with plans different from nature's way.
Similarly, we let the sky be, leaving the stars, moon, planets to be
enjoyed, the seasons to come and go as they do, the weather to
surprise us as it does: "Do not turn night into day nor day into a
harassed unrest."[50] I leave the reader to decide what our dwelling
under the sky is like at present. But it is obvious enough how things
are with the greenhouse effect, acid rain, and the radiation now getting through the deteriorating Van Allen belt, obvious as well how
far we have succeeded in preserving our days from being filled with
harassed unrest. To live in the awareness of the fourfold is to do far
more than to exist habitually, carelessly, heedlessly, unconcerned for
those species in danger and for the generations yet to be born. It is
to live as an integral part of the world that sustains us, under the
sky that nourishes and protects us as we save it and under the watch-
ful eyes of the divinities, the mysterious background to things, the
hidden causes of things, and the historical starting-point of our sense
of the sacredness and inherent worth of all things. In Heidegger's
picturesque phrasing,

In saving the earth, in receiving the sky, in awaiting the divinities, in initi-
ating mortals, dwelling occurs as the fourfold preservation of the fourfold.
To spare and preserve means: to take under our care, to look after the fourfold
in its presencing. What we take under our care must be kept safe. But if
dwelling preserves the fourfold, where does it keep the fourfold's nature?
How do mortals make their dwelling such a preserving?[51]

The answer is that we preserve the fourfold by incorporating it into
our building, and into our cultivating. We *live* the fourfold, and give
witness to the four in whatever it is that we give expression to. Heidegger's example of such living, dwelling, and building is that of a
bridge.

THE BRIDGE

Economic man asks how little we can build the bridge for and still meet minimum requirements of safety, design, and so on. Pragmatic man views the bridge as a means of getting over the river in a convenient and time-saving way. Technological man wishes to find ways of erecting the bridge quickly and simply. The Heideggerian conceives of the bridge as an expression of and a preserver of the fourfold (earth, sky, the gods, and mortals). The bridge does not simply provide a convenient way across the river by connecting the banks on either side. Rather, the bridge brings to awareness the existence of the two banks of the river, each with its own difference, yet now tied together by the bridge, which brings the banks and the river into a single "neighbourhood." "The bridge *gathers* the earth as landscape around the stream. Thus it guides and attends the stream through the meadows. Resting upright in the stream's bed, the bridge-piers bear the swing of the arches that leave the stream's waters to run their course."[52] It does not ignore the sky but is set against it, and it dwells differently in each of the seasons of weather.

The awareness of divinities is historically attested to by ceremonies of prayer and thanks at the dedication of the bridge, by the statues and plaques that we erect, often (it is hoped) to keep the bridge and its travellers safe from harm. Whatever the case, a finished bridge, a finished building, if we care about it at all, is thought of in special ways, for we think of it as contributing to the quality of our lives and of our neighbourhoods – unless it is conceived of as mere instrument of production or convenience. The bridge "gathers" the fourfold, is a site for the fourfold, is an expression of the fourfold, and reminds us of the fourfold every time we ride over it, walk over or under it, or look up at it. The site is a space, a location where the fourfold itself can appear. The bridge is on a site, but it is also itself a site, a location wherein or whereon we can travel from one side to the other, but also a site for the occurrence of the fourfold amidst our dwelling. Christo, by wrapping a bridge on the Seine, then, emphasizes the fourfold, as the Pont Neuf is wrapped (veiled) and later unwrapped (unveiled) in thousands of metres of gauze. The "neighbours" of the bridge say that they see it differently because of the wrapping and unwrapping, and never ignore it or merely use it again.

The bridge is a reminder of and an instance of the occurrence of the fourfold. The bridge dwells, and it dwells in our neighbourhood, and our neighbourhood dwells more fully because of the bridge, and the bridge could not dwell unless it dwelt in a neighbourhood, and together our neighbourhood, our dwelling, our land, our river, our buildings, our trees and flowers, and our bridge dwell in our sky in such a way as to enhance one another. There is enrichment rather than impoverishment. To build is to build for the sake of dwelling, and to dwell is to be mindful of the fourfold, of the effect of what we do on the quality of the neighbourhood, greater and smaller, and of the feelings we have for the things already there and yet to be built, for we are savers, preservers, and nourishers. For we too are *gatherers* of the fourfold, and we ought to express this in our living, our dwelling, our building, and our cultivating.

To nurture is to attend to something, to focus on its needs and requirements, its life-way, and to "improve" on that way only through sensitive *listening* to that which is being tended. Otherwise, the alteration will not be a preserving but a warping, a distorting, a destructive killing of the spirit of the thing, if not its actual killing. A listener is one who can meditate, who is able to contemplate "the meaning which reigns in everything that is" – that is, the fourfold.[53] To be a listener is to apprehend things in a more wholesome, a more holistic way, and no longer "only in a technical way."[54] To be meditative is to be "open to the mystery," open to the possibility of dwelling in the world rather than using it, or attacking it, or controlling it only. Not that technology is bad, or unnecessary:

It would be foolish to attack technology blindly. It would be shortsighted to condemn it as the work of the devil. We depend on technical devices; they even challenge us to ever greater advances. But suddenly and unaware we find ourselves so firmly shackled to these technical devices that we fall into bondage to them.

Still we can act otherwise. We can use technical devices, and yet with proper use also keep ourselves so free of them, that we may let go of them any time. We can use technical devices as they ought to be used, and also let them alone as something which does not affect our inner and real core. We can affirm the unavoidable use of technical devices, and also deny them the right to dominate us, and so to warp, confuse, and lay waste our nature.[55]

THE GROUND OF VALUATION

In spite of the several attempts to carve out an understanding of how meaning in life may be gained, how the phrase is to be understood, notwithstanding the analysis of valuation suggested, it may still be asked, "But why must I care about the subtleties of bridges, of dwelling, and of the nurture of the environment? It is a good story that you tell, but I think meaning in life is simply a matter of getting what you can out of it, and even at that we have to play it by ear." The challenge of such a response is twofold. First, it questions the particular value preferences that I have articulated and accepted, and second, it expresses implicit doubt about whether there is any basis for choosing one value over another, beyond one's own subjective preferences, and these are as variable as one's own condition and mood, and the changeability of the world.

The first question can only be dealt with by taking a lengthy journey through literature, history, politics, psychology, philosophy, art, religion, etc., in an attempt to expose the questioner to the factual issues that pertain and to the valuational possibilities of which s/he may not previously have had any clear knowledge. One learns to appreciate a walk in the woods by walking in the woods, preferably with someone who is able to enhance the walk by making one aware of the points of interest and delight all along the way. Similarly, Martin Heidegger cannot logically demonstrate that we ought to care about dwelling in the world, but only that dwelling is defined as a certain state of living, feeling, and thinking, which we must then contrast with our present way. Then we must choose. Even then, of course, it is not only a choice between the one and the other, but we retain the option(s) of modifying our present stance by incorporating within it certain aspects of Heidegger's view, or of some other.

The questioning of the "objective" basis for choosing any value over any other is a far more difficult issue to deal with. Perhaps nothing is really valuable. Perhaps there is no way of legitimately deciding that one value is genuinely preferable to another. In more traditional terms, if we live at a time when we have abandoned belief in a God who *reveals* to us what is valuable and what is not, and have abandoned as well any suggestion that the cosmos itself has a purpose and that we are a significant part of it, then what we choose is arbitrary, empty, groundless, a human burp in the face of the meaningless flow of time, life, and death. Even an appeal to "human nature" leaves the question totally unanswered, for even if it is the case that most of us value as we do *in common*, it can still be asked whether we do so because of our conditioning, and whether agreement in valuation, even if an innate fact of our physical and psychological being, achieves anything more than a mass opinion, where previously there was only personal opinion. Opinion it still is, and opinion, whether individual or mass, is in itself *groundless*. As in Albert Camus' modern rendering of the *Myth of Sisyphus*,[56] all human activity and valuation rests on no foundation whatsoever but floats on the breezes of taste, circumstance, peer pressure, and equally groundless law and political authority of whatever kind.

THE MYTH OF SISYPHUS

In this reworking of an ancient Greek myth, Sisyphus is a king of Corinth condemned by the gods to push a great rock endlessly up a steep mountain in Hades. With bleeding hands, muscles screaming with fatigue, and sweat running from every pore, he shoulders the rock to the mountain top again and again, and each time stands aside to watch his burden tumble back down the slope to the very bottom, where his labour began. He trudges back down the slope, only to be required to begin the painful ascent all over again. That is his lot, and it symbolizes the human situation generally. One never gets to the top, to one's destination, to a theory that makes so much sense that one knows that it will stand forever. Instead, all theories, all values, all reforms, all revolutions, all change, and all actions are built on the shifting sands of custom and opinion, and the winds of doubt and new circumstances and considerations are always blowing, always arising.

Unlike the rest of us, Sisyphus is condemned to an eternity of struggle and cannot find a way out. With power, conviction, determination, and courage, however, Sisyphus and Camus do find a way *in*. For if you can recognize the futility of life and its goals and at the same time consciously choose to live your life with vigour and undaunted determination, then you will have created a path worthy of your strength and talents; you will have the only happiness available to human beings who have confronted the experience of the absurd, as Camus refers to it.[57] You will hope without the help of external or transcendental reassurances, act without guarantee of external guidance, and love without the promise of fulfilment or constancy. In this you will fare exactly as did Sisyphus, for while you are not eternally condemned by the gods, you are condemned by the lifelong human situation, to accept inadequate or ill-fitting answers to life's most important questions. Choices will need to be made over and over again, with no hope of ever "getting it right," as we were taught unthinkingly to hope in school.

NIETZSCHE AND RECURRENCE

An even more pessimistic image is provided by Frederich Nietzsche in his "Myth of the Eternal Recurrence."[58] Imagine that the reincarnational theory is correct, except that what recurs is exactly the same world, the same you and the same me, the same mistakes and successes, preferences, and deaths. Everything must happen again exactly and in every way as it happened before, as in this life. And it will happen again and again, an infinite number of times in the infinity of eternity. Is the eternal repeating of every detail of your present life a cause for slumping regret or for bounding joy? Nietzsche's "yea-saying"[59] affirms with gusto that we can live in a world where "God is dead" and values are groundless by confronting the vista of possibility and the test of endless repetition. It is the ultimate in human maturation, for we are no longer awaiting parental, societal, spousal, or divine "permission" to do as we do. We are now on our own – utterly and completely on our own – to decide what is worthwhile and how we shall live our lives. Values arise from within us by dint of will silhouetted against a background of endless possibility and the *test* of endless repetition.

In fact the test is a profound one, for if you can choose to do as you are doing even though it would be to choose this same action, or person, or feeling over and over again throughout eternity, then you can say that it is the most worthwhile act for the here and now. When things are at their best, you *know* that you would do it again, even against odds, *for the worthwhileness is immediately apparent to you. It is an experience or a choice made that has yielded experiences of unmistakable and indubitable intrinsic value!* Its indubitability is contained within itself, as experience. The experience is not just any sort of experience, of course, for it is experience of value, of value so evident, so compelling, so rich in results that you would without a doubt choose it again.

The very groundlessness of valuation has revealed the rock-bottom inner ground of experiential immediacy. I think we are here at the limit of reasoning. Something is found valuable because we are capable of so finding it immediately and within experience. It may be, of course, that we have to forego this experience because it is not the right time or place, or because it will do someone else great harm were we to seek it just now, or because we are temporarily satiated and for a while we choose to experience or do something else. The rock-bottom "ground" is personal experience, indubitable in the having of it, and yet, as C.I. Lewis remarks, unless we were more or less the same in our likings and dislikings, in our valuings and disvaluings, we could never do each other any great harm or good.[60] Even on the personal level, Stace comments, "we are so constituted that we tend always to value certain things in roughly the same way, although even then there will be a shifting, changing, ebbing and flowing of the valuational feelings."[61]

As variable as the term "normal" is, and as open to oppressive misuse, it does seem that we do value a great many things in common. Lest this be grounds for oppressive legislation and force, however, let it also be noted that we do value quite different things, and differently at one stage of life than at another. In valuation it is important to encourage *difference*, if only to avoid the infectious stench of stale and rotting values of a time long past. Values change, just as the body of knowledge available to us changes, and it is imperative that we be not only open to the changes as they creep up on us but actually strive to play an important role in such valuational change. We live by changing our cells every few years, and we grow in spurts and stages throughout life. Living *well* requires similar change and exploration.

THE OPEN-ENDEDNESS OF MEANING AND VALUATION

If neither God nor the cosmos are assumed guarantors of objective values and the "right" meaning and purposes in our living, then it is up to us to learn to value in such a way as to increase the amount of intrinsic value in our lives. Our lives will be richly meaningful lives to the extent that we find the living of them, day by day, to be, on the whole, intrinsically valuable. And we know that we are in trouble when we cease to find our lives intrinsically valuable. I think it is also the case that what affords us a great deal of the intrinsic value in our lives is the result of our direct concern with the welfare and extent of intrinsic value in the lives of others. More about this later. If sources of intrinsic-value experience are to be sought, then something must be said about what sort of attitudinal stance is most conducive to the occasioning of such experiences. How does one prepare to be open to intrinsic values? What approach is taken by those who find their lives filled with meaning and the world itself filled with value? While I do not think that there is a single prescription that can even begin to do justice to these questions, I think one can sketch an attitudinal stance that does, for many, serve to render them more accessible to value possibilities.

The achievement of meaning in life is akin to the gaining of knowledge: neither can be simply handed on; we all must gain each for ownselves. Second-hand facts are what serve to make much of education dull and irrelevant. Vital education is education that poses questions and then seeks to grapple with those questions with whatever information and insight is available. The result is a response that engages us, for we begin with a genuine doubt and then seek an answer of some sort. Philosophical questions are even more to the point here, for in asking a question about the nature of reality, or about what the right thing to do is in a specific case, one does not expect a final authoritative answer, only a wise attempt at a solution that is the best of those envisaged.

One does the best one can, which, I would suggest, is the way we *do* live our valuational lives. We do not know what is absolutely best, by and large, but we do think we know what we ought to do, at least in most cases. Much of our ethical life is lived unthinkingly, for we do as we do by habit, custom, tradition, or because we have previously thought through the pros and cons of similar situations. We act on the basis of the best evidence available to us, and we rarely claim more, unless we are basing our claims on divine authority, law, or simply intend to emphasize the worth and importance of a decision. I think it is the same with meaning in life and intrinsic valuation. We must somehow be able to decide what is valuable at this moment while at the same time remaining open to future revisions in our valuational pattern. We revise because the old valuation no longer satisfies, or because the new one satisfies more fully, or is instrumental to other experiences that are of greater intrinsic value, and so on. This willingness to revise, to be open to new possibilities of value, is for me a key to life and value enhancement.

CHAPTER TWO

Kohlberg's Stage Seven

A MATTER OF HEART

I was the guest of a recently retired chief executive officer of a Japanese automobile manufacturing company. Without my asking, his daughter had responded to my correspondence on behalf of the family and had offered to meet me at the Tokyo airport and then take me to my guest apartment in their apartment building in Tokyo. I would stay there for two nights, until my room elsewhere in that gigantic city was available. I was greeted with warmth by the daughter, and later by her mother and father, whom I had not seen since their return home after nearly a decade in Toronto. I settled in, showered, and was then ushered upstairs to the apartment of my host family. We shared a magnificently prepared and graciously served meal, and then adjourned to the living-room – Western-style – where we sipped tea and liqueurs, and caught up on what had happened in our lives over the past months.

"We have talked often, and at considerable length, about what sort of present from us would mean the most to you. Of course we thought of a ticket to a Noh play, or a day at the Kabuki theatre, or even an evening at the once-a-year festival of the Geisha." I was touched by the care with which they had tried to imagine what I would most like to see or do, and recalled Lawrence Kohlberg's emphasis on "moral musical chairs" as an effective learning technique for assisting children in becoming sensitive to the needs and aspirations of others.

"But none of these seemed quite right. Please do not misunderstand. If you wish to attend any or all of these events, you should know that you need only say the word, and we will arrange it, and even go with you if you wish." In fact they did take me to each of these performances in the weeks ahead, as their guest, and to several others as well. Yet they had decided that none of these seemed quite what would likely be of most value to me, or so it seemed to them.

"It was just a few days ago that we found what we think is just the right gift for you," said my host. "We had to ask ourselves what was most difficult for us to do on our own when we first arrived in North America. Several tentative possibilities occured to us but were rejected. Then we all agreed that shopping for family and friends was the most difficult. We know how important it is to find just the right gifts, and to be able to do so within your personal budget. Not only do you have to know where to find what it is that you are looking for, but you need to know where the best examples and widest variety are to be found. Finally, you will want to find these items at the lowest prices." I thought of the hours I might spend looking for a Japanese sword for my son, or a Geisha doll in a glass case for my daughter. Then there were the pearl earrings, the camera, and the kitchen knives ...

The next morning the family car was waiting for me shortly after nine a.m. Both mother and daughter had decided to come, and as experienced shoppers they showed me a day that left me both exhausted and exhilarated. It included both whirlwind shopping and a leisurely and secluded lunch. They had been able to put themselves in my shoes, not only saving me time and frustration but turning a full day of shopping into one of intense pleasure and cultural exploration. Of the gifts they might have given, this was the least flashy and ostentatious but clearly among the most important and genuine of the many acts of hospitality I enjoyed while in Japan. It came from the heart, and was an everyday example of *kokoro*: acting from one's heart and mind out of concern for the other person, and with no thought of gain or personal reward.

THE MORAL STAGES

The late Lawrence Kohlberg was a developmental psychologist whose work in the field of moral education revolutionized our way of approaching the teaching of ethics and values in the schools and beyond. Basing his research on the work of the Swiss psychologist Jean Piaget and the American philosopher John Dewey, Kohlberg extended Piaget's work in particular to include a rather precise and sequential series of developmental stages in moral thinking, beginning with the egocentric viewpoint of the young child and extending all the way to the vision of the saint and the ethical reformer. From a philosopher's perspective, his findings, while richly suggestive, are far from definitive. Not only can we raise questions about the nature and composition of his longitudinal data base (his original subjects were all boys), but we can query whether the "stages" of development turn out to be what they are because of a male, white, Western (etc.) cultural bias that unintentionally "cooked" the "evidence" into this specific pattern of understanding.[1] Furthermore, there are serious questions to be asked about the status of the stages themselves. Are they anything more than empirical generalizations about how most American boys think and develop, or are they normative descriptions of how we *ought* to think and develop, stage by stage, always being pulled by the "carrot" of the highest possible stage of development? Again, are the stages so clear and distinct that we can classify children especially as being at one stage of awareness rather than at several stages at once, from moment to moment?

Carol Gilligan, a former associate of Kohlberg's, urges us to develop this point still further. If a specific group or race or culture or sex continually ranks lower in stage development, is it because its members are actually less developed, or are they merely different? If different, is the reason that they do not do well on the Kohlberg scale merely the result of a bias in favour of specifically male development inherent in the original research, which consisted of longitudinal studies of eighty-four American *boys*? To conclude that the stage-results of eighty-four boys are universally applicable to all other cultures and races as well as to females is to assume a great deal. Gilligan writes: "Prominent among those who thus appear to be deficient in moral development when measured by Kohlberg's scale are women, whose judgments seem to exemplify the third stage of his six-stage sequence. At this stage morality is conceived in interpersonal terms and goodness is equated with helping and pleasing others. This conception of goodness is considered by Kohlberg ... to be functional in the lives of mature women insofar as their lives take place in the home."[2]

Gilligan is rightly concerned that "the very traits that traditionally have defined the 'goodness' of women, their care for and sensitivity to the needs of others, are those that mark them as deficient in moral development."[3] In Kohlberg's work, the highest stages of moral development are defined in terms of the more mature awareness of rights and justice rather than in terms of caring for and about the needs of others. Such a view makes it inescapable that women will rank low. That they should rank *lower* than do men may be the result of the cultural emphasis on justice reasoning for boys and men, and the result of the Oedipal phase in male development, which demands separation from the parents and the acceptance of individuation and personal responsibility. Girls do not individuate by *rejecting* the parent of the same sex in particular but by accepting the mother as a more nearly mature model, with whom they are now increasingly able to enter into a more deeply caring relationship. This is the ideal, of course, and not always the case. But notice how the male "advantage" turns to disadvantage from the perspective of the caring and interrelated viewpoint of the developing woman: "If aggression is tied, as women perceive, to the fracture of human connection, then the activities of care, as their fantasies suggest, are the activities that make the social world safe, by avoiding isolation and preventing aggression rather than by seeking rules to limit its extent."[4]

In a world that is excessively violent and has been so as far back as the history of male domination is recorded, then it may be the case that the allegedly "higher" stages are actually "lower" and that an ethic of caring rather than an ethic of justice and rights is called for. If men mature in aggressive isolation and rejection, it may be that they need to compensate for this tendency by being encouraged to rediscover relatedness and to temper aggression and violence by the development of a sense of caring relatedness. Be that as it may with respect to Kohlberg's stage sequence, such questions only confirm my suspicion that a theoretical position should not be held too tightly and definitively. Rather, it should be held loosely and as but a guide to fresh insight, which will need to be considered again and again over time in order to be evaluate critically, modified, and incorporated it into the initial position.

Kohlberg's theory of moral reasoning describes moral development as the movement through six distinct stages of understanding, with the later stage being more "adequate" or "better" than the earlier. The sixth or most adequate stage is not reached by all people, or even by most, but serves as the norm by which the earlier stages are judged less adequate. Richard S. Peters provides a succinct summary of Kohlberg's six stages:

Children start by seeing rules as dependent upon power and external compulsion [stage one]; then they see them as instrumental to rewards and to the satisfaction of their needs [stage two]; then as ways of obtaining social approval and esteem [stage three, expanding to stage four as one moves from interpersonal relations as one's focus to the *system*, e.g. one's country]; then as upholding some ideal order [stage five], and finally as articulations of social principles necessary to living together with others – especially that of justice [stage six].[5]

Thus, when children or adults are asked to decide and explain whether it would be right to tell on a friend in specific circumstances, they will respond with reasons that reveal characteristic elements habitually associated with a specific stage of moral reasoning. They will emphasize punishment or reward at one stage, be concerned about their reputations at another, and only at a later stage – which they may never reach – concern themselves with whether it would be right for everyone to "snitch" on friends (or on anyone), or with how they would react if someone did or did not snitch on them.

The six stages are taken by Kohlberg to be *inductive generalizations*. They do not arise from a theory of human nature, he tells us, but are empirical abstractions.[6] As inductive generalizations, the characteristics of a stage cluster together as they do repeatedly and predictably in the actual reasoning patterns of actual people interviewed by Kohlberg and his associates. Each stage is a structured whole, or a closely organized system of thought, and each may be considered a separate moral philosophy, a distinct view of the social-moral world.[7] The stages are "hierarchical integrations," such that the next highest stage "includes or comprehends within it lower-stage thinking," but the higher stage is opted for because there is a "tendency to function at or prefer the highest stage available."[8] Stage six is the norm for the other five stages and the standard by means of which they are ranked.

Central to the theory is the evaluative grounding of the norm, i.e. the evidence supporting the claim that stage six is the norm of morality and that the process of development along the stage-sequence is true moral development as it ought to be, rather than merely as it happens to be. Put more simply still, we need to be shown that Kohlberg's description of empirically observed reasoning about moral problems is also normatively prescriptive. We need to be convinced that the "is" of human moral development is also its "ought."

How do you "establish" your norm, your "ought"? I think the answer is that you select, from the plethora of descriptions of which you are aware, those that you take to be "better," or "conducive of more positive value," or more "morally adequate," or that make most sense. You try to *support* your choices, as best you can, by telling the "whole story," or by providing an account of your *horizon of understanding* and not just a small part of that horizonal perspective. Whether you are a utilitarian or a formalist, a Christian or a Buddhist, you are only able to explain the decision you have taken when you describe to another the entire broad context that encompasses the collection of value-positions you hold. If pressed, you must present your outlook on the world as fully as you can, including a description of your *way of life* as a valuing, feeling, acting, and aspiring human being. And this is not merely to provide an intellectual account of your beliefs and your claims to knowledge. R.M. Hare's description of this procedure is worth attending to: "If pressed to justify a decision completely, we have to give a complete specification of the way of life of which it is a part ... if the inquirer still goes on asking 'But why *should* I live like that?' then there is no further answer to give him, because we have already, *ex hypothesi*, said everything that could be included in this further answer."[9]

WHY SHOULD YOU BE MORAL?

When Kohlberg asks, and sets about to answer, why it is that you should be just, or why you should be moral in the first place, or why you ought to care about anything at all, he moves to a postulated "stage seven" of his schema. He does so, I think, precisely because this stage serves as the normative ground and standard of his entire system. It is his whole story, his horizonal perspective, without which none of the separate stages and moral obligations seem to have a clear point or authority. Stage seven is the *bedrock* of normativity, and this is true even of stage-six justice. Stage seven constitutes the selection of an "is" cluster of values and ethical norms – more broadly, a way of living in the world – as its "ought," its ideal. Stage-seven thinking *is* the description of the broader context that serves as the grounding, the justification, and the motivation for adhering to any of the moral demands required by the earlier stages as you passed through them. It is faith-like in that it provides meaning, purpose, direction, and as much of a guarantee as human beings are capable of achieving. Faith carries the meaning "This is my understanding of the ultimate sense of things, and if this makes little or no sense to you, then you will be unable to understand why I think and act and value as I do." At the same time, to reveal to another your most comprehensive sense of things is to make clear what it is that you have faith in, and explains why you think, act, and value as you do. The word "faith" has a religious association, however, which "horizonal perspective" or "whole story" need not have.

STAGE SEVEN AS HORIZON

Whereas the first six stages describe "moral" development, stage seven goes beyond all this to provide additional metaphysical and religious assumptions necessary to help answer questions that morality itself cannot answer, and to motivate by making morality part of the meaningful whole of understanding that constitutes the "whole story." What Kohlberg calls "ethics" includes a much broader range of problems than does the justice reasoning of the higher stages (five and six) of "morality." The term "ethics," for Kohlberg, refers to a faith-perspective, a way of life, an entire horizon of knowing, feeling, and willing, whereas "morality" refers only to specific ways of reasoning about perceived moral obligation alone. Whatever whole story or world-view is chosen, whether theistic, pantheistic, or humanistic, what is necessarily included is an intuitive or direct grasping of the meaningfulness of your life and of the worthwhileness of the whole of things, of the cosmos. Once you have found "support in reality, in nature taken as a whole or in the ground of nature, for acting according to universal moral principles," then you are freed from the paralysis of knowing what reason requires of you but not caring about it, or knowing what reason says but not doing it. The assumptions of ethics give meaning to what you do and tend to assure you that what you do is both worthwhile in the total scheme of things and in accordance with the way things really are. By contrast, "the experience of despair calls into question the fundamental worth of human activity,"[10] and the assumptions of ethics place us in harmony with the order, unity, and graspable structure of the whole of which we are a part.

It should not be assumed, however, that this distinction between ethics and morality is ubiquitous in the literature. In fact it is quite idiosyncratic, and there may be considerable insight gained from asking why Kohlberg conceives of morality in this specialized way. Part of the answer might be found in the work of James Fowler, another associate of Kohlberg's. Fowler has applied the stage-developmental schema to religion and has found stages of religious development that are more or less parallel with the stages of moral development offered by Kohlberg. You might suppose that a stage-one moral thinker would have as her or his "whole story" a stage-one religion of authority based on punishment and reward. It is not the case, however, as Kohlberg emphasizes, that you must be moral and religious at the *same* stage-level. Nevertheless, every stage has a stage seven or whole story that supports, explains, and justifies the moral stage-thinking that you reason and act in accordance with. Therefore, as I have argued elsewhere, stage seven may not be simply a separate stage at all, but the ultimate (for Kohlberg) whole story of meta-physical/religious/valuational assumptions that forms the horizon or perspective from which the individual judgments of your stage-perspective, or way of living in the world, make sense.[11]

But then each and every stage has its whole story. It is just that some whole stories are more restricted, less encompassing, less adequate, than later or higher ones. Otherwise, the structure of stage seven appears to be a tag-on to Kohlberg's system rather than the limit or pinnacle of justification and explanation of the previous stages. It should be noted, however, that because Kohlberg limits himself to moral *reasoning* in his account of the first six stages, he does not make explicit the affective, caring, valuational, spiritual, and (possibly) religious dimensions of the stages *until* he provides his account of stage seven. Yet the first six stages do at least imply a perspectival or horizonal context – that is, a system of assumptions and principles by which you select from the data of experience and come to see the world, others, and yourself the way you do. Stage one is a philosophy of life, a metaphysical system, however ragged and simplistic it may be. Of course, the holder may not be able to articulate or even to understand the assumptions implied by the perspective, but this can happen to greater or lesser extent at any stage. All stages have stage-seven-like components on which they rest, but these components are rarely sufficient for mature analysis; they are regularly implicit rather than explicit, and often unsystematic, inconsistent, and incomplete.

In different words, if stage seven provides the context, broader justification for, and widest understanding of the place and nature of morality, then any and all other metaphysical, religious, and broadly philosophical systems that might be employed will be measured against this broadest and most adequate stage-seven perspective. Not all systems are equally sound or acceptable. Some systems are simplistic, egocentric in focus, easily caught in contradictions, militantly irrational and closed, and sometimes even "immoral" when judged from the perspective of a higher-stage morality, or of some other moral perspective. These and all other candidate-systems must be judged by the requirements of whatever moral situation has emerged, and are to be rejected if found wanting.

Of course, you would only be able to discern that your moral vision was inadequate if you had already begun the move to the perspective of the next higher stage, from which it begins to be seen that the existing moral perspective is inadequate. While seeing things through the "spectacles" of the existing stage, all seems fine, and the alleged inadequacies do not appear. One of Kohlberg's strategies for encouraging the move to a higher stage of moral awareness is to point out the inadequacies of the present-stage way of thinking morally by means of depicting the moral dilemmas resulting from it. You cannot continue to hit the child in the sandbox with your shovel, for the unsatisfactory result will be that you soon discover that no one will play with you. It is necessary to think beyond the limits of your own wants and begin to consider the needs of others, even if only far enough to get the instrumental result that you want: companionship. But if you encounter little or no difficulty with your moral perspective, then you rest satisfied with the way things are. There is no need to look beyond the present stage of moral understanding.

In any case, each stage-viewpoint is, at least in principle, able to justify itself as an adequate and acceptable outlook on others and the world. In this sense, every stage has its own stage seven, or comprehensive account of why you, who think and act that way, do so. It is the broader rationale for thinking and acting as you do. As Fowler writes,

Every moral perspective, at whatever level of development, is anchored in a broader system of belief and loyalties. Every principle of moral action serves some centre of value. Even the appeal to autonomy, rationality, and universality as justifications for Stage 6 morality are not made *prior* to faith. Rather they are expressions of faith – expressions of trust in, and loyalty to, the valued attributes of autonomy and rationality and the valued ideal of a universal commonwealth of being. There is, I believe, always a faith framework encompassing and supporting the motive to be moral and the exercise of moral logic.[12]

Fowler assumes that "we require meaning," and that in order to gain it "we must have some grasp on the big picture." Tying this sense of the big picture to *imagination*, he provides a series of alternate labels and descriptions for what I have been calling one's horizon, or the whole story. In addition to tying it to the imagination, he also further specifies that imagination, when used in this whole-story sense, is imagination as faith. Thus, "faith forms a way of seeing our everyday life in relation to holistic images of what we may call the *ultimate environment.*" If the term "ultimate environment" is too formidable, "*comprehensive frame of meaning that both holds and grows out of the most transcendent centres of value and power to which our faith gives allegiance*" is an alternative. Fowler recounts that early on in his teaching career he had described "the big picture" idea in words similar to the above. It was evident that he was not getting his idea across, and after several students succeeded at best in recounting only aspects of Fowler's conception of the "ultimate environment," a retiring woman student summarized the idea as follows:

"I think you mean, Professor, our images of that largest theatre of action in which we act out our lives. You might say that our images of the ultimate environment determine the ways we arrange the scenery and grasp the plot in our lives' plays." And then she added, "Furthermore, our images of the ultimate environment change as we move through life. They expand and grow, and the plots get blown open or have to be linked in with other plots."[13]

This simple account is a helpful description of horizonal or whole-story notions, and the student's emphatic stress on the changeability of such "ultimate" images is especially to be underscored. You hold a stage seven in the way that you do not normally hold a horizon, I suppose – horizons we just have; they are like lenses that we look through, and it is difficult, and takes the utmost effort to turn our glance inward in such a way as to be able to see the otherwise transparent and unseen lenses – namely as an "ideal" whole story, a story that we find to be more adequate than any other to date. Knowing that it, too, will undergo change, however, will likely cause us to hold it with less obstinacy, less unwillingness to change it for a better, although it will be held none the less firmly and passionately in the meantime.

Stage seven is, therefore, stage-like in this regard, and yet it does not function in nearly the same way as do Kohlberg's other six stages. Rather, it is foundational in that it serves as the ground, not only of stage six but of all valuation whatsoever. Yet there is nothing to preclude a future development of a stage eight or a stage nine. Nevertheless, for right now, at least for Kohlberg, stage seven is as comprehensive a perspective as is available, and so serves as *the* normative, most encompassing, and ultimate source of all moral motivation. Without stage seven, there is a tenuousness about all valuation, moral or otherwise, in that you can easily ignore all value requirements by simply asking why you should bother or care about such things. An example of such an evaporation of moral motivation, or caring, is the mental crisis of the brilliant and steadfastly socially minded John Stuart Mill, who, at the age of nineteen, in 1826, feared the existential vacuum that overwhelmed him:

I was in a dull state of nerves, such as everybody is occasionally liable to; unsusceptible to enjoyment or pleasurable excitement; one of those moods when what is pleasure at other times, becomes insipid or indifferent ... In this frame of mind it occurred to me to put the question directly to myself: "Suppose that all your objects in life were realized; that all the changes in institutions and opinions which you are looking forward to, could be completely effected at this very instant; would this be a great joy and happiness to you?" And an irrepressible self-consciousness distinctly answered, "No!" At this my heart sank within me; the whole foundation on which my life was constructed fell down.[14]

Fowler remarks that such life crises often result in growth and development in faith, for "each of these brings disequilibrium and requires changes in our ways of seeing and being in faith." It is even more to the point, given the Mill example above, to read Fowler's critique of Kohlberg for not having "conceptually separated cognition or knowing from emotion or affection."[15] Mill was brought up rather as a psychological experiment by his father, James Mill, who wished to demonstrate that children could learn far more than they seem capable of, and at far earlier ages than was thought. While other children were playing tag and hide-and-go-seek, John Stuart was learning Greek, geometry, political theory, philosophy, and logic and mathematics. Never having had a childhood, as he later remarks, the feeling side of him did not keep pace with his enormous intellectual potential. In fact, it quite withered.

Mill reflected deeply upon his situation and, finding no way out of his unfeeling state, sought its cause. With the same honesty with which he first admitted his uncaringness with respect to his highest ideals concerning the improvement of mankind, he now maintained that "the habit of analysis has a tendency to wear away the feelings." Feelings are the "natural complements and correctives" for reasoning. He was but partially equipped to undertake the tasks he had set for himself: "I was thus, as I said to myself, left stranded at the commencement of my voyage, with a well-equipped ship and a rudder, but no sail; without any real desire for the ends which I had been so carefully fitted out to work for; no delight in virtue, or the general good, but also just as little in anything else. The fountains of vanity and ambition seemed to have dried up within me, as completely as those of benevolence." From this point in his life onwards Mill placed emphasis on creating a balance among the needs of the developing individual and affirmed that "the cultivation of the feelings became one of the cardinal points in my ethical and philosophical creed."[16]

To know that something would contribute to a better state of affairs does not necessarily imply that you actually care about it, or will do what you can to bring it about. To value something does imply that you will seek to have it, or to bring about a desired state of affairs, all other things being equal, and assuming that something else is not more desirable. But since stage-seven thinking includes the knowing, feeling, and willing aspects of the human person, to know what is best is to do it, for knowing that something would be better includes valuing it and acting to bring it about. To this extent Plato was right in maintaining that to know the good is to do the good. This follows only if you include in "knowing" that something is the case both caring about it and being already committed to bringing it about to the extent that you can. Platonic and Kohlbergian knowing include spirited caring and effective willing.

THE "MORE" IN ETHICS

That there is more to ethics than justice reasoning is particularly evident in Kohlberg's stage-seven conception, as I shall describe shortly. But there is more to ethics than *reasoning* even at stage one, else you would not value and act as a more or less whole human person. That is to say, even at the stage-three level of nice boy, good girl peer-group orientation, you care about being accepted, and are highly motivated to dress and act as does everyone else within the group. At the level of stage seven, the something more might be expressed quite simply as the search for greater fulfilment, or for life's higher meaning, or for the *summum bonum*, or for wisdom, or for a holistic way of being in the world. It includes group-oriented thinking and concern but stretches far, far beyond its confines to the cosmos as the most inclusive conceivable whole.

EXAMPLES OF STAGE SEVEN

The chief examples of stage-seven thinking offered by Kohlberg are four in number: the Roman emperor and philosopher Marcus Aurelius; a contemporary American woman, Andrea Simpson, who became involved as a lay person with the treatment of mentally ill patients in hospital; the seventeenth-century philosopher Spinoza; and the twentieth-century Roman Catholic theologian Teilhard de Chardin. All of them are described by Kohlberg as belonging to the *mystical* tradition. I think it unnecessary for Kohlberg technically to label all four in this way, for I suspect that he only intends the term "mystical" in a rough-and-ready way. They do all affirm "a consciousness of the Oneness of everything."[17] The unity grasped is transformative in that the whole is now the dominant realization, against which the parts make sense for the first time. This new "cosmic" perspective of consciousness represents "a shift from figure to ground, from a centering on the self's activity and that of others to a centering on the wholeness or unity of nature or the cosmos." We now identify ourselves with the cosmic perspective, and "we value life from its standpoint."[18] Indeed, I suspect that we now do all our valuing from its standpoint, for it is the foundation of valuation itself, its whole story and horizon. Perhaps it is well to pause long enough to point out that "mysticism" is not so simply defined, and to suggest that Kohlberg is not really calling upon a mystical perspective at all, but upon a cosmic perspective.

MYSTICISM

F.C. Happold, himself obviously influenced by William James's account of mysticism in *Varieties of Religiousous experience*, repeats the four criteria of mysticism that James identifies: ineffability, noetic quality, transiency, and passivity. Happold adds to James's account the criterion of a consciousness of the *oneness* of things, a sense of timelessness, and the realization that the everyday self is not the real I.[19] Of these additional criteria, a consciousness of the oneness of things is particularly important for the present analysis of Kohlberg's position. What has to be decided, however, is precisely in what sense this realization of "oneness" is to be taken. Paul Friedländer concludes that Plato, for example, was not a true mystic because Plato's apprehension of the Forms is not an actual merging with them. Rather, the most that could be said for Plato is that he had an intellectual awareness of the oneness of things.[20] Mysticism is more than intellectual awareness, for it is a direct experience of the oneness of self and cosmos, or God, and it is likely more a matter of passionate feeling than it is of intellectual awareness. Mystics do not speculate about the oneness of things; they experience it *directly*, and they report accompanying feelings of overwhelming identification with the greater whole, akin to the self-forgetting merging of human love.

Kohlberg is not proposing a detailed theory of mysticism, of course, yet it is instructive to see just how far he is willing to go in his account of stage-seven consciousness. He does quote Teilhard, who admits to "an intuition that goes beyond reasoning itself,[21] but he also includes Aurelius, whose "rational mysticism" does seem to be an intellectual awareness of the oneness of things, with no claims to having had an *experience* of oneness, or to needing an emotional or non-rational capacity (often termed "intuition" or the "heart" in mystical literature) with which to apprehend your merging with ultimate reality. If mysticism is a direct non-rational awareness of your merging with the greater whole, or with divinity, then Aurelius is not an obvious candidate. Certainly Teilhard and Simpson are, and likely Spinoza, although he may be a borderline case. Without going into more details about each historical figure selected by Kohlberg, let me state what difference all of this may make.

First, it is not mysticism that Kohlberg advocates but a grasp of the figure/ground oneness of the cosmos, i.e. both figure and ground, individual and the whole of things are perspectives on one and the same picture, but at one time with the foreground *individual* in focus and at another with the background *whole* as the focus. Second, were Kohlberg to chain himself to a fully mystical description of stage seven, he would have a great deal more work ahead of him, for the non-rational, intuitive, emotional feature of mysticism would make it just that much more difficult for him to speak of stage seven as a stage of *reasoning*. Aurelius is helpful precisely because he is not a mystic but a rationalist who takes the cosmic perspective of things. If it is the cosmic perspective rather than the cosmic *experience* of oneness and merging that is important, then stage seven may sometimes be mystically derived, but it is always rationally describable. Because apprehension of the oneness of things may be a rational state of awareness, it need not be mystically based.

Perhaps Diagram A below will help to fix the point. It is the embraciveness of the perspective that is important, I think, and you can easily see how it comes to be thought of as required by virtue of the partial and uncomprehensive nature of the previous stages. If you set out on the path of increasing your awareness of your relation with another, with the group, with a larger community, and then with all human beings, it is as if you would need a reason to *stop short* of considering the widest possible context – the cosmos, or God. This, however, is a stage of reasoning, albeit the apparently final stage, at least in terms of its extent and comprehensiveness.

WHY BE MORAL?

Ask yourself the question, "Why do I care about my neighbour, or even about the cosmos?" If you were to wear Kohlberg's spectacles you would see that you are a part of it all. You actually reflect the cosmos yourself – macrocosm within microcosm. You would be unable to ignore what is now tantamount to your own pain and destruction, since you and the cosmos are one and the same. Your neighbour, too, is part of the "divine" whole of things. We are all separated by our individual perspectives from the cosmic whole in which we find ourselves. At the same time, however, we can discern our identification with it. I am my neighbour, and s/he is me, and so again I

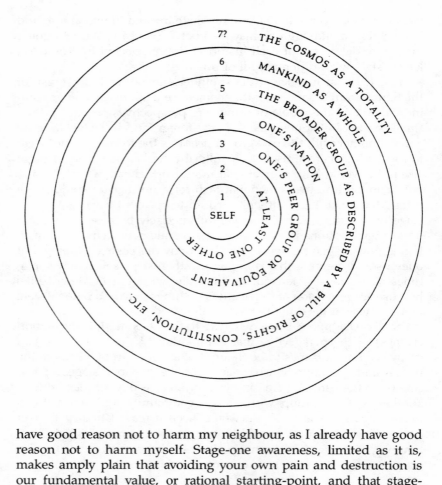

have good reason not to harm my neighbour, as I already have good reason not to harm myself. Stage-one awareness, limited as it is, makes amply plain that avoiding your own pain and destruction is our fundamental value, or rational starting-point, and that stage-seven thinking has simply substituted a comprehensive cosmic "I" where once there was only our individual phenomenal ego.

THE CHARACTERISTICS OF
STAGE SEVEN

The characteristics of stage-seven awareness include: (1) realization of the oneness of mind and self with the whole of nature; and hence (2) the taking of a cosmic perspective ("as opposed to a universal, humanistic Stage 6 perspective"); (3) a shift of focus from figure (or foreground) to ground (or background, i.e. the whole is not the focus, and the individual is seen as but standing out of the whole to which it remains connected); (4) an identifying of yourself with the cosmic perspective; from which (5) both peace and *life-meaning* arise; and hence, "to see life whole is to love and accept life because it is to see ourselves as necessarily part of life."[22] And this last, as I have suggested already, is why we can now answer the question "Why be moral?" We are now not value-neutral towards the whole of things or towards the individual things that go to make up this whole, but rather we love them in a way that is at least akin to the way we love and value ourselves (other things being equal).

It is somewhat surprising that Kohlberg takes such a long path to come to the answer to the question "Why be moral?" I think he is on an important track, let me hasten to say, yet it is also abundantly clear that he might have dealt with the matter very differently. After all, the question is a major one among contemporary ethicists. Kurt Baier, whom Kohlberg quotes frequently, argues that being moral is the only rational thing to do. When we adopt the moral point of view, we already commit ourselves to accepting the best answer that we can arrive at, the one that takes into account all of the relevant consequences, circumstances, people, and hopes and aspirations of those affected.[23] Reason is *the* human tool, and the only and best one available for resolving disputes and moral confusions. To use reason is implicitly already to have previously committed yourself to being moral. Not to be moral, after having accepted the moral approach to life, is like asking why you should be reasonable (for which question-raising reason is the essential agent, and therefore is already presupposed in the very asking). To ask is to answer.

Or again, Kohlberg might have answered the why be moral question by adopting a strategy something like that of W.T. Stace. Stace argues that you are *naturally* social, and equally naturally compassionate:

What, then, are the special parts of human nature which give birth to morality? They are, in my opinion, two ... The first is *the social nature of man*. The second – which is closely connected with the first, but not identical with it – is his *capacity for being made happy in some degree by the bare fact of the happiness of other persons* ...

This social nature of man ... is the most primitive source and perhaps the most important. It is this which in the first instance forced morality upon us ...

The other reason is now before us. That I am, willy nilly, made directly happy by the happiness of others, and unhappy by their unhappiness, means that I can only attain complete happiness for myself through unselfishness, through seeing others happy and making them happy.[24]

It is my contention that Kohlberg is not satisfied with any of these solutions because they are neither broad enough nor fundamental enough to constitute stage-seven awareness. Baier limits himself to what Kohlberg terms "morality" and so leaves out of consideration issues such as what is the good life, the good person, ideal human nature, the ideal human condition, the ground and nature of meaning and purpose, and the *summum bonum*. It is, by and large, precisely such issues that are left out of meta-ethics because they are the stuff of normative ethics, metaphysics, and religion. That Kohlberg wishes to restore the broader context is much to his credit. That most contemporary discussion about ethics and morality leaves the normative, the metaphysical, and the religious aside helps to make apparent what it is that Kohlberg wishes to incorporate into his unusual choice of terms, "ethics."

MORALITY, ETHICS, AND RELIGION

The trouble with the quest for the broader (or broadest) context of awareness is that it is not easy to see how to separate it from the narrower context of *morality* itself. Kohlberg adopts a parallelist stance when describing the relationship between morality (culminating with stage six) and ethics/religion (stage seven):

Moral and religious reasoning may be investigated as separable domains. However, we believe that there is a parallel development of structures of moral and religious reasoning. Reaching a given structure of moral reasoning is "necessary but not sufficient" for reaching a parallel religious structure. The ethical function of religious thinking is to support the structures of moral reasoning that develop in some autonomy from religious structures.[25]

And he is no doubt correct that they are separable domains, for you can stand at stage six (or any other) and never move beyond to stage-seven considerations, where, within Kohlberg's scheme, metaphysical and religious concerns arise. In another respect, however, morality and religion are inseparable in the same way that stage six is the norm and moral end-point of lower-stage thinking. Stage seven is the "whole-story" justification of stage six, and it is often, though not always, religious in form. Without something like a whole story, you are not as fully aware a human being as you might be, nor are you as fully ethical, as fully matured, and so on.

In what precise sense, then, is stage seven "parallel" to the other six stages? Is stage five parallel to stage six, or is stage six merely implicit and undeveloped in stage five? Stage seven is what is required to bring to completion the progress up the stages that ends with the seeing of the whole context out of which morality itself arises and is for the first time justifiable. It provides the "ideal" of a unified society and an "ideal" of a harmonious and integrated cosmos, as both Kohlberg and the other cognitive-developmentalists to whom he refers (Baldwin, Dewey, and Mead) require.[26] A progression is not a parallelism but a developmental typology that begins, progresses, and arrives. Stage seven is an embodiment of what Kant would call the quest for the unconditioned. The "ideals of reason" in Kant are posited to *complete* the story he unfolded in such detail. God, Freedom, and Immortality are not parallel but are the endpoints without which you could not tell in which direction the beginning stages were headed. Stage seven is the "ideal" norm that allows us to sort out moral phenomena into stages. These stages are discernable in terms of their own inner logic, of course, but the ranking of them leads us to justice and beyond, else each stage-morality would float relativistically as but one more alternative moral stance among many others. Stage seven is the normative guidepost that provides the criterion of "adequacy" found only completely in stage-seven awareness.

THE INADEQUACY OF JUSTICE

Assuming that James Fowler's stage six of faith is comparable to Kohlberg's stage seven of moral development, the following description, written by Fowler in the language of the "ultimate environment," is helpful:

Stage 6 is exceedingly rare. The persons best described by it have generated faith compositions in which felt sense of an ultimate environment is inclusive of all being. They have become incarnators and actualizers of the spirit of an inclusive and fulfilled human community ...

The rare persons who may be described by this stage have a special grace that makes them seem more lucid, more simple, and yet somehow more fully human than the rest of us. Their community is universal in extent. Particularities are cherished because they are vessels of the universal, and thereby valuable apart from any utilitarian considerations. Life is both loved and held too loosely. Such persons are ready for fellowship with persons at any of the other stages and from any other faith tradition.[27]

With this description in mind, let me turn to Kohlberg's analysis of Andrea Simpson's vision of the world.

If Marcus Aurelius "represents a version of natural law thinking," then Andrea Simpson represents a version of natural being, or loving, or cosmic "flowing."[28] The ethics of stage seven are more than mere reasoning. They are clearly existential in that the whole person is involved and the result is an expression of the integrated personality. As a mystic, Simpson would undoubtedly agree with Evelyn Underhill that it is not merely the integration of the ordinary self that is at play here, for in fact "the self is remade, transformed, has at last unified itself."[29] What has been added and integrated into the self is your own deep self, or "divine spark," the realization of which brings peace and meaning to your life, and the integrated capacity for selfless love. In any case, it is evident that Andrea Simpson's cosmic consciousness was not arrived at through a process of reasoning and intellectual insight alone but through direct experiences achieved through contemplation and meditation: "In meditation, her experience was that you stop using your mind, deliberately, like a flower that opens itself to the sun, and let this dimension in. Whatever dimension you call it, that is not just overhead in the sky but in the heart and the whole surrounding world, it's in everyone. You open yourself to that which surrounds totally and is totally within."[30]

In a way, there are whispers of this ultimate integration of self, and the arising of the deep self, all along the path of the stages of development. The blossoming occurs only at stage seven, however, and if the mystics are correct, only when the old self, including the rigid control of the intellect, "dies" and gives way to love.[31] Perhaps Kohlberg has created an integrative, rationally cosmic stage seven and a further non-rational cosmic annihilation-of-self stage *eight*, which he has unwittingly rolled into one. Whatever you think about this, it is clear that the post–stage-six stage or stages move us beyond reasoning to agapistic loving, to selfless empathy, and to acts of supererogation.

SUPEREROGATION

Supererogation, or the doing of actions that are clearly beyond the call of duty, e.g. sacrificing yourself for the sake of others, is for Kohlberg post-moral. Yet for Simpson or Christ or Buddha, I suspect, what Kohlberg calls "morality" would simply be reinscribed "pre-ethical," or "on the way to the fully ethical," with the implication that morality was but the preamble to genuine and full-blown ethical living and decision-making. This reinscription emerges not merely from a parallel position but from a new perspective that has actually transcended justice. This is not to say that justice is left behind, any more than any other higher stage leaves behind the lower stages. Rather, at each new stage positions are taken up; problems are overcome for which lower-stage reasoning is inadequate. Is justice ever insufficient as a guide to ethical (or, if you prefer, fully moral) living? Kohlberg maintains that the answer is "no," but I would like briefly to try to develop a workable "yes" response.

Could a conflict arise between justice and agape (selfless love)? If the omega point of justice reasoning is the universalization of principles (as Rawls suggests), the omega point of agape is uncompromising particularity, grasped selflessly. Taking the captain's dilemma as our example, we must decide whether the right form of response would be significantly different for agents at stages six and seven. Kohlberg's justice position, he tells us, requires us to draw lots, thereby recognizing "the equal value of human life." As for agape, he writes that even though "an ethic of agape goes beyond justice to supererogation, it still requires principles of fairness to resolve justice dilemmas."[32] Surely this is precisely what is in question. The agapistic perspective no longer conceives the issue as one of justice, for justice is now inadequate. The dilemma asks us to choose how to decide justly who will be put overboard if the life raft is to have any chance of making its way to a shipping lane and to safety. To refuse to jettison someone is to ensure the death of all.

Is it difficult to imagine the mystic viewing justice as the *wrong* path to follow morally? For one thing, justice's advantage is its greatest flaw; it is *impersonal*. It doesn't matter who goes overboard so long as someone does, of course *fairly*. The agapist, however, not only wishes to treat everyone fairly but also uniquely, i.e. differently as appropriate, and as a centre of intrinsic worth in him/herself. If only one person needs to be removed, undoubtedly the selfless saint would jump. If another had to be chosen – for instance, if the mystic was the only capable navigator – s/he would interact with those on board, spontaneously serving as an example and perhaps observing whether some might be able to handle their selection better than others. Such personal factors might weigh more heavily than arbitrary and strictly impersonal justice. The drawing of lots is to discriminate only in the crudest of ways. To draw lots is to use an impersonal, automatic mode of decision-making. This is not selfless love but a kind of impartial expediency.

The same sort of simplistic thinking attaches to all life-raft and desert-island examples. You pretend to be sure about the factors involved, but you never *are* sure in real life. You can continue to hope for the impossible even as the raft sinks, and sometimes rescue actually occurs, at the last moment. We assume that only the captain knows enough to have even a chance of getting us to safety. We encapsulate the complex personalities of the others as "old man who had a broken shoulder" and "young man, strong and healthy."[33] There is usually a pregnant woman on board, as well, just to make certain that the reader is actually moved to consider the case with some degree of seriousness and interest. Even worse, we assume that all transformative dialogue has already occurred.

Yet a psychiatrist interacts with a patient for years in an attempt to find the key to reorientation and transformation. The agapist makes goodness happen in a less than good world. And this is accomplished by being transparently personal, i.e. loving, and by being relentlessly discriminating among the factors present, and as they arise. Real life is forever unfolding, and so rules, principles, universalized formulas, and mechanisms of fairness come and go as the circumstances change. An agapist would know what to do only one moment at a time, as the scene changed. Agapism would be a form of situation ethics, and so from the stage-six perspective, the agapist would, sometimes, appear to be immoral, and certainly unjust. She or he would be a candidate for the cup of hemlock, or the stake. Was it "just" for the prodigal son to receive so much more praise than the son who stayed at home and worked? Should the latecomer to the vineyard have been paid as much as the man who worked a full day? Was it fair? Surely the New Testament (and the Old) is filled with instances where the treatment accorded is based on the particularities of those involved and not on universalizations. We sometimes refer to this as a "higher logic." Love is personal, not general. It searches out of and for uniqueness and cannot assume some arbitrary *equality*.

The morality of stage seven is not parallel but *fundamental*. It transcends justice and serves as the ideal ground out of which justice reasoning arises, but only as an abstract and stripped-down version of the richness of agape. Nevertheless, an analysis of agapistic behaviour after the fact would likely reveal a "new" pattern of morality: a breaking-free from the old understanding of justice and the emergence of a new "justice." It is not that justice and morality are forever lost but that they are transcended in the instance or circumstances, and eventually transformed in light of the cumulative experience of genuine caring and identification.

RECONSTRUCTION

Perhaps the most curious aspect of the foregoing is that the elements of personal integration do not appear to be clearly visible at the early stages of moral reasoning. No doubt Carol Gilligan's critique of Kohlberg's seemingly exclusive emphasis on justice reasoning may be explained in part by the noticeable absence of any sustained emphasis on love and caring in his first six stages.[34] He contends that it is there and elaborates his position in detail,[35] but you still come away with the suspicion that it is not easy to derive feeling, or even willing, from an account of knowing per se. Kohlberg views himself as within the Platonic tradition, and yet Plato was adamant that the foundations of morality were first, the three parts of the soul (roughly corresponding to the rational, the emotive or feeling side, including will, and the appetitive or sensorial) in integrated harmony; and second, the assumption that the form of goodness is already within. The form of goodness is at least akin to the mystical spark of divinity, and it is not available until justice, the soul as integrated, has already been achieved.

It should follow from this, I think, that part of moral education is to train the will and to sensitize or "educate" the emotions (feelings) as well as to develop the powers of reason. And over and above all this, you would care mightily about the *integration* of these "parts of the soul" all along the educative way. Perhaps, as Plato says, you do this by giving each part its proper sphere of influence, yet you can do this only by vaguely sensing – recollecting – what its proper place and function is. The norm of justice is the good itself, or the system of the forms, which is *innate* in us. Plato's recollection may be akin to Kohlberg's stage seven, but preparation for it would include far more than "justice reasoning." The goal of the moral educator is to develop the three fundamental characteristics of human conscious activity – knowing, feeling, and willing – and to render these harmoniously integrated into a self that is morally responsive. The norm of such moral goodness is stage seven – not stage six – as the ideal towards which we "ought" to strive, and by means of which we measure our development.

WHY ADOPT THE STAGE-SEVEN PERSPECTIVE?

Why ought we to adopt stage seven? Two sorts of answers need to be given to this query. First, we ought to strive for a stage-seven state of consciousness because it is the/our whole story of morality, ethics, meaning in life, metaphysics (religion), and epistemology. It is the limit of reason – that is, it is the whole story rendered as completely, as integratedly, and with full awareness of the depths of human capacity (including mystical experience) as possible. Every comprehensive account of human nature, the world, and the cosmos has been a stage-seven account. Nevertheless, it remains to ask, why accept Kohlberg's account of stage-seven in particular?

I think the correct answer to this is to observe that there is no reason aside from and beyond those given by Kohlberg. He is building us a system to investigate, and he is defending and describing it in all the ways he can. We can do no more than be critically open, to put our own story *at genuine risk*, and he can do no more than work out the details and the defences, the evidence and the network of available support. If we are still unconvinced, he must, as Hare remarks, simply tell us the whole story again, and we must tell him ours.

We might remain unconvinced for the same reason that a Buddhist is unconvinced that s/he should become a Christian – because the starting-points are different, the evidence is different, the preferred and chosen way of living in the world is different, and the "ideal" is different. Yet her/his stage is also post-justice, for s/he speaks of compassion, of union and oneness, of direct experience of a higher and more valued reality, of the emergence of the unitive self and the death of the ordinary ego of selfishness. Her/his self is integrated, peaceful, loving, and transparently open to whatever and whomever is before her/him. There are, however, several candidates to choose from: Spinoza, Aurelius, Simpson, Schweitzer, Martin Luther King, Jr, Christianity, Buddhism, Judaism, Confucianism, Shintoism, Islam, humanism, etc. This is not to say that the visions are equal, but rather that they all emerge from stage-seven awareness as it has been delineated above.

Of course, any religion or metaphysical position or morality may be formulated or expressed as being at any of the stage-levels. It is rare for one to be a stage-seven Christian or Buddhist. If the mystical requirement is added (my potential stage-eight), it is rarer still! For the purposes of this exploration, however, it is enough to note that the characteristics of stage-seven consciousness emerge from an encompassing concern and love of cosmic proportion. Stage seven is also value-foundational in that it is, or it contains, the value assumptions, or "oughts," that transform all appropriate "ises" into "oughts." An *ought* is an *is* that measures up to the ideal.

MEANING

Stage-seven consciousness raises and attempts to answer the questions relating to "the meaningfulness of one's existence as a rational being – a question at the heart of religion – and [one which] in some sense requires a religious answer."[36] Stage seven, I have suggested, specifically describes the conditions of and the environment conducive to a richly meaningful life. It is a blueprint that yields a life worth living; one found valuable in the living of it here and now. If meaning is translatable as the intrinsically valuable, then, as I have argued at length elsewhere, we must take the term "intrinsic value" to mean *basic* or *foundational* value experience, in that it and it alone stops the regress, otherwise infinite, of extrinsic valuation.[37] Something is extrinsically or instrumentally valuable only in so far as it will or may lead to another value that is extrinsic ... until finally you come to the bedrock of your system of value, i.e. to that which is valuable "for its own sake" and not because of something else to which it leads. Only experiences may be intrinsically valuable, and therefore meaning in life is to be found in life's experiences.

One such source of the intrinsically valuable experience is morality. The moral life is rationally required, and conceivably grounded in our nature and in the nature of the cosmos. Yet there is far more to life, meaning, and value than morality. Meaning arises from loving interaction with others, with the world's animates and inanimates, and through identification of yourself with the entire cosmos, of which you now feel yourself to be an inextricable part. Meaning in life arises out of acts of self-realization, self-expression, the appreciation of beauty, intellectual achievement, and even good food and a congenial environment. In this sense the theory of value requires the articulation and living of life in specific ways – it describes a way of life, as almost all religions have observed, and as normative ethical positions used to do. And while morality is generally – indeed regularly – an indispensable condition for the moral life, it is the case that stage-seven thinkers may depart from even the best intellectually graspable morality.

Perhaps this is why Kierkegaard insisted that the ethical stage was but the middle developmental stage, with religion being the third and highest. In his usual extreme way he spoke of the "suspension of the ethical,"[38] and while I would follow Kohlberg and Fowler in affirming that stage seven "must be compatible with principled morality"[39] and not rendered incompatible, as Kierkegaard seems to do, I can understand what it is that Kierkegaard has caught sight of. Even justice itself is limited by the rules of the intellect, and it should be evident that any position that goes beyond reason may at times seem unreasonable. We should therefore be far more careful about whom we condemn as being immoral, while at the same time remaining steadfast in our allegiance to what Kohlberg, Baier, and the rest of those working in the field of ethics take to be the most adequate formulation of the moral point of view.

Part of the reason for the occasional discrepancy between the morality of stages six and seven may be simply that we know so little about ourselves and our world even now, and that reason and language are never adequate to express the deepest of insights without distorting or reducing them in some way. As James R. Horne maintains in his book *The Moral Mystic*, there is a continuing tension between moralist and mystic:

No sooner do we reach a vision of God, or the Good, no sooner do we articulate such a vision, than we find that we have been thrown into moral dilemmas, in which the ideal and the demands of actual social situations clash and give rise to something like the mystical decision process again. If God appears to give us moments of moral certainty and reassurance, at other times he appears to perplex us, and to tell us that we are called to new visions of our destiny, and to further spiritual growth.[40]

The visionary can sometimes be the prophet who calls us to a higher righteousness, and in the process exposes our highest ideals as but tentative and partial glimpses of a whole that still far exceeds our grasp. Fowler, too, gives stress to the "subversive" nature of his stage-six individuals:

Even as they oppose the more blatantly unjust or unredeemed structures of the social, political or religious world, these figures also call into question the compromise arrangements in our common life that have acquired the sanction of conventionalized understandings of justice. King's "Letter from Birmingham Jail" was written not to "Bull" Connor or the Ku Klux Klan, but to a group of moderate and liberal religious leaders who had pleaded with King to meliorate the pressure his followers were exerting through nonviolent demonstrations on the city. King's assault on the more blatant features of a segregated city proved subversive to the genteel compromises by which persons of good will of both races had accommodated themselves in a racist society.

   ...

In these persons of Universalizing faith these qualities of redemptive subversiveness and relevant irrelevance derive from visions they see and to which they have committed their total beings ... they are visions born out of radical acts of identification with persons and circumstances where the futurity of being is being crushed, blocked or exploited. A Martin Luther King, Jr., prepared by familial and church nurture, by college, seminary and doctoral studies, influenced theologically and philosophically by Gandhi's teachings on nonviolent resistance, gets drawn into acts of radical identification with the oppressed when Rosa Parks refuses any longer to let her personhood be ground underfoot ... In the direct experience of the negation of one's personhood or in one's identification with the negations experienced by others, visions are born of what life is *meant* to be. In such circumstances the promise of fulfilment, which is the birthright of each mother's child and the hope of each human community, cries out in affront at the persons and conditions that negate it.[41]

Perhaps no account of the negations of personhood, and basic human dignity and freedom has been better articulated, or more poignantly and directly conveyed, than that provided by Dr Viktor E. Frankl in his restorative book *Man's Search for Meaning*.[42] Whereas Kohlberg's attention is on the general and universal structures of human reasoning and the principles of ethical decision-making, Frankl, the therapist, attends to the needs of the individual striving, sometimes even struggling, to make sense out of and to breathe meaning into the living of life.

CHAPTER THREE

Viktor Frankl
and Logotherapy

As early as 1946, when Frankl's *Man's Search for Meaning* was first published in English, he saw clearly that "long ago we had passed the stage of asking what was the meaning of life, a naïve query which understands life as the attaining of some aim through the active creation of something of value."[1] Frankl writes that "to look for the general meaning of man's life would be comparable to asking a chess player: 'What is the best move?' There is no such thing as 'the best move' apart from the one that is best within the context of a particular situation of a particular game."[2] What is meaningful for an individual, and worth seeking, alters from person to person, day by day, hour by hour, and situation by situation.

Meaningful living is to be contrasted not with negative meaning, or evil, but with *boredom*. Even evil, as dis-meaning or negative versus positive meaning, can present us with something to overcome, to resist, to set out to destroy and eradicate: in sum, it can provide us with a meaningful and worthwhile cause. I often wince at those who have served well in the military and then find that everything that follows after those years of life- risking challenge, of cameraderie, of pushing themselves to the end of their strength and capacity, and then reaching even beyond that, is humdrum and a let-down. If they could find something that engaged them as did the war, that spurred them to reach beyond their anticipated limits, presented new challenges, and encouraged them to enter into relationships as deep and genuine as those encountered in the trenches of war, then they would be able to achieve more than most in civilian life, for they would be people already honed by the demands and hardships of war. Instead, what often happens is that apathy sets in. The civilian world is not as glamorous, nor does it necessarily challenge you. The assembly line is dull, repetitive, and often characterized by avoidance rather than commitment. Much of work in our society is repetitive, monotonous, and for most people nearly devoid of creative expression and innovation. You simply "put in time." And your interaction with similarly bored and apathetic people is not likely to be of a lively sort, nor is it likely to reach particularly deep levels of human exchange. You tell jokes, recount the doings of the "idiot box," and look forward to a weekend of an all too often similar boredom. Frankl refers to this state of apathy as "the existential vacuum":

While speaking of the will to meaning, I referred to meaning orientation and meaning confrontation; while speaking of the meaning of life, I must now refer to meaning frustration, or existential frustration. This represents what could be called the collective neurosis of our time. The dean of students at a major American university has told me that in his counselling work he is continually being confronted by students who complain about the meaninglessness of life, who are beset by that inner void which I have termed the "existential vacuum." Moreover, not a few instances of suicide among students are attributable to this state of affairs.[3]

This state of inner emptiness is fillable only with meaning.

LOGOTHERAPY

Frankl calls his school of psychotherapy "logotherapy" because his profound and horrendous experiences as a death-camp prisoner in Nazi Germany convinced him that what kept people healthy and alive, even in such extreme and de-humanizing conditions, was both the continued experience of meaning and the anticipated meanings of a possible life after the death camps. The Greek word *logos* means a number of things in English, including reason, speech, account, definition, proportion, rationality, argument, thought, etc., but it also denotes *meaning*. Logo(s)-therapy is meaning therapy, and it is based on the assumption that there is a primal urge or fundamental need within us that is even stronger and more fundamental than the will to power or the will to pleasure – namely, the need for meaning in our living and thinking. The *will to meaning* is our primary concern, our ultimate drive.[4] Frankl vehemently rejects Freud's opinion that "the moment a man questions the meaning and value of life he is sick." By contrast, Frankl contends that one who does question the meaning and value of life is "truly a human being."[5] The weight of argument passes from Freud's intellectual theory to Frankl's horrendous experiences in a death camp:

the precept *primum vivere, deinde philosophari* – first survive, then philosophize about it – was invalidated. What was valid in the camp was rather the exact opposite of this precept, *primum philosophari, deinde mori* – first philosophize, then die. This was the one valid thing: to give an accounting to oneself on the question of ultimate meaning, and then to be able to walk forth upright and die the called-for martyr's death.

If you will, the concentration camp was nothing more than a microcosmic mirroring of the human world as a whole. And so we may be justified in applying what is to be learned from the experiences of the concentration camp to conditions in the world today.[6]

The extreme conditions of the death camp taught Frankl that life *can* remain *unconditionally meaningful* even under the most extreme conditions, and that life "remains meaningful literally up to its last moment, up to one's last breath."[7] While logotherapy does not see itself as antagonistic to any of the more orthodox forms of psychotherapy, so long as they are used to deal with issues they are well adapted to handle, it does identify itself with the existential movement. This is an important alliance to note, for existentialism rejects the view that there is a single right perspective or horizon of understanding and emphasizes instead that each of us must find a meaningful and workable way of being in the world. As humans we do not come into the world with a preordained nature, except in a biologically limited sense, but create our nature in the very process of choosing, valuing, and living. We are fully responsible for who it is that we become. In the final analysis, there is no one else to blame. It is totally our own doing, and the blame we put on others for "making us what we are" is misplaced. We could have unburdened ourselves of this negative influence at any point. We are always already *free* to remake our present and future by disencumber ourselves of unwanted and unhelpful aspects of our past history. Freedom, choice, and responsibility are the ethical watchwords of existentialism.

THE EVERYDAY WORLD OF MEANING

In everyday life we *mask* the felt meaninglessness of our existence. We find ways of papering over the despair and emptiness by means of diversions, spectacles, and entertainments, as Pascal warned,[8] or through drugs or alcohol, or by exercising the will to power and/or the will to pleasure, in order to hide the existential vacuum, the ennui within:

In "Executive's Disease" the frustrated will to meaning is vicariously compensated by the will to power. The professional work into which the executive plunges with such maniacal zest only appears to be an end in itself: Actually it is a means to an end, that of self-stupefaction. What the old scholars used to call "horror vacui" exists not only in the realm of physics but also in that of psychology; man is afraid of his inner void, of the existential vacuum, and runs away into work or into pleasure. The place of his frustrated will to meaning is taken by the will to power, though it be just economic power, that is to say, the most primitive form of the will to power, the will to money.[9]

The bored and abandoned Executive Wife, by contrast, flees from the void she feels to drink, or drugs, or a round of cocktail parties, bridge parties, and so on, or to sexual fulfilment and relief from the dispassionate boredom of being at home alone. All of these masks are a retreat to the will to pleasure, and again the result is to gain some pleasure, to be sure, but at the expense of papering over the deeper need, that of coming to grips with the will to meaning, which is crying out for attention. Other masks that Frankl specifically identifies include our obsession with speed, with motorization that impresses others – a Camero or a BMW may be imagined to confer on me a specific image or special status – and whose speed and noise alone can distract us, and, alas, those around us for a considerable time. If we believe the ads, certain products will also make us somebodies, attractive to the opposite sex, and to be taken as successful, as having arrived.

As I have argued throughout, the ultimate criterion of meaning in life is the value accruing from the direct and immediate experience gained as a result of living. However complex the background of a so-called meaningful life, the meaning itself is directly experienced. And the ultimate ground or place of *meaning arising* is the individual human being, in the specific situations of his or her life. While the sources of meaning are almost predictably outside the individual self, the experiences of meaningfulness are necessarily someone's experiences.

LOGOTHERAPY AS PLURALISTIC

The vanguard of contemporary intellectual theorizing is stridently pluralistic in stance.[10] The liberalism that more or less died in the Western world sometime during the last decade or so was often a liberalism of uncritical toleration without much in the way of hardheaded evaluation – or so it has come to be caricatured. Pluralism has far more in common with liberalism than it has with any of the conservatisms of the present decade. Pluralism differs from liberalism, however, in critically focusing on *differences*, and in making clear what is gained and lost by adopting one *ism* over another. Liberalism *reduces* differences to a thick porridge of *sameness*, maintaining that all paths really lead up the same ultimate mountain peak, and that all people value the same (few) basic things, whether they are aware of it or not. Conservatism argues that there is but one mountain peak, that all people ought to value the same things, and that there is but one right way of proceeding up the path. Conservatism is an ideology with a single aperture. It is non-hypothetical, and proceeds from a world-view erected firmly on "axioms" which themselves must be taken to be both self-evident and necessary for the life that one leads is qualify as a moral life. Any claims to truth under this ideology must be based upon these axioms if they are to have any validity.

Pluralism asserts that any world-view is but one of many possible world-views, even though each may be convincingly self-consistent and self-evident from within its own perspective. Whether you adopt a particular world-view or not will, for the pluralist, depend on the degree to which it produces insight and yields value in the living of your life. Something has value for someone when it is *experienced* as meaningful – that is, when the tone of its direct experience is selected as preferable to the other alternatives available at the time, or simply when it is found directly worthwhile in itself. A pluralist assumes that you choose your world-view on the basis of the direct evidence of the meaningfulness of the value-cluster derived from it, and not because it is the only one, or the sacred one.

Frankl has noted that logotherapy has been accused of hovering "close to authoritarianism" and of "taking over the patient's responsibility and diminishing him as a person."[11] I suspect that such charges are, in Freudian psychoanalytic terms, "projections." Surely it is more often the case that traditional psychoanalysis and psychotherapy are more likely to operate in an authoritarian manner. Kisch and Kroll have effectively argued this point in an article entitled "Meaningfulness versus Effectiveness," in which they maintain that psychotherapy has become an "emotional imperialism" through exploiting patients "by rendering them vulnerable to the needs of the therapist. The therapist is established in an emotionally superior position; the patient believes and accepts the notion that the therapist has answers derived from superior knowledge and greater emotional stability." It is precisely such emotional power and authority that lead "therapists as well as patients to accept interesting ideas as established truths." Because of the emphasis placed on such descriptions as "normal," "able to function well in society," and "exhibits socially acceptable behaviour," there is ever present the danger of confusing theory with ideology: "The ideological therapist is indoctrinating the patient into a world view that he or she believes to be a superior mode for personal living. In this respect therapy can degenerate into a form of brain washing. Frequently therapeutic method is determined by the therapist's adherence to a particular technique irrespective of the patient's presenting problem."[12] The specific selection of methods of treatment and the interpretation of the nature of the problem, together with the end results preferred, are all expressions of "the therapist's own school of thought" and are imbedded in his or her overall world-view.

By contrast, Frankl, in describing logotherapy, warns that "a doctor cannot give meanings to his patients" and that meaning arises out of "one's whole being – one's life is itself the answer to the question of its meaning."[13] Even more to the point, Frankl writes that "it is never up to a therapist to convey to the patient a picture of the world as the therapist sees it; but rather, the therapist should enable the patient to see the world as it is,"[14] or, as I would prefer to say, as the patient finds it reasonable and meaningful. Questions about what is meaningful can only be answered by the patient, and the logotherapist is to interact with the patient in heightening and enhancing what is already latently meaningful to that person. You are responsible for your own meaning:

The logotherapist leaves it to the patient to decide what is meaningful and what is not, or, for that matter, what is good and what is bad ... but he may well show the patient that there is a meaning and ... that life not only holds a meaning, a unique meaning, for each and every man, but also never ceases to hold such a meaning – that it retains it, that it remains meaningful literally up to its last moment, to one's last breath.[15]

A liberal, as therapist, might wish to "water down" differences in world-view to a handful of universal or common values; a conservative would see to it that the right values were sought, and in the right manner; the pluralist would focus on the patient as a unique individual whose meaning arises out of his or her own world-view and whose world-view is to be accepted for what it is (that is, as a source of unique meaning in the world) as long as it does not bring serious harm to the patient or to others. If the patient's world-view alters, it will be because he or she has grown to see that a different world-view, or a modification of the previous world-view, yields more meaning in his or her life, or in the moral sense is the course to follow, or in the sense of what it is that s/he wishes to become "ideally" that this step is an important one to take. Frankl seeks to *preserve* the creative *tension* between the "being" or the "is" of a person and the "ought" or the ideal that that person also posits for her or himself.

Indeed, "if this tension is to be preserved, meaning has to be pre-vented from coinciding with being. I should say that it is the meaning of meaning to set the pace of being."[16]

Part of what is means to be a "healthy" person is to have goals or aspirations, or to do better with your human encounters, at your work, and so on. Both in and out of the death camps, those people who have something to work towards, to strive for, to achieve in the next minute, day, or decade, continue to find their lives meaningful, whereas those who have no such "ideals" confront the existential vacuum head on. Frankl suggests that "he who can cling to no end point, to no time in the future, to no point of support, is in danger of allowing himself to collapse inwardly."[17] The end point envisioned, and the imagined future will likely change in the process of living, but none the less point the way out of the existential vacuum. The individual remains the ultimate judge of what is, in fact, meaningful. What is required on the part of the therapist is the ability to deal with the patients who have a spiritual or philosophical "knot" to untie, or whose world-view is inconsistent, or woefully unexplored, or frightening (perhaps by being out of accord with the world-view of the family or group to which they belong), or appears to them to be "sinful" or "immoral." To quote Frankl,

What is needed here is to meet the patient squarely. We must not dodge the discussion, but enter into it sincerely. We must attack these questions on their own terms, with the weapons of the mind. Our patient has a right to demand that the ideas he advances be treated on the philosophical level. In dealing with his arguments we must honestly enter into these problems and renounce the temptation to go outside them, to argue from premises drawn from biology or perhaps sociology. A philosophical question cannot be dealt with by turning the discussion toward the pathological roots from which the ques-tion stemmed, or by hinting at the morbid consequences of philosophical pondering. This is only evasion, being a retreat from the plane upon which the question is posed – the plane of the mind.[18]

Frankl's emphasis on the *philosophical* is important, for it makes clear that any and all positions, however partial they might be, are, or should be seen to be imbedded in a wider perspective, or horizon, or whole story about human beings, the world, the cosmos, and the various relations among them. All of us live from, or are in search of, *a philosophy of life*. A "neurotic" world-view needs to be listened to, genuinely encountered, for it may in fact yield more meaning than another. But it may also be responsible for the patient's guilt, or psychic pain, or emotional and physical suffering, and so will have some-how to be altered or integrated with other factors in her/his life.

Such probing is typically philosophical and *meaning*-oriented, and it is evident that Frankl's writing and practice is drenched in what has historically been termed normative philosophical theorizing, or the search for a philosophy of life. Logotherapy is wilfully and inextricably involved in assisting individual patients in the creation of a somewhat systematic and meaningful *whole story* that will serve to provide answers to the questions of importance in an individual's life and tangible directions for living. A person who is in despair, who is at the edge of suicide, is not, of course, in search of an entire philosophy of life at that very moment. Yet s/he will begin the journey back to fullness of living by providing at least one answer to the question "But why do you not commit suicide?" This powerful question is not meant to trigger the act, for it actually pulls in the opposite direction. The fact that the person has not yet tried to snuff out life indicates that s/he perceives, however dimly, some reason or reasons for going on. Frankl often rehearses the range of possibilities, and it is easy to imagine the list as reaching ahead indefinitely: you are not yet ready to give life up, for all of its pain, or you do not wish to leave forever someone whom you love, or you still have a hope that things will get better, or you cannot bear the thought of another spring arriving, with its birds in greening trees, without being around to enjoy it. Any single thread will suffice, for on it and around it will be woven a considerably larger and richer tapestry of meaning. Any reason for living is enough to get the process underway. What matters is that a cluster of meaning be found and not that the meaning coincide with the therapist's or anyone else's meaning-cluster: "What matters ... is not the meaning of life in general but rather the specific meaning of a person's life at a given moment."[19]

LOGOTHERAPY AND FREEDOM

Viktor Frankl, a dissident thinker in psychotherapy, has broken with the Freudian-implied claim that all therapy is therapy for psychological complexes. He has broken with behaviourism in rejecting the thesis of pan-determinism, the view that we are nothing more (in principle) than the predictable result of the specific confluence of past events and purely physical inheritance. But he has thrown out neither Freud nor Skinner with the bathwater. Instead, like a resourceful Archimedes, he has focused on the bathwater, the tub, and even the reservoir beyond the faucets. His view is holistic, and as such is able to accept and use the more established and orthodox principles and techniques and yet go beyond them to distinctive logotherapeutic principles and techniques. He insists that logotherapy treats *aspects* of human psychology that the other psychologies have ignored. They have focused on the unconscious, on behaviour, and he on meaning and consciousness. Rather than assuming that the sense of meaninglessness is a cover-up for what is really and unconsciously bothering you, or that consciousness is an inner subjective and biophysical feeling that arises as an inner awareness that you *are* doing what you *must* do, he takes freedom and the will to meaning seriously.

The determinist, by contrast, argues that it is not self-consciousness that is an illusion but the belief that you can freely choose to do what you do. Freedom is to us what a program would be to a computer if it were to become conscious: the necessary and automatic would "feel" or appear to be free, self-chosen, even debated over. Freedom is an illusion, and self-consciousness is but the inner observation of the necessarily occurring. We are not free to intervene, but we continue to think that we are. Right-minded thinkers will now see that we ought to move *Beyond Freedom and Dignity*[20] to efficient environmental engineering and behaviour control and modification. Frankl, it might be further argued, claims a psychological insight that is spurious, or ill-thought out, and he has developed techniques for pampering that illusion. It is not doubted that we *feel* as though we were free, but it is denied that this feeling is anything more than an unfounded warm hope that makes us feel better about ourselves. The charge is a strong one, and must be rebutted.

THE NECESSITY OF FREEDOM

A necessary precondition of logotherapy is the existence of and the capacity to use human freedom properly. As the death-camp experiences or a myriad of crisis situations make amply clear, we can find meaning in and enrich our lives even when our *external* freedom is taken away. *Inner* freedom is ever ours, however restricted our external situation may be. As Joseph Fabry writes, "even under the most restrictive circumstances we have an area in which we can determine our actions, our experiences, or at least our attitudes; and this freedom of self-determination rests in our noetic realm."[21] I will expand on the noetic and the noölogical in the next section. For now it is enough to say that the noetic, for Frankl (and for Kant), is that dimension of the human being to which freedom may be attributed. Frankl contends that the noetic is the spiritual dimension, the capacity to have meanings, the *depth* of self rather than its surface. The doctrine of psychological and biological determinism holds only in the domain of ordinary psychology and biology, whereas the doctrine of human freedom holds in the noölogical domain, which is the uniquely human domain. How may both views be held at one and the same time? Psychological and biological conditions do not *completely* condition us: "the humanness of human behaviour cannot be revealed unless we recognize that the real 'cause' of a given individual's responses is not a cause but, rather, a reason." In more accessible and pointed language, "things determine each other. Man, however, determines himself. He decides whether or not he lets himself be determined, be it by the drives and instincts that push him, or the reasons and meanings that pull him."[22]

The distinction between saying that all choices are caused and that some choices are caused by the chooser through the exercise of selectivity is enormous. It is one thing to say that all choices are caused and quite another to say that among those causes are those that the individual her/himself contributes. However, it still remains to deal with whether or not even these latter contributions are determined, forced up on you by forces *beyond* your control, and not freely and self-determinedly decided upon.

THE NOÖLOGICAL DIMENSION

The thrust of the term "noölogical" is that the mind (in Greek, *nous*, and pronounced "noos"), or the human spirit, is a conscious activity concerned with meaning (*logos*).[23] We are capable of "self-transcendent" activity – that is, we are able to conceive of alternative meanings, and to reach out to them in the very act of stretching beyond our present condition.[24] We are also self-transcendent in that we can have purposes and goals, and find meaningful that which far exceeds the limits of our own skins. We can have hope for the rain forest and its peoples, love our families and those beyond, cherish the natural environment generally, and envisage our place in the scheme of things as transcending the everyday.

The development of the consciousness of our own freedom is central not only to our discovering that we can exercise it but also in guarding against manipulation. Indoctrination is the technique of stilling the critical capacity to think beyond formulas, orthodoxies, and habits or of stunting its awareness and development in the first place. Fear, reward, punishment, ridicule, charges of immorality are but some of the ways of influencing people to back away from non-preferred thinking and acting. B.F. Skinner is probably right that much education and psychotherapy is indoctrination, for educators and psychotherapists all too often claim that they know what the appropriate ways of thinking and acting are, rather than encouraging the student/patient to investigate different paths to meaning, to weigh the evidence, and to make a final decision in the light of a genuine exploration. Yet if all our thoughts, actions, and responses are controlled by inheritance, history, and environment, then are we not simply going through the motions when we appear to or feel that we are making decisions of our own? Frankl, like every other thinker in history who has not begun by accepting a fatalistic or pan-deterministic view, keeps separate and alive the human capacity to control our attitudes towards circumstances, and towards the inevitable, at the very least.

Historically, even the Stoics, who argued for a strict pan-determinism of events, continued to hold that one's attitudes were all-important in finding peace and blessedness in life (*ataraxía*, i.e. tranquillity of the soul). While the Stoics often did not see the implications of such a stance, they did hold that the strict determinism of all things and events did not apply to one's *attitudes* towards them. Even Nietzsche, whose account of determinism led him to formulate the extreme version of it in his doctrine of the eternal recurrence, presupposes that we can overcome our negative and hopeless attitudes towards this endless repetition.[25] If we do suppose that whatever is or will happen has existed before in exactly the way it is happening now, and will recur again and again in exactly the same way an infinite number of times, then the actual detailed acts of my writing, the printer printing, and your now reading these words are but the repeats of a cosmic videotape in which we have acted an infinite number of times before, are acting now, and will act again, *without deviation*, throughout eternity. For Nietzsche the real point of the doctrine is to cause his readers to grasp that part of the responsibility of being human entails that we willingly accept whatever happens to us as having "unconditional meaning," unconditional value, or "intrinsic meaning," as Arthur Danto puts it.[26]

But if literally *every* aspect of our being and experience is predetermined, then we are determined also to take a specific attitudinal stance towards what happens, and Nietzsche's words, and the professed comfort of Stoic peace of mind, do nothing for us, ever, for we are unable to break out of the predetermined stream. On this account even Nietzsche and the Stoics speak and write – even live – as they do because they must. And we must listen or not, as we are determined to do. In telling us that his "formula for greatness in man is *amor fati*: that you should not wish things to be otherwise not before and not after, in the whole of eternity,"[27] Nietzsche is aiming to move us psychologically, emotionally, and it is as if he strikes us with the small triangular rubber hammer of the physician directly on the reflex-points of our attitudes, our values, our meaning. He strives to jolt us to attention, to strike us on that precise nerve that will jerk us to responsible attention and affirmation. We can freely alter our attitudes towards things, even though all else is determined. Not even the extreme in circumstantial and biological meaninglessness can render life devoid of inner meaning.

CONSCIOUSNESS

It is in *consciousness* that freedom lies, coiled like a snake in sleep, invisible to the ordinary eye.[28] For many people, perhaps even for most, it does not stir most of the time but sleeps on through the chilled boredom and habituation of their lives. The awareness of your freedom can be awakened, however, and the therapist, the teacher, the parent, the friend, the lover all have the power to awaken the sleeping serpent. The image of the serpent is an auspicious one, not only because its implied sexuality helps to make you aware of how you can awaken one morning to a new and burning awareness of the heretofore dormant within you, but also because the serpent is feared and killed by those who are afraid and are not up to the risks of the awakening of that part of the self, or of another. If you want to control another, you must eradicate his or her sense of freedom! But is there freedom?

Imagine that you have a fear of swimming. The friend or therapist probes, and it happens that you were thrown into the water as a child by a father who was convinced that you would learn to swim the hard way, as he did. You struggled, went under, panic swept over you, but you made it to shore. Your father thought that he had caused you to lose your fear, but in fact you swallowed it, or sublimated it because you feared him, his ridicule, and the sense of unworthiness and cowardice that hurt so much it could not be faced. To a Freudian or a logotherapist, it would be essential to bring to the surface of consciousness the original causes of your condition. To a behaviourist, it would be sufficient to bring about a pattern of positive reinforcement whenever you swim, which would eventually take priority over your fears and your sense of having failed. Indeed, your father was a behaviourist who was able to change your behaviour by substituting the fear of drowning, the fear of ridicule, and the potential loss of parental esteem for the fear of the water. Either way, as cause or "cure," behaviour modification would not come to grips with the alleged state of consciousness, only with the behaviour and its mod-ification. For the psychotherapist or logotherapist, however, to sub-stitute one behaviour for another night well be to leave the original state of consciousness unaffected and unimproved, and therefore untreated. Through the unconscious or the conscious mind, you bring to centre stage whatever is troublesome in order to face it, and to dredge up its *causes*. Then and only then can you work to change your attitudes towards those causes, your feelings about them, or your perspective on the event(s) of the past. Herein arises our free-dom. It still stands as a fact that we cannot alter the past or its physical effects up to this point. We can, however, alter its hold on consciousness, and therefore its hold on the unconsciousness. By understanding the father, his intentions and limited vision, your background fear, and your sense of having failed, you may then trans-form or *transcend* the old meaning and alter its hold on your present horizon of understanding. You can only look back at history from here and now, for all consciousness is consciousness in the here and now.

History does get rewritten every time we encounter it, for it is always a slightly different history as we are ourselves always in a different place, with a different horizon of understanding and with a slightly different focus of attention and capacity for grasping his-tory's importance. In this sense history, and its *causal influence on us*, is continually remade, or can be transformed if we reflect upon it seriously. You can actually affect the entire chain of causal influences, from childhood to now, and as each of these lets go of its hold, the resultant domino effect will apply to an indefinitely large number of causal conditions as well. As you exercise the *reflective* capacity to stand as an observer to yourself, the effects will continue for as long as you are both awake and alive. Each new insight or major experi-ence, each telling comment, marriage break-up, or death of a loved-one may be an occasion to review your past, and hence your present, in a different light, thereby altering the past's causal effect on you. Thus it is that Frankl reminds us that "existential analysis aims at nothing more and nothing less than leading men to consciousness of their responsibility."[29]

PRESCRIPTION AND DESCRIPTION

The significance of the continuous revision of history for freedom and meaning is that the *final* reflective alteration in an active and critically aware mind takes place in the instant of death, and not before. Therefore, all of the information about a person, all events as well as all of the reflections upon those events, and the re-reflections, the re-re-reflections, will be causally complete – finished – only at death. It is then and only then that you can actually *predict* which causes have actually produced which string of effects, in their final completeness, when all shifting and modification have come to a standstill. Then you can predict what must necessarily have been the results – the total string of results – of an event, and therefore what you would do as a result. *But to predict after death what effects there have been from a given cause is, in effect, not prediction at all, but description.* When you have taken into account the autonomy and the potential never-endedness of reflection, the final causal budget cannot possibly appear so long as reflection and some consciousness of freedom are apparent, until reflection and consciousness have ceased to be altogether.

Anyone can "predict" what has already happened: the trick is to forecast, to read the signs before the results have hardened into fact. The behaviourist or reductionist can appear to do this because s/he deals with those whose power of reflection is virtually inactive, or else simply reduces or writes off allegedly conscious and reflective power altogether. People are in fact excessively controlled every day, and probably most of us much of the time. We can, however, awaken the serpent within and thereby realize our capacity to take our destiny into our own hands. It is the task of the logotherapist to assist in "bringing the individual to the point where he can of his own accord discern his own proper tasks, out of the consciousness of his own responsibility, and can find the clear, no longer indeterminate, unique and singular meaning of his own life."[30] Meaning is now your own responsibility, and you no longer deny it, or merely endure it, but rather cherish it and welcome it.

With freedom goes responsibility, and from responsibility comes the possibility of life enrichment. We are now able to decide for ourselves. But lest this account prove too sugary, let it be emphasized that Frankl includes within the category of the meaningful and the worthwhile the capacity to find meaning even in pain and suffering. The chronically ill and the terminally ill, the crippled and the grieving may all find ways of enduring their incredible misfortune by determining that life is meaningful and unconditionally worthwhile in spite of what it is that must be endured. Those who entered the Nazi death ovens in prayer, in song, and hand in hand somehow found the power to go on, to overcome, to endure, and to find meaning even in this, right to the bitter end. Logotherapy dwells on the Holocaust not because it is typical life but because it places in strikingly bold relief much of ordinary existence as banal and trivial, and offers to those who suffer and endure the strongest possible example for continuing to endure and to hope, however hopeless one's circumstances way seem. The Holocaust has something of the same role that Nietzsche's myth of eternal recurrence has: both serve as extreme images of lives that might easily be deemed worthless but were found both worthwhile and meaningful none the less, and in spite of the overwhelming evidence to the contrary. The Holocaust victims are to be wept for but are also to be learned from. They can teach us to say "yes" to life even under the most adverse conditions. Life is unconditionally meaningful.

SELF-DETERMINATION

Is the defence of freedom finally in hand? Is the possibility of a freedom of attitudes and the capacity to reflect on who you are an unassailable fact? A part of what is meant by "free will" is *self-determination*. And the fact that you continue to speak of "determination" implies that you do suppose that here too causes are operative, but from within rather than from without. What must be accounted for next are the causes of these causes. Self-determination might be described as the determination of the indeterminate.[31] When we reflect back upon a happening, it is already determined, fixed, and knowable as determinate. Any act of consciousness yet to occur is indeterminate in that its form and content is as yet not determined, or fixed. In addition to consciousness itself, there is always a deeper you, looking at the "you" that is your present object of focus. And to look at this deeper you is to have a still deeper self still looking at the you looking at you ... and so on to infinity. *The self can never be caught, can never be objectified so long as it is active, precisely because it is a process, and not a static thing in the first place.* Thus it is that your *reaction* to yourself, to your past history, and to your "personality-as-it-has-developed" is always *in process*, never hard and brittle, unless you allow it to become so. To the degree that the dialogue between the objective, surface you and the indeterminate you in process and continual, unending determination remains a healthy and vital dialogue, then self-determination is occurring. Your *process self*, by virtue of its indeterminacy, is forever capable of determining what your *objective self* will be at any moment in time. You are who it is that you have decided to become. You are responsible for who you are.

In mathematics, the largest currently thinkable number can always have yet another unit added to it, and the last occurring or first occurring cause in your personal history can always be altered by still another subsequent thought or reflection. Stop the process and you have a determined history, and description in this now fixed, *dead* state has become possible. Prior to this there were only *trends*, tendencies, likelihoods, statistical probabilities and traits. We can overcome or transcend any or all of these by remaining reflectively self-critical. Only at death is the time right for uncritical senility, and not a second before death.

It should also be evident from the above that it is the philosophical or spiritual or meaning-inquirer, and not the measurer of physiological effects and overt behaviour, who is able to attend to the facts of internal consciousness. The contents of consciousness cannot be measured directly by others because the method of observation is that of self-experimentation in the form of *introspection*. Having recognized this, it is then possible to enrich your appreciation of meaning in various ways, from the inside out, as it were. In doing so, you make evident on each occasion the nature and function of *freedom* in your own richly reflective life. Freedom is the capacity for *interiority*, which reveals an unlimited potential for understanding, interpretation, evaluation, and meaning. The *noölogist introspects; the reductionist extrospects*. The therapist, in the best sense, is at least sensitive to both dimensions of awareness. For it would be as difficult to find the data of behaviour and physiology by introspecting as it is to find the introspective data in the physical or behavioural realm. The true locus of meaning in life is both within and without, both body and mind, both fact and value, both reason and emotion.

IMPLICATIONS FOR EDUCATION

Because of the difficulty of finding external evidence of self-reflective activity, the reductionist dogmatically concludes that this capacity must be spurious. In fact it is detectable all around the edges of the presuppositions and assumptions of reductionist theory, but the signs are not noticed because they are not apparent from within this point of view. In the interest of system self-maintenance, only those facts considered to be self-evident are recognizable. People adhering to a reductionist system of thought wear lenses that render them incapable of seeing anything lying outside their structure of accustomed security. They ignore or simply do not see anything that does not conform to the prescriptions of the system. An extreme version of this is the disease of black-and-white thinking, which results from an obsessive fear of the otherwise indeterminate greyness of things. It is evidenced by mechanical thinking that renders all things precise, fixed in purpose, predictable, and eminently controllable.

As will be recalled from the discussion of Heidegger earlier, mechanical thinking sacrifices wholeness and richness of human and non-human environmental qualities for controllability and expediency of quick and precisely limited achievement. It is in the very nature of the struggle to see things clearly that we strive to avoid blindness by claiming perfect, or 20/20 vision. That we are less myopic than we were in the past may be all that we can ever claim or hope for, and quite enough to yield increasing meaning in our living, working, and loving.[32] But we often sacrifice even this in order to be able to control and manipulate limited information for strictly limited purposes. In doing so we hide our myopic vision by donning a restrictive lens that blocks out all informational input except for that which is precise, and required for the expedient task at hand. All else is beyond our vision and remains unseen because it does not relate to our pre-arranged scheme of selection. Frankl's phrase, an "open-door policy," which applies to the therapist as facilitator of meaning rather than imposer of meaning, could be fruitfully applied to an open receptiveness to input and peripheral vision heretofore ignored, or rendered unseeable due to our strict focus. An open-door policy with respect to sources of meaning, value, and understanding might prove transformative.

It is not by chance that the reductionist is extraordinarily effective educationally. S/he has seen well that positive reinforcement, immediate feedback, and a clear step-by-step program of learning bring sustained results. We have all benefited from these insights, and we likely use these techniques in our own lives, consciously or unconsciously. The danger is, however, that the very effectiveness of these principles encourages us to think that the form is also the content. In other words, if you wish to teach the "facts" of history, you must spell out what facts are to be known, and in what order. So far, so good. But the easy assumption is that these facts are all there is to know about a subject and that they are indeed the "facts." But this is to deny that history is a creative and an interpretive activity. It might be better not to teach these dates, alleged causes, and events as anything more than interpretive conclusions based on assumptions. It may be that a good student will reject the "facts" and even come to alter the sequence of learning and understanding. History and education are selective, and therefore "ideological," in that all principles of selection and emphasis are themselves value-laden. The reflective teacher will induce her/his students to focus not on the facts selected but upon the principles of selection themselves. You build such critical capacity to look at the assumptions, and to re-evaluate and reinterpret the facts, by calling attention to the open-endedness of all human inquiry, human institutions, and to the tentativeness and prejudices of all interpretations, including those deemed "facts."

Frankl maintains that "in an age such as ours, that is to say, in an age of the existential vacuum, the foremost task of education, instead of being satisfied with transmitting traditions and knowledge, is to refine our capacity which allows man to find unique meanings."[33] Fabry recounts a videotaped interview of Frankl by Huston Smith:

Smith asked Frankl how professors in universities can teach values to students and give them something like a meaning. Frankl answered that "values cannot be taught; they must be lived. What we can give our students is not a meaning but an example, that is to say, the example of commitment to a cause worthy of such a commitment; for instance, science, truth, scientific research. This example we are giving will be watched and witnessed by our students."[34]

Emphasizing that we ought not to confine ourselves to the transmission of traditions and knowledge, Frankl urges us to "refine man's capacity to find those unique meanings which are not affected by the crumbling of universal values." It is education's task to equip men and women "with the means to find meanings." Unfortunately, it is more often the case that students are presented to with a reduced, edited version of history that amounts to "an indoctrination along the lines of a mechanistic theory of man plus a relativistic philosophy of life."[35]

RELATIVISM

What of the claim of relativism? Frankl does not mince his words in warning that our "original and natural concern with meaning and values is endangered by the prevalent subjectivism and relativism. Both are liable to erode idealism and enthusiasm."[36] Yet it is not clear what alternatives to subjectivism and relativism there are. Often the alleged solution is the substitution of objectivism and absolutism. Indeed, Frankl has been taken to say just this. Reuven P. Bulka, in *The Quest for Ultimate Meaning*, argues that, for Frankl, "there is an objective value world, a world filled with meaning. This meaning is beyond us in our subjective situation and exists outside and independent of us." Further, Bulka quotes Arnold and Gasson, who conclude that "if values are not only objective but absolute, as Frankl further contends, they must be given to us, discovered by us, but cannot have their origin in us. In that case, the question is legitimate: What has created them?"[37]

Bulka takes this to confirm his own understanding of Frankl as affirming an "ultimate meaning," and presumably interprets Frankl's "unknown God," or equivalent, as the ground of this ultimate meaning. But I am not convinced that Bulka has read Frankl correctly, and much hangs on the issue. Earlier in his book Bulka observes, and I think correctly this time, that "Frankl uses the term 'objective' to indicate that values *exist unconditionally*, and that no person could ever be deprived of the possibility for actualizing values."[38] My interpretation of this claim is that Frankl calls attention to the fact that your own found meaning is just that: meaningful as found, and unconditional. Furthermore, this formulation is meant to call attention to the fact that no amount of torture, brainwashing, indoctrination, or "retraining" can ever necessarily achieve the eradication of such values. Human values are unconditional, and even the short wait in the gas chamber but confirms that the interiority of meaning is, at least in principle, unassailable. Logotherapy underscores this point because it affirms the possibility of finding meaning in life whatever the circumstances and however bad things may have become. But it does not seem to me correct to conclude that Frankl is calling attention to objectively unchanging, absolute, and eternal values. This reading flies in the face of Frankl's openness to change, both personal and social, and of his emphasis on the validity of the individual's own sense of meaning and worth. The logotherapist works *with* the individual rather than imposing a pre-existent and absolute set of values on to the patient: "Existential analysis must not be concerned with what the patient decides for, what goals he sets himself, but only that he decides at all."[39] What is "objective" is that there is always a source of meaning to be found, even in suffering and death, not that any specific meanings and lifestyles are required. What matters is whether or not a choice does in fact bring meaning to living and whether some other choice would have brought more meaning. If the latter is the case, then you will seek the more meaningful path next time.

The issue of relativism is not a simple one to decide, however, since Frankl does not take the easy way out and deny relativism in order to establish a value-absolutism. Rather, he seeks to walk between the extremes of values as pure caprice and values as already established, unchanging, and awaiting discovery as fixed standards. What he actually says is much more subtle and intellectually acute:

But are meanings and values as relative and subjective as one believes them to be? In a sense they are, but in a different sense from that in which relativism and subjectivism conceive of them. Meaning is relative in that it is related to a specific person who is entangled in a specific situation. One could say that meaning differs first from man to man and second from day to day, indeed, from hour to hour.

To be sure, I would prefer to speak of the uniqueness, rather than relativeness, of meanings ... From what I have said, it follows that there is no such thing as a universal meaning of life but only the unique meanings of the individual situations. However, we must not forget that among these situations there are also situations which have something in common, and consequently there are also meanings which are shared by human beings across society and, even more, throughout history. Rather than being related to unique situations these meanings refer to the human condition. And these meanings are what is understood by values. So that one may define values as those meaning universals which crystallize in the typical situations a society or even humanity has to face.[40]

Frankl identifies a tension between the world (the "objective"), and the experiencing, willing, valuing, choosing person (the "subjective"). He appears not to wish to eliminate this tension but to maintain a creative tension between the two. This contradictory valuational tension is permanent, whereas any specific value may or may not be.

THE WORLD AS RESISTANCE

Frankl also writes of yet another tension, with meaning to be fulfilled on one side and the individual who is to fulfil it (or not) on the other.[41] Tension moves us, keeps us from slumping, renders us taut, poised, and ready for achievement and creative and unique reconsideration both of ourselves, and of what we encounter in specific situations. That there is a situation, and that it can directly affect us, he takes as evident. That we may respond to it in a variety of different ways he takes as evident as well. What is "objective" is not a single, correct reading of the situation but the recognition that there is a concrete situation, which significantly affects each person. The world and its situations are not mere subjective (projective) fantasy but are centres of resistance, or circumstances. The tension between the subjective and objective poles must be kept intact, just as the tension between "is" and "ought" must be maintained and encouraged. What is spiritual or religious about the quest for "ultimate meaning" is not its ultimateness but its open-endedness, yet trustworthiness.

Human beings are spiritual beings in that they are aware of the "realm" of potential meaning as transcending any and all existing human meanings, reaching beyond conscious meanings to unconscious meanings not yet encountered or even imagined. Frankl terms this "unconsciousness religiousness," maintaining that it "stems from the personal centre of the individual man rather than an impersonal pool of images shared by mankind." Logotherapy seeks to "re-mind" the individual of his or her "unconscious religiousness – that is to say, to let it enter his [or her] conscious mind again." This is the ultimate ground of logotherapy and completes what I would call the exploration of the whole story, for it underwrites meaning inquiry as an activity that stretches all the way to some perspective on the ultimate whole of things. To fall short of this, to exist with a stunted or "crippled relation to transcendence," is a formula for neurosis.[42] That the transcendent is an "unconscious transcendence" makes abundantly clear that Frankl does not wish to claim that any one whole-story perspective is the correct one. To quote Bulka again,

This theology of the unknown and the unknowable as a basic corollary of the notion of unconditional meanings is for Frankl an all-inclusive one that can even be espoused by the so-called non-religious. Frankl subscribes to Einstein's idea that finding an answer to the question "What is the meaning of life?" is to be religious. With this view it is easy to fit humanity into the category of religious.

What then of atheism? The answer, as might be expected, is that the atheist, too, possesses religious underpinnings. "The pathos of atheism is based on an implicit religious ethos; and the passion of the unreligious includes a hidden love of God."[43]

It might have been better not to have spoken of a hidden love of God, or of an implicit religiousness, but I suspect that the emphasis is there because of the avowedly "godless" stance of Nazism, and much of modern Communism. The religious dimension is the sphere of *nous*, I think, and the claim is not that we are all religious in any straightforward sense but that we all ought to expand our horizons to include the widest search for meaning and understanding, as symbolized by the ongoing and never-ending exploration into the unknown and the heretofore unconscious, known as life.

FREEDOM VERSUS CONTROL

One of the greatest risks resulting from denying the ongoing unfolding of meaning, and the exploration of the unconscious and uncharted potential meanings and understandings of existence, comes from the assumption that you already know what is best, what human nature is, and what the limits and specific characteristics of the universe likely are. Most forms of cultural engineering require that you already know the specific values to be implemented for people and institutions. At their worst, teaching machines teach that there is an end to all learning and that that end is represented by something like "getting it right." Teaching machines are programmed on the assumption that there is something definite and limited to be learned, whereas critical education questions the assumptions and principles of programming themselves. Even Kohlberg's seven stages can be taken to describe the complete path which humans have followed and will follow in their exploration and personal development. But if we hold the stages more loosely, as rough-and-ready guides to categorization for the purposes of understanding, based on the best evidence available at this time, then we will less likely pigeon-hole those whom we study, teach, and love. The only defence against cultural or personal control (determinism) is the exercise of your own independent capacity for reflection. It is the one capacity that is uncatchable, invisible, and unmanipulable, at least in principle. Therein lies its greatest meaning, for nothing need ever be dull or boring again. Your knowing can be perpetually and indefinitely enhanced, as can your ability to feel, your strength of will, and your expression of love. Development as a possibility reaches out in all directions, and therein lies the infinite possibility for the enrichment of meaning for each of us.

Enrichment of meaning is the result of valuational and developmental growth. It usually begins by seeing possibilities where before there were thought to be none, or by seeing old things in new ways, or by becoming sensitized to that which you have predictably overlooked. All three of these senses of potential value-enrichment are premised on seeing differently from before, or on expanding your capacities to see or to feel. Value-enrichment includes the ability to value intrinsically the uniqueness of people, other things, and events. As in Saint- Exupéry's The Little Prince, every rose is different, special, distinctive, and a genuine source of value and meaning for an individual capable of loving roses – one at a time.[44] Even pain and suffering may be used in their uniqueness, as occasions for reflection and resultant change, as something to grow on. Given the fact of evil and tragedy in our lives, we may either succumb or profit. Little wonder that the Japanese, to look ahead to the remaining chapters of this book, have found in the sweat and discomfort of rigorous training in the martial arts, or in the subtle refinements of the tea ceremony, a disciplining and sensitizing that opens the practitioner to the depth of the art and of her/himself. The master is the one who has come to develop the discriminatory powers that allow even details to be seen, and the determination to persevere at learning the art over an entire lifetime. The master-figure is a searcher who has discovered that freedom is the development of deep seeing, which has only a beginning, never an end. Mastery is the whole-hearted and lifelong commitment to set out on the path of growth and development, to walk into the unknown and the unconscious, and to persevere, come what may. You have to learn to make tea even when it rains, as the Japanese saying goes, for while most can do what needs to be done when the going is easy, only those with developed personal awareness and control can achieve greatness under difficult circumstances. To be a master of meaning and value is to know that you can never become such a master. You must forever become and enrich who you are, as itself the ongoing meaning-filled activity. The joy is in the passage itself. The process is a meaningful activity, enriching who you are. The ongoing activity is a way of forever becoming. The process in itself is a meaning-filled activity enriching who you are.

DISCONTINUITY IN TIME

■■■ The late Professor Nishitani Keiji was then in his mid-eighties, and on the hot summer day that we met to discuss Japanese philosophy, he was quite evidently in the midst of deep sorrow. His wife had died only three days earlier, and I had anticipated that he would send word that he could not meet with me as we had arranged. Instead, he sent word that he was expecting me that afternoon as planned. This was my third visit to his home, and it was two years since my last journey to Kyoto. The earlier conversations had gone on for many hours at a time, but on this occasion a mutual friend had asked that I be brief because of his recent personal loss. His wife had been his companion for more than six decades.

He met me at the door, greeting me warmly, and seated me in his study–living-room. Several family members were in the house, evidently providing comfort and assistance, and no sooner had I expressed my sorrow to him than tea was set before us both. He poured, looked up, and with strength and control, as well as with blunt honesty and deep feeling, said, "Coming to grips with death is a difficult problem." He repeated this again after a meditative pause: "I have thought

about death for many years, but it remains a difficult problem
– it is very difficult." The theme of death would reappear
often in the time that followed.

We talked of each other's research and writing, and soon
the conversation turned to the philosophy of Nishida Kitarō,
Japan's most famous modern philosopher, whom Professor
Nishitani had succeeded at the University of Kyoto, and he
seemed to be relieved to have his mind at least partly on
other things. "The logic of *basho* is not ordinary logic," he
said. "It is logic which allows you to say 'one *soku* many,' and
'many *soku* one.'" "*Soku hi*" means "is and is not," and symbolically represents the vanishing point where one thing turns
into its apparent opposite, the moment of transition where
forward motion (at its zenith) becomes receding motion, and
which again in turn (at its nadir) becomes forward motion
again. It is akin to the almost imperceptible flow through the
point where the upper sand in an hourglass becomes the
lower sand, and then, when the glass is turned over, the
lower becomes the upper, only to flow through the vanishing
point of opposition once more, becoming the lower yet again.
Things become other than what they are in the flow of time.

"'Basho' means not just 'place' but the place where something is, in its suchness. It is the place where something is
seen, or known, indeed where everything is seen or known.
It is like Heidegger's 'clearing' except that it is the largest universal and not a limited place surrounded by the dark forest.
Thus, rather than a clearing, it is *clearness*, suchness, where
whatever is seen is seen as it is – or, if that claim is too great,
where everything seen is seen more clearly than it has ever
been seen before.

"Action, whether human or otherwise, is the *character* of
place. *Basho*, or place, is always historical. It is where history
comes to be *as* history. Our bodies are also historical. Action,
body, and place are just as they are because of everything
else. All is interconnected such that whatever is and whatever
arises does so because it is a historical expression of that
totality. At the same time, it is wonderfully unique, and therefore free, for there has never been, nor will there likely ever
be another moment, body, or happening exactly like this one.
The arising is unique."

Nishitani-*sensei* picked up his tea cup, then continued.
"This cup is always this cup, and for it to reappear, the whole
history of the cosmos must repeat itself such that this place,

this moment, and this history arises once more afresh. *Individuality* implies a kind of absoluteness of existence. It is always one of a kind, and it is one of a kind in each and every moment. In this sense everything must be seen as an individual and as unique. Even the smallest fleck of dust is unique and absolute, for in the whole history of the cosmos there will never be this same dust again. Otherwise, the cosmos will have to repeat itself in its complexity and completeness! Of course, an individual, like the cup, or perhaps a tree, is and is not a cup or a tree, respectively. It is not a cup because, as every Buddhist knows, the doctrine of impermanence teaches that the cup is ever changing, is without substance and permanence, and is but a temporary expression of the *whole*, which is itself unseen yet seen in this cup, in this moment, in this place. But it is also a cup, *this* cup, *right now*, here, and precisely in *this* place. So it is that all history is of the present, and is in the present. History is a continuity as seen from the discontinuity of the *now*, the moment. The present is a mode of time that cuts or breaks time as a continuity, as a continuum. Hence, the present is the origination point of all time, of all history, of the past and the future. Continuity is negated in order that specific times, specific histories, specific events may arise. They stand out of the flow as *discontinuities*."

He sipped from his cup, breathed deeply as though reflecting both about what he would say next and about the ache of grief that "lined" his thinking and acting in the now of his life. I asked him about enlightenment experience, in which the subject/object distinction is overcome, and he responded that *basho* was "some deeper ground from which self-consciousness and all other distinctions spring. You can step out of the place of distinctions, of intentionality, into the place where the place mirrors itself. Of course, to speak of a mirror is already misleading. There is no mirror, nor is there anything to be reflected."

At this, we began to laugh like kids, as we savoured this delicate and hard-to-hold Zen kōan together. Perhaps it was his first full moment away from grief for some time. "The farmer must catch his spade by the handle, firmly, and yet continue to have an empty hand. On the one side, there is no farmer and no spade, and yet there is a farmer who, when he comes to grasp the true nature of work, will do so with

empty hands. This is *soku hi*. This is also the egoless spontaneity of Zen."

As Nishitani-*sensei's* home was now filling with the aromas
and noises of his family preparing the evening meal, it was
evident that our intense conversation had to be brought to a
close. I asked one last, but large question – whether Nishida
had ever made the turn in his mature writings from ontology
(an account of what *is*) to axiology (an account of what value
and valuation is). The answer given was no surprise. "There is
no such distinction, either in Nishida or in Japan. Consider a
Japanese rock garden, like Ryōan-ji, for example. Most people
look at the surface of this great garden, at the beautiful rocks,
the rippled patterns in the sand, the moss, and the earth-col-
oured walls. But the garden is the expression of the landscape
architect's own enlightenment! Indeed, now that there *is* this
enlightenment expression in the world, it is as though the
garden is in fact looking at us. Underneath our feet, where we
are, at this place, the garden is looking at us, for we are a part
of the garden. We are within the garden and are not just
spectators, for we have ourselves become part of the actual
manifestation of the garden architect's expression of his own
enlightenment experience. The garden is my Zen master now,
and it is your Zen master, too. So it is, axiologically speaking,
that values arise, and remain to aid in the transformation of
human awareness, and render us open to higher values. Your
encounter with another's achievements may yield transformed
and enhanced value possibilities for you. The 'transvaluation'
of values occurs only when your understanding of reality has
been radically altered."

Nishitani-*sensei* pointed to a painting of plum blossoms on
the wall next to me, and read the verse that was there
inscribed: "By the roadside, along the Yangtze River, wild
plum trees grow, filling the air with richly fragrant blossoms."
Interpreting the poem, he continued, "We admire the fragrance, for we are in the very midst of it." He stared at the
painting, then said, "For the poet or the painter to be as
aware as it seems each was, both had to be totally there,
totally involved in the *now* of this experience. As a result of a
transformation of being, this ontological shift, each was able
to have a 'pure experience' of this moment. The poet and the
painter, at different times, were in the midst of the fragrant
blossoms, or better, there was no poet or painter but *only*

awareness of richly fragrant blossoms. This was the whole world of the moment, and the subject-object distinction is not present, for this is awareness apart from or prior to such distinction. All values arise in such immediate experience, and if they are of the sort to which Nishida, or the garden architect and the poet, gave expression, they arise out of the pre-intentionality of 'pure experience.'"

It was with these words found on the painting of plum blossoms by the Yangtze that he inscribed my copy of his *Religion and Nothingness*, so that our philosophical encounter, our "discontinuity" in time, would be well marked. It was now three hours later, and Nishitani-*sensei* walked with me from his house, seemingly as reluctant to end our time together as I was. He walked with me up a steep and long stairway near his house to an old Shintō shrine, where we talked of life and death for a few minutes more. We walked back down to the street, where the taxi that he had called was waiting for me. He looked like an authentic Yoda from a *Star Wars* set, a wise and profound instructor in matters of both philosophical and spiritual depth, standing in his grey-black *yocata*, cane in hand, waving goodbye in the Kyoto dusk. I shall not soon forget this man, whose life illustrates better than most just how uniquely worthwhile a human life can be.

CHAPTER FOUR

Relatedness

This chapter and the one following are essays in comparative (cross-cultural) thought. In order to try to express the importance of the sense of relatedness, of caring, and the resultant experiences of joy, I will dwell on sources both Western and Eastern (primarily Japanese). No one tradition has a monopoly on insight, and none is without significant difficulties resulting from its way of being in the world. Often, however, you can better capture the significance of an idea or practice by going beyond the habitual and expected approaches of your own tradition to those of a foreign and less well-known and understood tradition. The result can be a deepening of understanding.

Heidegger's sense of *dwelling* in the world, and not just existing in it, arose out of a recognized capacity for receptive rather than manipulative awareness. He described in detail what it meant to be open to the surrounding environment in the building of a bridge that would tie together two river banks. He sought to envisage a bridge that would enhance the near and distant sense of appropriateness in the humanscape and the landscape rather than violate the *neighbourhood* by forcing a passageway from one side of the river to the other, without regard for the creation of an event that *gathered* the *fourfold* together in this *horizon* of possibility and opportunity. If the building is successful, the resultant sensation or emotion or feeling is one of joy, arising from our increased sense of relatedness, because the disparate elements of our horizon have been brought together. The bridge occasions an increase in our sense of relatedness, of tying together the disparate elements within our horizon. A joyful building engenders a joyful recognition when the task is completed, and it will continue to be a source of meaningful satisfaction each time the bridge is used or viewed.

As the bridge becomes an enhancement within our horizon, a neighbourly event, so our sense of our relatedness to the broader horizonal awareness, the world, is also a source of joy. In his hauntingly profound and beautiful book *The Saviors of God*, Nikos Kazantzakis expresses the sense of belonging in this wider sense, with considerable passion:

37. Joy! Joy! I did not know that all this world is so much part of me, that we are all one army, that windflowers and stars struggle to right and left of me and do not know me; but I turn to them and hail them.

38. The universe is warm, beloved, familiar, and it smells like my own body. It is Love and War both, a raging restlessness, persistence and uncertainty.[1]

You care about others, about your neighbourhoods large and small, and about the world because you have sympathetically or empathetically identified with it. As in Kohlberg's *stage seven*, you both know and feel this kinship. Yet if someone asks why anyone should care about the cosmos, and accuses those who hold this and related positions of being "bleeding hearts" or overly emotional mystical trippers, it is not easy to know how to respond. It is not easy for the same reason that it is not easy to tell someone why one ought to be moral. In the final analysis, the *whole story* must be told for the fullest justification to be given. Even then, there is nothing in the telling of it, even two or three times, to prevent the hearer from remaining unmoved, unresponsive to the subtleties of an allegedly "higher" vision of things.

Even more troublesome is the imaginable lack of success you might have in telling a hardened individual why she or he should care about those in her or his closest neighbourhood. Bernard Williams describes this well in his introduction to *Morality*: "Does he care for anybody? Is there anybody whose sufferings or distress would affect him? If we say 'no' to this, it looks as though we have produced a psychopath. If he is a psychopath, the idea of arguing him into morality is surely idiotic, but the fact that it is idiotic has equally no tendency to undermine the basis of morality or of rationality."[2] The psychopath as psychopath is morally hopeless because s/he does not care about anyone or anything else. Williams contrasts the psychopath with the nearly as hopeless *amoralist*, whom you can imagine as "having some affections, occasionally caring for what happens to somebody else."[3] The amoralist is not concerned with issues of fairness, justice, or other general moral considerations, nor is s/he particularly consistent about anything, except for a fluctuating self-interest. Still, the amoralist affords us a glimpse of

what morality needs in order to get off the ground, even though it is unlikely in practice to get off the ground in a conversation with him.

He gives us, I think, almost enough. For he has the notion of doing something for somebody, because that person needs something. He operates with this notion in fact only when he is so inclined. Even if he helps these people because he wants to, or because he likes them, and for no other reason ... what he wants to do is *to help them in their need*, and the thought he has when he likes someone and acts in this way is "they need help," not the thought "I like them and they need help." This is a vital point: this man is capable of thinking in terms of others' interests, and his failure to be a moral agent lies (partly) in the fact that he is only intermittently and capriciously disposed to do so.[4]

In order to glimpse the moral point of view, the amoralist needs to "extend his sympathies" to others, not necessarily to those immediately around and before him, in order to achieve some sense of fairness and the ability and willingness to generalize his stance towards others "equally." Williams warns that ethics is not simply a matter of the development of the capacity for sympathy, because consideration of issues of desert, just distribution, rights, and the value of the human person all need to be worked out in considerable detail as well. In a provocative summary identifying the role that sympathy plays in ethics, he writes: "It does not follow from this that having sympathetic concern for others is a necessary condition of being in the world of morality, that the way sketched is the *only* way 'into morality.' It does not follow from what has so far been said; *but it is true.*"[5]

This conclusion interests me because it parallels some of what I have sketched out earlier on with respect to valuation. The basic requirement of valuation is that we are capable of valuing, and unless there were some primitive or given sense of euphoria and dysphoria, it would be hard to know how to get the business of valuation started. Similarly, unless we already have the capacity and the sensitivity to care, to be sympathetically concerned about another, then there is no way into ethics except as the formal study of moral reasoning, divorced from caring and valuing. You would then know, perhaps, how you ought to act, but you would neither care to so act nor would you so act consistently, at least not necessarily. One who already cares, however, is predisposed to work out how she or he ought to act, in order to act in precisely this way. She or he is already committed to ethics and, in general, to the now self-imposed requirements of ethical living. She or he already cares, and the details and extent of that caring continue to be worked out over a consistent and dependable lifetime.

The place to begin to understand the basic requirement for originating ethical awareness is with anyone or anything that is, in fact, cared for. This is the starting point of purchase, and with persistence and considerable luck you may be able to expand the range of caring to include a great deal more than you originally included. Whether the final reach of caring will include a sense of the relatedness of all things is unclear because of the complexity of the pathway(s) to be followed en route.

RELATEDNESS AS FOUNDATIONAL

In her provocative book *Caring: A Feminine Approach to Ethics & Moral Education*, Nel Noddings outlines an understanding of human nature as characterized by the fact of *relatedness* rather than separation, or being *alone* in the world. She describes the "ethical ideal" as arising from two sentiments: "the natural sympathy human beings feel for each other and the longing to maintain, recapture, or enhance our most caring and tender moments."[6] And it is the accompanying sense of *joy* that results from the awareness of relatedness, and the resultant *caring* for those things to which we claim to be related, that encourages the maintenance and growth of and the steadfast acting in accordance with this ideal.

Noddings refers to "joy" as an "affect" or a "feeling" rather than an emotion, since affects or feelings are reflective modes of consciousness, whereas emotion is non-reflective. We often have feelings about our lives in a specifically self-conscious way. We can look at ourselves feeling, and we can take joy in the sweep of past and present emotions, knowing, feelings and doings that we gather together in an assessment of how things are going for us to this point. Quoting R.S. Peters, Noddings concurs that emotions usually have *objects* – for example, you are angry with someone in particular, and not just generally angry.[7] I can be fearful of the car bearing down upon me as I cross the road, but I am unlikely to be fearful-in-general as I do so. Of course, you can have a phobia, or be so depressed that nearly everything causes you to fear both in a specific and in some general sense about your being in the world. But these are abnormal states. To be sure, Jean-Paul Sartre described in detail a general and non-specific *angst*, a "lonely emptiness" as Noddings recounts it, but she prefers to call this a feeling rather than an emotion. In fact this feeling of lonely emptiness is the direct opposite of her own posited joy.

Joy is to relatedness what Sartre's lonely emptiness is to his radical aloneness, or unrelatedness. I would add that the *existentialists'* stress on the alienness of the world to us, on its being slimy (a metaphor for such unconnectedness) and dense (incomprehensible), is the direct horizonal cause of their emphasis on "nausea," "angst," and the generally pessimistic stance they appear to take. It is true that they turn it around and, by standing firmly and robustly *against* the meaninglessness and alienness of the world and of others, are able to affirm a positive viewpoint with both joy and conviction. I stand with those who view existentialism as an unusually positive and life-affirming philosophy. Nevertheless, it remains the case that the positive is built on a long story that explores the extent to which human beings are both alone in and estranged from each other, and from the world itself. Noddings recommends that we take a second look at the assumption that we are *basically* estranged and alone. She concludes, I think rightly, that we are basically related rather than alone, and as a result fundamentally caring rather than alienated and fearful. The result is that we experience, except in justified specific instances, joy rather than angst, all along life's way.

WATSUJI TETSURŌ AND SOCIAL RELATEDNESS

The modern Japanese philosopher Watsuji argues at length that what is distinctive about the Eastern perspective on ethics is the fundamental assumption that we are first *in relation*, and only secondarily individuals. While much of Watsuji's work has never been translated, what little there is suffices to demonstrate the fundamental starting-point of *relatedness* as typically Far Eastern. Watsuji asserts that the "place of ethical questions really lies in the *between-ness between men*, not in consciousness of the isolated individual."[8] The term "between-ness" has several connotations for Japanese readers. "Between" can refer to the various sorts of contacts, encounters, duties, obligations, co-operation, struggles, enmity, and so on between one individual and another. This sense of between is the relational sense, and in the Orient it automatically draws to the surface the network of relational duties emerging from the Confucian heritage: father/son, father/mother, father/daughter, mother/daughter, brother/sister, friend/friend, ruler/subject, and so on. Yet there is a second sense of between that must be mentioned as well. What is between one person and another is *emptiness*, *nothingness*, a *space* or *field* in which we can meet, talk, love, hate, hurt, nurture, encourage, and otherwise engage in ethically significant activity with one another. The between is the place wherein we are able to interact with one another, and it is a field of possibility, an opportunity as much as an emptiness to fill.[9] Leaving the notion of emptiness to one side for the present, the betweenness of men and women works itself out in the *way* called "ethics," which occasions and is the description of the consensual rules and structures of social existence.

Utilizing the somewhat startling conception of the "identity of self-contradiction" (or the "unity of opposites"), a notion that is ubiquitous in modern Japanese philosophy, Watsuji insists that we are individuals, and yet we are individuals only in so far as we are foregrounded expressions of the background whole, which is society at large, or humankind. It makes no sense to speak of an individual except as the individual stands out from the whole of which s/he is a part. Of course, to speak of the whole is to be an individual who stands out from it and reflects back on it as well. We are individuals only in so far as we recognize that we are related to the social whole, and there is the social whole only as there are individuals who both constitute it and stand apart from it, in reflection, in order to assess its worth and to direct it. What results is a "relational unity of opposites," for we conclude that we are not only part of the social whole, and not just individually distinct, but are also related to the *other* person because we are "one in communal existence."[10]

The importance of this brief excursion into Japanese ways of thinking is that it calls into question a common Western assumption that we are first individuals and then move our way into group consciousness and social skills, and that the group is nothing more than the sum of the individuals who make it up. By contrast, the Japanese assumption is that we are always already related *as well as* individual, and that unless that were so, we would not know that we are individuals. Individuals are individuals necessarily against a background of social relatedness. To recognize yourself as an individual is already to recognize your individuality as compared with your existing social relatedness. Furthermore, there cannot be first individuals and then a group of individuals, for if that were so, many or even most people would stand outside the relatedness of society, finding that they have no interest in giving up the freedom and contentment of their own individuality. Yet wherever there are and have been human beings, they have *associated*, grouped, organized ways of living with each other, become intimate, formed families of sorts, desired a *network* of relationships, and suffered from prolonged periods of isolation from other human beings. Watsuji concludes that we are individuals as related, related as individuals, and that this "double structure" alone can account for both human individuality and human relatedness. The one does not follow from the other, for the one already implies the other.

Perhaps one final point needs to be made concerning "between-ness." Just as the individual and the social whole are not to be separated from each other except for purposes of thinking and speaking, so mind and body are not to be separated. The betweenness is, after all, not just the bridging of mental space between lovers, for example, but it is also the bridging of physical space. We need to cross the between and make contact in the most intimate space of closeness. Yuasa remarks that Watsuji often writes of the "carnal body" in his work on Japanese ethics, and his brief translation of a passage from Watsuji's *Ethics* is important in this regard:

The carnal interconnection is always found wherever there is betweenness, even though the manner of conjunction may differ. We find it not only between husband and wife, but it is also clearly visible even between friends. To feel like seeing a friend is to tend to go physically near him ... Seen in this light, the interconnection between carnal bodies contains the moment of experience, a moment that will naturally develop into a psychological relationship. It is, therefore, clearly a mistake to regard the relationship simply as a psychological relationship without the interconnection between carnal bodies.[11]

Mind and body, too, are a unity, and perhaps a unity of opposites. But ethics is an ethics of the whole person, in relationships in the between where intimacy is to be found, both personally and socio-culturally

NODDINGS ON RELATEDNESS

What Noddings takes to be normal is the realization that we are always already in relationship to many things, and that we are naturally *caring* towards those people (and things) for whom we have the sense of relatedness: "We love not because we are required to love but because our natural relatedness gives natural birth to love. It is this love, this natural caring, that makes the ethical possible." In order to be in a position to care we must be aware of our relatedness, and in order to be in a relationship we must "commit ourselves to the openness that permits us to receive the other." We must be open, "available," willing to take on the *risks* of a relationship. Relatedness, rather than aloneness, is our basic and fundamental reality, Noddings contends, "and not just a hopelessly longed-for state." It is important to follow her in her analysis, for her point is that we are not only related but that a great many of our most profound, positive value-experiences arise from the "recognition or fulfilment of that relatedness." She articulates with force and tenderness the range of joyful relatednesses:

There is the joy that unaccountably floods over me as I walk into the house and see my daughter asleep on the sofa. She is exhausted from basketball playing, and her hair lies curled on a damp forehead. The joy I feel is immediate ... This joy arises out of an awareness of the caring relation. It is not something in this moment that brings the joy, even though my daughter is the direct object of my consciousness. Rather, it is something beyond the moment – a recognition of fulfilment of relatedness – that induces this joy.

Must there be an object of joy? Suppose I am working in my garden or lying on the beach under a starry sky. A seedling uncovered beneath the mulch may trigger joy (as my daughter did), or a shooting star may induce the feeling; but, then again, there may be no particular object of my joy. There is a sense of well-being, but more than that. I am not focusing consciousness on myself, but am aware peripherally of myself-perceiving. There is joy experienced as a real quality of the world – not as a state resulting from an appraisal of my situation in the world.[12]

The experienced joy may have no particular direct object as its occasion, but neither is it devoid of indirect sensual content. It is, whatever else, an experience, and not merely an intellectual awareness. Perhaps this general sense of well-being is *both* an intellectual awareness *and* an experience of belonging in the world, as well as a sense of relatedness to it. But it is not primarily or exclusively an ideational response. Feelings, unlike emotions, are reflective awarenesses of the meaning and value of a sensual field.

In a like vein, Yuasa says of the Japanese, quoting from Watsuji's early study of *Ancient Japanese Culture*, that "there is no distinction between the mind and the flesh, so there is no clear consciousness of the distinction between the self and the modes of external beings in one's bodily sensations." The result is an embrace of nature as that with which you are conjoined in the meeting-place of the between: "They loved nature, becoming one with its whirling life ... This intimate embrace with nature does not allow one to make nature into an object of thinking."[13] You come into the world already related to nature, and already encountering nature and others in the between.

It is in the between that you come to experience the "becoming one with" another. In this mode of relatedness, the space and moment of betweenness almost vanishes, virtually disappearing into a seamless blending of self and other, or lover and beloved. Yet individuality persists, and the betweenness persists, intact, although shrunk to its smallest possible extent. It is in the between that we come together.

Noddings' language is remarkably similar on this point. Consider the following reflection on the "place" of joy arising: "It is connected to me and to the object that triggers it, but it is focused somewhere beyond both, in the relation or in a recognition of relatedness."[14]

A significant part of what it means to be human is to discover the space between ourselves and the other, and to learn how to shrink this space to a point of *intimate* relational possibility. The traversing of this psychological and physical space, as with the bridging of Heidegger's physical river-space, may yield either alienation (and even intensify our separation) or relatedness (to the point of an *intimate* coming together through caring identification). The choice appears to be ours, in each moment of each day that we spend in this world, alone and together.

CRITIQUE OF KOHLBERG

Like Carol Gilligan, about whom I will say more in a moment, Noddings is in process of sketching out an alternative approach to morality and moral education to that offered by Kohlberg. Noddings and Gilligan wish to demonstrate that his emphasis on moral reasoning, justification, and justice are less representative of the ethical lives of girls and women, although both emphasize that they are not writing about an ethics that is strictly for women but one for men and women whose moral experience does not fit neatly into the Kohlbergian schema. None the less, women are less likely to engage in abstract reasoning about morality as moral justification, and more likely to discuss morality in terms of more "concrete situations."[15] These concrete situations are situations of specific relatedness. As Gilligan writes,

Thus women not only define themselves in a context of human relationship but also judge themselves in terms of their ability to care. Women's place in man's life cycle has been that of nurturer, caretaker, and helpmate, the weaver of those networks of relationships on which she in turn relies. But while women have thus taken care of men, men have, in their theories of psychological development, as in their economic arrangements, tended to assume or devalue that care. When the focus on individuation and individual achievement which extends into adulthood and maturity is equated with personal autonomy, concern with relationships appears as a weakness of women rather than as a human strength.[16]

Gilligan and Noddings warn that a caring approach to ethics, undervalued because it is not reasoning and justice oriented, may well lead to conclusions supportive of Kohlberg's allegation that women often appear to be "stuck" at stage-three reasoning.[17] Stage-three "peer-group" moral reasoning gives primacy to the group, towards which you wish to be "seen" as acting in a way that will please, hence the so-called "nice-boy, good-girl" orientation. But stage three (or at least some variation on it) is taken by Noddings and Gilligan to be an alternative route to morality. The roots of this may well be found in the adolescent breaking-away from mother and father that characterizes the individuation process for boys, as contrasted with the girl/mother identification that is typical of girls. Because of these contrasting patterns, "girls emerge from this period with a basis for 'empathy' built into their primary definition of self in a way that boys do not."[18] Boys emerge with sharper, more separate ego boundaries, keeping the between clear and distinct. Boys learn to play in more competitive situations according to strict adherence to the rules of the game, while "girls' play tends to occur in smaller, more intimate groups, often the best-friend dyad, and in private places."[19]

This need not imply that we are *either* justice *or* care oriented in our ethical decision-making, for there is no *necessary* incompatibility between the two for the most part. Gilligan and Attanucci confirm this judgment in the conclusion to an article describing these alternative moral orientations: "If moral maturity consists of the ability to sustain concerns about justice and care, and if the focus phenomenon indicates a tendency to lose sight of one set of concerns, then the encounter with orientation difference can tend to offset errors in moral perception."[20] In caring, we need to consider rationally whether we are being just, appropriate, and fair, and in being just and fair we ought to care about those involved and about the subtle nuances of the case that do not quite fit the general rules and precedents, and for which an exception might well be made. Failure to express a balance between justice and caring in our judgments is a result of the "focus phenomenon." This state is characterized by a tendency to operate from one perspective or the other. What we need to do is to apply both perspectives to a situation and try to work something out to include the insights each approach affords. We need to maintain the *tension* between these approaches, letting neither overrun our sensibilities to the other.

It may well be that no easy way can be found to reconcile justice and caring, but then no one ever claimed that ethical action was easy to discern. Just as we often wish to discuss our pending decisions with others, there is an advantage in being able to turn to our own inner dialogue, listening carefully to the insights of caring and justice, concern and duty, love and obligation, before deciding what is to be done. Our age is far too heavily an age of justice, lawyers, rules, and a decidedly "male" sense of order and fairness. It is distinctively an age when men are not encouraged to care, to nurture, and to preserve a sense of dwelling in their neighbourhoods. But an uncaring "justice" is inevitably unjust, and the moral prescription of the moment must be a temporary *overdose* of caring and an empathetic identification with others in order to redress the imbalance and restore the tension between justice and caring. The longer-term perspective will likely be one that reduces the overdose to a more normal one, where justice and caring will be considered the two sides of the moral coin of the day.

In a summary contrast between Kohlberg's stage-six justice reasoning and a *caring-based* ethical perspective, Gilligan states that,

Whereas the rights conception of morality that informs Kohlberg's principled level (stages five and six) is geared to arriving at an objectively fair or just resolution to moral dilemmas upon which all rational persons could agree, the responsibility conception focuses instead on the limitations of any particular resolution and describes the conflicts that remain.

Thus it becomes clear why a morality of rights and noninterference may appear frightening to women in its potential justification of indifference and unconcern. At the same time, it becomes clear why, from a male perspective, a morality of responsibility appears inconclusive and diffuse, given its insistent contextual relativism.[21]

Mary Field Belenky et al. have also provided a summary of the work of Carol Gilligan and her colleague Nona Lyons, as follows:

They have shown how the responsibility orientation is more central to those whose conceptions of self are rooted in a sense of connection and relatedness to others, whereas the rights orientation is more common to those who define themselves in terms of separation and autonomy. Although these differences in self-definition do not necessarily divide along gender lines, it is clear that many more women than men define themselves in terms of their relationships and connections to others.[22]

Caring implies an enhanced sense of connection and interrelatedness and a reduced emphasis on separation and individual autonomy. And such connectedness allows a "way of knowing," at the heart of which is "the capacity for empathy."[23] Belenky et al. call this way of knowing "constructivism," and describe those who adopt it as stretching "the outer boundaries of their consciousness – by making the unconscious conscious, by consulting and listening to the self, by voicing the unsaid, by listening to others and staying alert to all the currents and undercurrents of life about them, by imagining themselves inside the new poem or person or idea that they want to come to know and to understand." The result is an empathetic identification with the thing known, a "passionate" interaction with that which you wish to understand: "Constructivists become passionate knowers, knowers who enter into a union with that which is to be known."[24]

If I am correct in my analysis of Kohlberg's stage-seven thinking, then there are aspects of stage seven that closely resemble the caring stance. First, emphasis is placed on the individual, on the person, rather than on the observing of the general rule, or the abstract and impersonal casting of lots, or the general rather than the specific. Second, the focus is on the context or situation rather than on some abstract and stripped-down generalized ideal account. Third, emphasis is placed on relatedness itself rather than on the obeying of principles or rules, or on the extent to which a moral decision is abstractly justifiable. This does not imply, of course, that women who care are necessarily stage-seven moralists, only that Kohlberg has packed so much into stage seven that it may well include much that ought to have been included in various stages along the way as essential ingredients in the moral-maturation process. Such things as a caring attitude, an emphasis on relatedness, on attention to the details of the situation at hand, and on the development of a wider whole-story context may serve to temper considerations of justice and other more impersonal and rigidly abstract moral principles. Unless you are a psychopath, you *have* cared, at least to some small extent and at least about someone, and one of the chief distinguishing features of stage-awareness is the *range or extent of that caring capacity*. At stages five and six you rationally include the entire human race in your deliberations (about which you ought to care), and at stage seven about the world of beings and things that form the entire greater environment, and about which you do care deeply.

ANIMALS, PLANTS ... AND ROCKS?

Precisely in this connection, it is not by mere coincidence that Noddings includes a chapter on caring for *animals and plants, things and ideas.* She affirms that an ethic grounded in caring "must consider our relation to animals. For us, there is no absolute source of life, meaning, and morality that separates the species neatly according to some preordained value hierarchy." The experiential truth of the matter is that many of us do care about our pets, our plants and gardens, and look beyond the limits of the domestic, to the wilderness, and include the well-being of the elephant, dolphin, whale, and panda bear in our caring. Some of us care about rocks and pebbles, water and outer space as well. Hence, "we need to account for these feelings and come to grips with the question whether our relation to animals can ever be properly described as having an ethical aspect."[25]

I do not wish to explore the issues of ecological ethics here, for that forms the subject matter of the next chapter. What does interest me here and now is Noddings' emphasis on concern for the wider context as part of the whole story, the expansion of one's horizon of caring to include more than the human. She is insightful in adding to this broadening of the ethical sphere of consideration the "sensitive and aesthetic" capabilities as well.[26] If we concede that "greatness of mind is measured by the extent of our concern,"[27] then part of what is required for ethics to be more developed rather than less is a concern for things, in the widest possible sense, in the light of which we attempt to devise an adequate ethical position.

John Macmurray was cited earlier as one who identified the importance of educating the sensibilities, and he specifically encouraged sensual sensitization. To be related – a basic ontological fact about our way of being in the world – is to value that to which you are related, and to disvalue whatever stands in the way of the maintenance and enhancement of that relatedness. The ethical mode of valuing is called caring, while the aesthetic equivalent is also *caring*, but in the sense of being found inherently or fundamentally worthwhile, not in the sense of occasioning the same degree of reciprocity as is required in ethical encounters with human beings. Rocks do not love back – pet rocks though they may be – nor do they raise questions about the meaning of rocks, or the ideal system of relations among rocks. Plants, rocks, and even animals do not *respond* in the way that humans do, but this indicates a difference in the sort of relationships that we can have with them, not a barrier that keeps us from caring, from nurturing, from exercising our stewardship, or from *dwelling* among the world's non-human richness rather than conceiving of it merely as a valueless resource except as material-at-hand to be expended as we wish.

A telling account of what is termed "respect for things" has been given by Henry Bugbee. Again emphasizing receptivity towards the greater surround, rather than exploitation of it, he writes,

By "leaving things be" I do not mean inaction; I mean respecting things, being still in the presence of things, letting them speak. Existing is absolute. Things are of infinite importance in existing. But as Kant says, existing is not a character of things; it is their givenness. And since the givenness of things is what I take to be the foundation of respect for *them*, I cannot see that emphasis on things of a certain character, as opposed to things lacking this character, affords an ultimate purchase for interpreting the possibility of respect ... I have been unable to follow that tradition of thinking personality to be a necessary character of anything deserving respect.[28]

Bugbee goes so far as to conclude that the "religious attitude is one of truly universal concern for things." And this concern is not a concern for things generally or abstractly taken but "a concern which is concretely an experience of things in the vein of individuality." To have respect for things, to express a reverence for things results from comprehending that all existences are "gifts," and by maintaining an attitude of "being embraced by a significance that is all-embracing; as a significance found in them uniquely and originally it is the essence of their individuality."[29]

The world is filled with meaning if you are but open and receptive to it, but it requires a fundamental and transformative capacity to appreciate things as inherently worthwhile in themselves and as sources of intrinsic meaning in our lives. "Let it be!" is the increasingly amplified cry of those who can enjoy the magnificence of existence and who care about whether any of it will be left for the already born and yet unborn generations to come. There is an additional twist to this cosmic caring at this very point in the history of things, for unless we learn to care, to protect and nurture, and to strive to find ways to live well without heedlessly expanding the economy, we will destroy ourselves, our children and grandchildren, and countless species that are already perishing on a daily basis. Aesthetic and metaphysical caring are not usually a necessary condition for basic human survival. At this precise moment, however, they appear to be just that: conditions of existence.

ZEN MEANING

Zen Buddhism recommends that we lose ourselves in the richness of the moment; that we learn to become as though a raindrop, a flower, or the gnarled pine that we see, touch, smell, and hear before us. The claim that we should *become* a tree or a flower may appear to be illogical, or impossible except as a metaphor of the same intention as comparing your love to a red, red rose. Thus, it might be concluded, such comparisons are not to be taken literally, but are a kind of poetic licence that expresses intensity of feeling. But something very different happens on the Zen account. As an artist expressing the stance of Zen Buddhism, you must attend to the landscape or the pine tree or the human body immediately before you for its own sake, i.e. intrinsically. Learn how to make it your whole world of the moment; lose yourself in the richness of the experience. Look at things for the *joy* of seeing them, as the musician and the student of birdsong likely chose their vocation because of their love of music and song, and of nature. John Macmurray captures this aesthetic sensitivity well when he writes:

Sensitive awareness becomes then a life in itself with an intrinsic value of its own which we maintain and develop for its own sake, because it is a way of living, perhaps the very essence of all living. When we use our senses in this way we come alive in them, as it were, and this opens up a whole new world of possibility. We see and hear and feel things that we never noticed before, and find ourselves taking delight in their existence. We find ourselves living in our senses for love's sake, because the essence of love lies in this. When you love anyone you want above all things to be aware of him, more and more completely and delicately. You want to see him and hear him, not because you want to make use of him but simply because that is the natural and only way of taking delight in his existence for his sake. That is the way of love, and it is the only way of being alive. Life, when it is really lived, consists in this glad awareness. Living through the senses is living in love. When you love anything, you want to fill your consciousness with it.[30]

And in filling your whole consciousness with it, there is, at least for the moment, nothing else of which you are aware – not even your own breathing. Your whole consciousness is the tree, your loved one, and the only you that is left is the consciousness of the loved one, or the bamboo, or the music. You have become that of which you are aware, by which you are filled, at least in the sense that your ego-sense (with all its busy-noise) has disappeared, leaving only the immediate experience itself. You are totally absorbed in such awareness, abandoning any attempt to be objective or dispassionate about what is being attended to, as inevitably distancing.

Rather than speculating about what might be meant by an artist's or anyone else's becoming one with another by means of the power of identification and absorption in the situation, Zen has long *practised* this capacity, and has made it an integral part of disciplined cultural training. The Japanese are widely known for their good taste in things aesthetic, and the subtlety of their sensual discernment is often noted. The philosophical underpinning for this cultural capacity is provided in large measure by Zen Buddhism. Zen requires that you learn to let go of your ego and then forget your assumptions about the object's "being out there." Do not separate yourself from the object. Instead, make yourself open to the fullness of the immediate experience itself. Through meditative practice the mind becomes concentrated and stilled, quieted, receptive rather than active and grasping. The mind ceases to be an ocean of distractions and emotional and intellectual turbulence. The winds of the mind die down, and the surface becomes calm, tranquil, like a *mirror*.

The mirror-mind of receptivity is able to reflect more of that which is apprehended, and it does so in a less distortive and forceful way. Things float along on its quiet surface rather than being dashed to and fro and distorted out of shape by fears, wishes, cravings, and graspings. Kishimoto describes the results of a receptively meditative mind beautifully:

Suppose a tree is chosen as the object of mental concentration. A Zen meditator tries to reach Zen experience by means of concentration of his mind upon the tree. At first, all the ideas and emotions associated with this tree, acquired during his past life, come up on the surface of consciousness. Gradually, as the mind becomes tranquillized, such mental activities associated with the tree die out. Then, nothing but the tree stands in the conscious realm. If the practice of concentration goes successfully, *the tree occupies the entire conscious world as the object of concentration*.

Finally, when the last touch of ego-consciousness disappears, the meditator loses even the self-consciousness that he is concentrating on an object. The tree alone exists in his mind without his ego-consciousness. He becomes totally identified with the tree. The tree is no more the outside object of concentration. *What exists in the realm of experience is nothing but the pure awareness of the tree*.[31]

Lose yourself in the immediate awareness such that it is no longer "your experience," nor is it an experience of "that" tree "out there." Instead, there is but the experience itself, the givenness of treeness. You lose your impermeable ego-boundary walls by reaching out and embracing the tree, the other, and then by concentrating your awareness on the tree embraced, opening to it, exclusive of all else. Consider the following account by Izutsu as a depiction of the aesthetics of receptivity:

The painter sits in quiet contemplation, intensely concentrating his mind upon the ideal image of the bamboo. He begins to feel in himself the rhythmic pulsebeat of the life energy which keeps the bamboo alive and which makes the bamboo a bamboo, becoming gradually concordant with the pulsebeat of the life-energy which is running through his mind-body complex. And finally there comes a moment of complete unification, at which there remains no distinction whatsoever between the life-energy of the painter and the life-energy of the bamboo. Then there is no longer any trace in the consciousness of the painter of himself as an individual self-subsistent person. There is actualized only the bamboo. Where is it actualized? Internally? Or externally? No one knows. It does not matter ... The sole fact is that the bamboo is there, actualized with an unusual vivacity and freshness, pulsating with a mysterious life-energy pervading the whole universe. At that very moment the painter takes up the brush. The brush moves, as it were, of its own accord, in conformity with the pulsation of the life-rhythm which is actualized in the bamboo.[32]

The same phenomenon of total absorption and complete identification is regularly expressed through the martial arts. You may have read of, and might be able to imagine yourself to be, a samurai swordsman who, by learning to focus mind and energy on the circumstances of the encounter, is no longer separated from his sword. Spontaneously, the sword seems to block a blow, and without any thinking, body and sword together thrust home the decisive blow. In a way, by concentrating on the whole context of the battle, you actually begin to think, stand, anticipate, and feel as your opponent does. Looking for any weakness, any break in concentration, any flaw of stance, sensing the differences in reach and quickness, you pounce as if in telepathic communication with the enemy's mind and purposes. For your own part, you must not worry about whether you are as good as your opponent, for if s/he is any good, this will signal the break in your concentration that leaves you momentarily vulnerable, and objectively separate. Nor do you have time to think about the positioning of your feet, or the appropriateness of your grip on the sword handle, or about your children at home, or the lessons given by your teacher. You must be in the battle totally, undistractedly, and your mind must be quiet enough to reflect the details of your opponent's mind and body.

For the moment, this *is* your entire world. The samurai is a lethal living weapon precisely because, in the moment, that is *all* that he is. The point is not whether there ought to be samurai, for theirs is but another *way* of development, like the tea ceremony, judo, aikido, karate, the writing of poetry, painting, landscape gardening, swordmaking, or the *kendo* of sword-using. If you are a samurai, haiku poet, brush painter, potter, musician, sports figure, manager, assembly-line worker, then you are taught from the beginning to apply yourself single-mindedly to the experience of the moment. Be fully there such that when you wash dishes, you do just that; and when you love, do only that. How unwelcome it is to be intimate with someone who is thinking about tomorrow's schedule. How deadly it is when confronting a sword-wielding enemy. The inappropriateness and diminishment of the possibilities for life and love are equally severe, either way.

IMMEDIACY

An important aspect of that which is given in direct experience is its immediacy. Ordinary cognitive activities are heavily mediated by language, by concepts, by stereotypes, and by the imposition of order and regularity such that exceptions are not even seen. Often, when you look at a pine tree, the term "pine tree" comes to mind, at least at the background of consciousness. Reliance on the term and the habits of expectation associated with it often shut off the freshness and novelty of first-time seeing, and you look without looking, see without seeing. For example, you navigate the front steps to your home as you have every day for years. How many are there? What are they made of? Are they worn, well-painted, scratched, chipped, covered with pine needles or leaves, snow or freshly cut grass clippings? Habitual seeing does not seek out such fresh information because it has already seen, and it sees now only in the routine fog of basic navigation. Of course, habit does have its place in the Zen tradition. You can only forget where your feet are in a samurai battle or martial arts performance because you have established a habit of correct placement. Discipline leaves you open to a single-minded application, and to creative and original espression. In this Japanese Zen sense, spontaneity comes after intense and practised discipline, and not before.

By way of contrast with the mediocrity of habitual and uncreative awareness, a certain Zen Buddhist temple in Japan is renowned for the manner in which it teaches children how to write seventeen-syllable haiku poetry, while at the same time teaching the characteristics of concentration: the emptying of mind until it becomes like a mirror, meditative quietness, and the capacity to see as though for the first time. Children are brought into the temple yard – itself usually quite sparse – and are led to a goldfish pond, or to the landscape garden, or to a tree in bloom, or to an interesting shadow. In this instance the pond is itself a miniature landscape, backed by a heavily planted rock garden. The twenty or so pre-teens gather around the edge of the pool, laughing at the swimming goldfish awaiting a feeding, and the poet-monk tells them that they will today write poems about the goldfish pond. Not just one, or two, or five, but maybe ten poems, each different, each capturing a different immediacy, a fresh perspective, a never-before-seen nuance. They are told that they could write twenty, or forty, or a hundred such poems in and of this one place and never exhaust its possibilities, for its depth and our limitless responses to it are inexhaustible. And this newly discovered world of infinite richness and depth opens to us, if we are receptive, without our needing to move even an inch from where we are initially seated.

The pine tree may be but habitually seen, or even mis-seen (for conditions may have changed over the years without your having noticed), because of the anticipation that it will have just those features common to your earlier encounters with pine trees. I suppose this could be glibly summarized by the ugly quip "If you've seen one, you've seen them all." The ugliness of this utterance is aggravated by the fact that it is an oft-used way of referring to women by men who point to a physical conformity and ignore the uniqueness of a person by homing in on a single feature. This language of reductionism derives from our ability to limit our interest in another to his or her sexuality and to reduce that sexuality to terms of generic consumption. Viktor Frankl records that he has encountered such attitudes in the use of the sorry phrase "masturbation on a woman."[33] Non-reductionistic relatedness is a considerable journey from this "using" of a person, yet without it there is but limited pleasure at the expense of the other rather than ecstatic joy in intimate relatedness with the cared-for. The magic is in the mutuality of the caring-for that each person bestows, as a wonderful gift, upon the other. It is this mutuality which transforms sexuality into ecstatic and joyful loving.

In any case, the Zen master tries to guard against habitual seeing by reminding himself that each time a novice enters his room for his brief audience with the master, it is essential to think that this very day could be the day of breakthrough. Alas, this student is slow, unmotivated, lacking insight, a slacker, and perhaps even a troublemaker. But he does not pigeon-hole the student, for that would be to miss progress in the making, if it were to happen. To write the student off would be to thereby render himself closed. He would no longer be able to perceive the subtle openings-to-change in the student's heretofore life-hardened pattern through which the aware teacher can begin to introduce learning opportunities. So he leaves behind the habits of expectation and greets the student as though for the first time. He focuses on every movement, every glimmer, every gesture, every word, every pause or stutter. Is this the day?

AESTHETICS, JAPANESE STYLE

One of the more intriguing modern accounts of Japanese aesthetics comes from the pen of Japan's most influential modern philosopher, Nishida Kitarō (1870–1945). In a recent article Steve Odin outlines the main arguments of an early essay by Nishida on the subject of aesthetics. Nishida begins by attempting to formulate an adequate definition of *beauty*. The approach he takes is "to reformulate the Kantian sense of beauty as disinterested pleasure or artistic detachment, by means of a key notion of Zen, *muga*, which can be translated as either "no-self" or "ecstasy."[34] We must classify the notions of *no-self*, *ecstasy*, and the related notion of *nothingness* in order to be able to grasp the aesthetic stance being described.

It is by now well known that the centrepiece of Zen is *satori*, i.e. enlightenment as the awakening of the awareness of your *formless self*, the self that is encumbered by or covered over by the noisy, superficially busy ego of everyday life. Satori is said to be the realization of your own Buddha-nature, which means that you come to know that the non-illusory self is always already as perfect as the enlightened Buddha, and that this inner realization or discovery ever awaits your realization of it. Satori is the state of being freed of all duality. "Buddha is the name applied to a person who has achieved this Non-duality."[35] Buddhahood, as Yanagi expresses it, "is the 'state' in which that which creates and that which is created are undifferentiated. The Undifferentiated, the Non-dual, is assumed to be the inherent nature of man."[36] But not only is that of which you are aware non-dual or undifferentiated, or "non-thinged," but even the mind, as self-consciousness, is without form. The self in this sense is never an object for itself, for it necessarily "defies and eludes differentiation and objectification."[37] It is formless. The "I" and the "that" of ordinary experience are now gone. In Zen terms, "body and mind have fallen away."

Applying this to aesthetics, Yanagi writes, "A true artist is not one who chooses beauty in order to eliminate ugliness, he is not one who dwells in a world that distinguishes between the beautiful and the ugly, but rather he is one who has entered the realm where strife between the two cannot exist."[38] In the realm of no-mind, where all distinctions have vanished, there is only awareness of that which is right now – except that the distinction between right now and eternity has also vanished, except in the telling of it. Realizing your own nature is to become a Buddha yourself. A Buddha is an incarnation of non-dual awareness. And it is as non-dual awareness "that we have the creation of a uniquely Oriental art."[39] Such abandonment of the intellectual and phenomenal self, the emotional and volitional self, is also the description of the religious state, and, we might add, of stage-seven awareness as well. In Nishida's words, "True religious feeling must be an absolutely humble attitude. It must be an attitude in which one has wholly effaced the self ... Sacred religious feeling appears when one has abandoned one's entire person. When we know truth, we must abandon the self and conform to truth itself. To view a thing aesthetically must mean to submerge the self within the thing in itself."[40]

Aesthetic feeling is selfless awareness of a non-dual sort such that whatever is perceived is taken as arising from the emptiness, the nothingness, that underlies all subsequently discernible things. Just as aesthetic awareness is awareness as an activity of the formless self, so a tree or a tea bowl "is no ordinary tree" or bowl but a "wonder-full" tree or bowl "seen as the self-expression of the formless self."[41] In other words, all things take on a depth, a *meaning* that they did not previously have for us, for they are now seen in their *suchness* as "divine" expressions or manifestations arising out of the heretofore undifferentiated source of things. It comes as no surprise that the point is often made in poetic form: "This means that the colours of the mountain are those of the Buddha, and that the murmuring of the mountain stream is his voice."[42]

Nothingness-as-divine is found underfoot, as it were, as the ground, figuratively and literally, of everything in the world. In Zen terms, nirvana (the divine, sacred) is samsara (the things of the ordinary world), and samsara is nirvana. Nothingness, or the divine, or the sacred is only knowable in the phenomenal world of experience *as* every *thing*. Each and every thing is an expression of (a manifestation of) nothingness itself. The phenomenally real of experience is not a creation separate from the creator, nor is it simply made in the image of the absolute. Rather, it *is* the absolute, expressed as the absolute expresses itself, i.e. phenomenally: "If one is really overwhelmed by the consciousness of absolute Nothingness, there is neither 'Me' nor 'God'; but just because there is absolute Nothingness, the mountain is mountain, and the water is water, and the being is as it is."[43] The function of the concept of emptiness or nothingness is to shatter the ordinary and habitual way of looking at things. Shatter the habits of language, of anticipatory seeing, and of your own purposes and preferences, and the object of consciousness will likely appear in a new and more ample light. Anticipations strip down what is before you to an expected cluster of properties. Empty-mindedness or "no-mindedness" affords a fresh glimpse at the richness of experience prior to the anticipatory structuring that impoverishes that which is "there" to be experienced.

Nishida refers to nothingness as a field or "place" (*basho*) out of which distinctions arise. The enlightened, sensitive, true-seeing individual, for Nishida, is one who has attained non-dualistic consciousness and yet, of course, is dualistically able to operate in the everyday world of distinctions. This twofold awareness yields stereoscopic vision; you see the richness of differentiation, but now it stands out against the background of the formless, of nothingness, of the vision of the greatest whole as creative source. You must learn to look at things, savouring every detail, and at the same time through things, towards the not-yet thinged richness beneath the habitually seen surface they present. Like a vial of colour spilled into water, patterns are always already detectable, *and yet* they change from glance to glance, swirling from the recognized to the novel. The stability of a privileged single viewing is rejected, and the encouragement to look again and again takes its place. There is some stability, moment to moment, but there is also possibility and openness to unending alternative perceptions. It is this depth, this inexhaustible profundity that leads beneath the surface of things, beneath the expected, and is a prime source of genuine beauty and meaning for us.

DEEP BEAUTY

On this account of Zen aesthetics, surface beauty alone is likely to be seen as gaudy, showy, or trendy. Deep beauty is beauty that displays or reveals an inner radiance, a simple, subdued, restrained, quiet expression of that which is bottomless and inexhaustible. Yanagi expresses this well when he states, "All works of art, it may be said, are more beautiful when they suggest something beyond themselves than what they are. For that reason objects that were considered 'complete' were not used as Tea-bowls: having shown all that they are and having nothing further to suggest, they give an impression of rigidity and coldness."[44] In this sense beauty is rich in afterflavour, in "deep reserve," and in suggesting or hinting at that which is like the lining of a well-tailored garment: the lining cannot be seen at the surface wearing but is indirectly visible in the hang of the garment, in its sculpted folds, and is easily discerned by a more sensitive and knowledgeable eye. Nishida uses the image of a kimono, whose lining of precious silk cannot be seen, and yet the lining is visible in the way the kimono hangs and keeps its shape. The lining is only hinted at by the outer surface hang of things.

Perhaps the nature of the scroll, on which the Japanese, Chinese, and Korean people inscribe both works of art and literature, will help in extracting points of comparative importance. The scroll is rarely completely opened at one time, for the viewing technique is to re-roll on one spindle while unrolling from the other. What results is a continuous passage of material without end, and for that matter without discrete beginning. You can begin anywhere, as you can with a book, of course, and then unwind in either direction, as is less likely with a book. The symmetry of one-directional pagination in the book is matched by an asymmetry of a continuing two-directionality in the scroll. You may pass and repass the entire text again and again. The whole text is available at all times. Throughout, the viewed inside is always *lined* by the outside, and the outside becomes better known as the inside is progressively revealed. Actually, the outside, as rolled-up remainder, *becomes* the inside as the scroll is unrolled. Inside and outside are relative terms, and the one becomes the other as the process of rolling and unrolling proceeds.

Writing in the Far East is often considered to be a higher art than painting. The calligraphic forms are already "pictures," called picto-graphs. Pictographs were by and large representative of external forms (for example the character "man" has two legs and a head). Not only have they become stylized over the centuries, but there is also considerable room for creative deviation in the depicting of pic-tographs. The calligrapher can abandon her/himself, choosing from several traditional styles, and particularly in Zen Buddhist writing style it does not matter whether or not the characters are somewhat distorted. Yet whether distorted or traditional in conception, the pic-tograph is totally present in one glance. When you read any word in this text, your mind builds the meaning as your eye moves from left to right assembling the sounds of each letter to form a word, "man." The pictograph 人 (nin) 間 (gen) is taken in at once, in its entirety.

Furthermore, the power of a word or phrase rendered in picto-graphs is not merely the cerebral reverberation that results from understanding what is said but includes as well the aesthetic look of a pictograph, its shape and texture, and the way it emerges out of the empty background of the paper or silk. No wonder paper and cloth are so important in Japan, for the power and richness of a word cannot be separated from the material ground out of which it arises. The texture, colour, and absorbency of the paper are all part of the language. If the paper also displays rough, imperfect edges, you grasp the incompleteness of the paper as symbol of the indefinite flow of things back into and out of the emptiness of the metaphysical background to the paper as background. Trim edges give the appearance of completeness, and blemishless paper implies a perfection in the text itself that must be guarded against. The distinctions between a literal meaning of a term, its background, its form, its style, and the size, texture, substance and edge-quality of the paper, the details of the ink and brush, let alone the mood and the accomplishments of the artist-writer, are blurred. The result is a gestalt of communicative appreciation of an evidently aesthetic sort that encourages you to reach beyond standardized, habitual, expected, univocal, and machine-reproducible expression. In writing too the inexhaustibility and bottomlessness must shine through, and be nourished.

The scroll, with beautiful backing as a central ingredient in its presentation, is returned to its box, which is equally suited to the scroll-whole of which it is a contributor. The putting away of the scroll and box is equally a part of the total experience of understanding and appreciation. It is done mindfully, not as an unwelcome task but as an aspect of your contribution to the *meaning* of *this* specific reading and viewing. The box rests on a shelf and is itself artful, beckoning the appreciator to try again, for an indefinite number of readings and responses, appreciations and context-creations still await. The surface merely hints at the depths of a form, and you must learn to look at it as an expression of the profound depth with which it is lined. The flux of experience, of the universe, and of ourselves opens up the possibility of the enrichment of meaning and the development of a sensitivity to others and to the things of this world, without end, limit, or pre-established form.

SHIBUI

The adjective *shibui*, a central concept in Japanese aesthetics, describes the subdued, subtle, austere, restrained, quiet depth of enlightened art. Great beauty is understated, yet as unmistakable as thunder; black and white in its restraint, yet as dazzling in its shades and contrasts as a rainbow. The surface merely calls attention to the profundity of the great depth, the deep reserve, which is but hinted at, whispered, pointed to with the most subtle of gestures. The aim of artistic creation includes the attempt to give form to the formless, to the non-dualistic, and to "line" all creations with the unfathomable rich potentiality of nothingness, called to consciousness by a surface hint. To express in the objet d'art that which is beyond surface and which somehow reveals great depth, various techniques are used.

For example, lines in a drawing are almost never straight, since straight lines are shapely and evidently formed, whereas crooked lines are in process, incomplete, and move you beyond their crooked expression. Odd numbers do the same, whereas even numbers are thought to be complete in themselves. Deep reserve is inexhaustibility, bottomlessness. Hence, shoji screens, so ubiquitous in Japan, are covered in white rice-paper, and they let in bright yet diffused light. You are made calm, tranquil, meditatively open to that which lies beyond the shoji screens, which is only hinted at. Such tranquillity, observed the late Zen scholar Hisamatsu, "is expressed in every work of true Zen art,"[45] for satori itself is achieved by *zazen*, that is, by means of meditational practice. The tea ceremony, to choose yet another example, emphasizes such tranquillity: "Sitting alone, away from the world, at one with the rhythms of nature, liberated from attachments to the material world and bodily comforts, purified and sensitive to the sacred essence of all that is around, a person making and drinking tea in contemplation approaches a sublime state of tranquillity."[46]

Asymmetry, incompleteness, tranquillity, the simplicity of shibui, and the empty spaces of painting, the blank whiteness, the empty silence, the non-distinct background sand in Zen rock gardens – each is expressive of the ground of all, of the unseen "beneath," of the "lining," of nothingness as undifferentiated. All art emerges from and leads to this deep reserve. The almost imperceptible movements in the Noh drama are gestures towards the stillness. The serenity on the faces of the ubiquitous statues of the Buddha engender and encourage this tranquility. This "beneath" is a saying without saying, yet for one who can hear it is as loud as thunder. "The beautiful is the revelation of the absolute through the medium of personality."[47] Art's foreground points to or is lined with the background of nothingness. In Robert Schinzinger's words, "This 'enveloping last' becomes perceivable as the metaphysical background of a piece of art. To see a piece of art which is an expression of the artist's personality, is to perceive at the same time that which stands behind the artist."[48]

FROM ART TO LIFE

Whether the art form is painting or the performance of the tea ceremony, of haiku poetry or Noh drama, the martial arts or meditation itself, the *way* that is taught is the way of *daily life*. To take the example of tea again, a contemporary tea master has written that "the principles of the Way of Tea are directed toward all of Your existence, not just to the part that takes place in the tearoom. In practice, the test lies

in meeting each occurrence of each day with a clear mind, in a composed state. In a sense, even your smallest action is the Way of Tea."[49]
Master Sen practices Tea by encouraging the four principles of harmony, respect, purity, and tranquillity.[50] *Harmony* requires that you
attend to the seizing of the opportunity to achieve a very special once-
and-only-now interaction between host and guest, by means of the
food prepared for this occasion, at this season, the utensils used, the
decorative flower arrangement and/or scroll chosen to blend with the
whole scene, all mindfully gathered and expressed here and now.
Respect demands that we "look deeply into the hearts of all people we
meet and at the things in our environment. It is then that we realize
our kinship with all the world around us."[51] *Purity* requires a sincere
attitude, a cleansing of the environment, including a symbolic retreat
from the "dust" and cares of the everyday world. You enter the doorway to the tea room in a crouching position, for it is about half as
high as an ordinary doorway. All who enter enter a different world,
and regardless of their stature they enter no higher than anyone else.
Tranquillity comes with the constant practice of harmony, respect, and
purity both in the tea ceremony and in everyday life. Tranquillity is
the finding of peace within oneself, and being calmly confident that
one can deal with whatever arises. You attend to the people, the sights
and sounds and the occasion of the tea ceremony afresh, separate
from the ordinary activities of the everyday noisy and cluttered world.

Tranquillity, harmony, respect, and purity are achievable through
the practice of the Way of Tea, and each is applicable to everyday life:
"At the center of a life based on harmony, respect, purity, and tranquillity is that inner peace that results from accepting your limits and
finding satisfaction within the incomplete. With this peace, dissatisfaction and anxiety vanish, replaced by self-possession and com-
posure."[52] Our own self-development opens us to others, and the
achievements of gaining a tea-mind allow us to attain insight into
our relatedness: "In my own hands," writes Tea Master Sen, "I hold
a bowl of tea; I see all of nature represented in its green color. Closing
my eyes I find green mountains and pure water within my own heart.
Silently sitting alone and drinking tea, I feel these become part of
me. What is the most wonderful thing for people like myself who
follow the Way of Tea? My answer: the oneness of host and guest
created through 'meeting heart to heart' and sharing a bowl of tea."[53]

SELF/OTHER

Through celebrating our relatedness to others and to the environment, we discover within ourselves the same deep reserve that is the

deep matter of art, the result of which is a lasting tranquillity in our lives as individuals. Paradoxically, through others we discover our own path, and the path to our individuality leads back to an enhanced capacity to interact well and meaningfully.

Noddings too encourages *ceremony* as a means to maintaining and enhancing your capacity and effectiveness as a carer – one who cares for:

Daily we have meals and dishes; cleaning and soiling; growing and cutting; making and using and making again; sallying forth and returning home. Each of these may be decried or celebrated.

The one-caring chooses to celebrate. Just as the Jew, or Christian, or Moslem chooses to celebrate that which is integral to his religion – that which represents its source – so the one-caring chooses to celebrate the ordinary, human-animal life that is the source of her ethicality and joy. She may find delight in her garden ... One may celebrate meals and food. It can be a sort of ceremony to start the water boiling before picking the corn, to offer home-made chicken soup to an ailing family member, to make chocolates at Christmas in one's own garage (coolness is needed), to sit down together day after day to share both food and thoughts. This most repetitious of all communal events – eating – may be either a festival or a matter of survival ... Thus repetition is not mere repetition, leading to boredom and disgust, but it represents opportunities to learn, to share, and to celebrate.[54]

It is, I hope, apparent that this inquiry into Japanese aesthetics, and in particular the Zen Buddhist religious background to it, has not been a proselytizing foray. Rather, it has been used as an example, albeit an example chosen in part because of the extraordinary reputation the Japanese have as a people of exquisite and profoundly sensitive aesthetic taste. Nevertheless, it need hardly be said that the Japanese do not have a monopoly on great art! Great art exists the world over, and each cultural tradition has a recognizable aesthetic history, along with a less recognizable avant-garde that reacts against the old in its effort to say the new. The Japanese story is an unusually suggestive one, for much within it can set off small explosions of recognition within each of us, and may often encourage adaptation from the Japanese experience to our own cultural and individual journey. Just as our encounter with Japanese business management has caused us to struggle to revise our own ways of doing business, so our encounter with a different horizon of understanding encourages us to wish to make a similar series of revisions aesthetically and philosophically. Note well, however, that the reverse is going on with intensity in Japan. The Japanese are learning daily about Western business practices, needs, and strategies for productivity, and it is difficult for us in the West to comprehend how "Westernized" Japan has already become – even in matters of aesthetics. To encourage comparative encounter is to occasion self-scrutiny, and even radical doubt about the limits and adequacy of your own horizon of understanding. It need not, however, cause us to abandon our "homeland" or our "birthright." Rather, in most cases, I suspect, it occasions a revitalization of our own cultural perspective, such that we come to dwell at home again, rather than just living there.

Note also that Zen Buddhism, Judaism, Christianity, and Islam are but the religious ways of coming to understand yourself, others, and the world by telling the whole horizonal story as best you can and in as much detail as you find possible. My thesis has been that each of these is, at its best, a stage-seven account of things, not that any one of them has the direct road to the truth. In addition to religious cultural views there are non-religious cultural views, philosophical positions, and variously incomplete positions in formation, each of which needs to be heard seriously, taken seriously, engaged in dialogue, and otherwise encountered. The result may itself be a major source of meaning in your life and a vindication of the thesis of human relatedness and the interrelatedness of all things. As George Burch wrote in his review of Bugbee's *Journal*, "Our concern is limited in practice by the breadth of our experience and the depth of our ability to respond, but it is not limited in theory by the unworthiness of things. The humility which refuses to judge other persons or other things as unworthy of our concern makes possible the respect by which we are committed to them, and this in turn makes possible the insight by which we discover the union between ourselves and all things."[55] This "declaration of interdependence" leads beyond the human, beyond plants and animals, beyond ecology taken in its narrow meaning, to the cosmos itself. Cosmological thinking is stage-seven thinking, and it is the ultimate in relatedness. It remains to sketch out this vision of things in the next chapter.

THE EMPTINESS OF THE MOSS GARDEN

▬ Emptiness, nothingness, silence, the blank space that predominates in Oriental painting, and the unseen silk lining of a precious kimono, which is only indirectly apparent in the well-tailored hang of the garment, all refer to the subtle background of everything, which in the West often goes completely unnoticed. The Haiku poet Bashō, in writing about the sound of the frog's splash upon its jumping into the old pond, actually sought to emphasize the deep silence evident to a perceptive listener both before and after the staccato noise of the splash-event. It is the silent frame surrounding the noise that allows that noise to stand out in its "suchness," in surprising intensity, like an exclamation point on a sheet of pure white paper. Below are two different translations of Bashō's famous poem, and if you emphasize the silence of the second with the silence-shattering splash of the first, the effect of a pin-point of sound in the midst of a surround of silence serves to heighten both the effect of the sound and our anticipation and reception of it.

> The old pond –   Breaking the silence,
> A frog leaps in,   Of an ancient pond,
> And a splash.[56]   A frog jumped into
>   water –
>   A deep resonance.[57]

Similarly, a Japanese temple bell, struck from outside by a wooden log suspended from a rope at both ends, rather than from inside by a clapper, as is customary with Western-style bells, is able to sound not simply because of its thin bronze shell but because that shell partitions the *inner space* from the rest of space, a marking-off of the unmarked, a dividing of the undivided, a shaping of the unshaped. You can actually imagine the sound of the soundless space, sounding because of the bronze bell and log striker, but nevertheless it is the soundless air that now sounds. It is almost a Zen kōan, or paradoxical puzzle, like "What is the sound of one hand clapping?" except that here it has become "What is the sound of the soundless?" It is the inner space of the bell that may be said to be the locus of the sounding, for were there no space there, or even an incorrect amount of or an inappropriately shaped space, the bell would offer only a dull thud rather than a vibrant ringing that ripples through the space within and around it for wonderful miles. The vast action is with and within the empty space, and not with or within the thin bronze shell, however beautiful and necessary it may be. In fact it is both, for just as everyday appearance is reality and reality is everyday appearance – *samsara* is *nirvana* and *nirvana* is *samsara* – so the sound is the result of both the space-air, which represents reality, and the bronze bell, which represents everyday appearance. The two are fused together in the incredible act of ringing, but it is a common shortcoming that we see but one of these and ignore the other. The everyday becomes humdrum, and not a new moment of shimmering beauty, or a profound source of joy and meaning.

The awareness of and growing sensitivity to the empty and the silent would serve me well in the weeks ahead. The amazing moss Zen meditation garden of Kyoto would enchant me with its more than one hundred different mosses, its deep green trees and plants, and its greenish ponds and pools. It was as wonderfully green on green as the cherry blossom festivals were pink on pink. I felt as though I had entered a living fairyland where everything and everyone was green, where the water flowed green and, I imagined, the oceans swept in as jade. The tree trunks were partly moss covered, the rocks were etched in moss, and old logs were nearly completely moss covered, identifiable only by their nearly indiscernible shapes. The garden was relatively large, and the early morning had brought few to the opening of the garden gates and the required period of meditation before entering. I was overwhelmed by the lushness, by the sheer beauty of the uniformity, which, when I looked more closely at the subtle details of textures, shapes, and shades, was far from uniform, and by the moist, almost heavy silence. As I wandered the paths, I heard the most beautiful dull *thump*, a wooden sound somehow muffled, which recurred every two or three minutes. I anticipated the repetition of the sounding and found myself concentrating on the empty silence that preceded each repetition, resonating beyond the moment and into the recaptured and emphasized silence that followed. I was nearing the sound, now totally entranced by the shimmering volume and intensity of the silence, which had now become the foreground. It predominated, for the sound lasted but a second or two, the silence for what seemed the longest time, both before and after. It was the sound that accented the silence, made it stand out like a three-dimensional figure against a two-dimensional background. The brief thump accentuated the silence, calling attention to the fact that it was *within* this mere receptacle for sound, this empty possibility, this formlessness that accepted form, that the sound occurred. The sound was so brief, so concentrated, so focused that it caused the nothingness of the empty silence to resonate with subtle whispers, tiny creaks, half-heard breaths, and periods of soundlessness so dense that it seemed that my eardrums had gone slack from lack of use.

Before me was a tiny trickle of water flowing through a hollow greenish-coloured bamboo pipe from a small moss-covered hillside. At the end of the bamboo pipe was a hinged piece of bamboo whose end was partly blocked so as to allow the water to accumulate. When the accumulation was sufficient, the hinged piece dropped downwards, lightly striking a rock strategically placed to create – indeed, almost to record – the heavy sound of soaked bamboo on stone. The water spilled out and the pipe gently swung upwards, relieved of its unbalanced weight, to its horizontal position. So simple, so ingenious, and so like the bobbing birds in water glasses in the windows of airport souvenir shops the world over. Yet here this simple mechanism was fitting, and helped to make clear how legendary awakenings could occur upon the hearing of a single sound, stories often told and retold in Zen Buddhist history. Like ripples in a pond, the sound continued to strike the depths of my being as I walked away from the point of impact, past ripple-ring after ripple-ring, until the silence regained was eventually interrupted by the sound of visitors, buses, and automobiles near the entrance gates to the moss garden.

Within the Zen tradition, a meditation garden speaks to anyone capable of hearing what it whispers to those who have quieted at least some of the surface noise of contemporary hustle and bustle. The garden is the tangible expression of the landscape architect's own enlightenment experience – or experiences. I had heard a whisper of enlightenment, but only dimly, for there was still too much static in my living and listening. I knew that I needed to become more transparent, more silent and quiet, more aware, more "here" than I was able to be at the time. Still, I was much closer to "here" and to "now" than I had ever been before. I had begun to sense my relationship with the garden.

CHAPTER FIVE

Where Is Here?

Margaret Atwood powerfully describes Canadians as a people who have struggled to *survive* in an environment that is perceived as threatening, if not hostile. She accepts Northrop Frye's insight that Canadians answer the question "Who am I?" with another question, "Where is here?"[1]

In societies where the environment is well-defined (i.e. already humanized), the question is not likely to be "Where is here?" but "Who am I?" precisely because "in societies where everyone and everything has its place a person may have to struggle to separate himself from his social background, in order to keep from being just a function of the structure." "Where is here?" is a different question because

It is what a man asks when he finds himself in unknown territory, and it implies several other questions. Where is this place in relation to other places? How do I find my way around in it? If the man is really lost he may also wonder how he got "here" to begin with, hoping he may be able to find the right path or possibly the way out by retracing his steps. If he is unable to do this he will have to take stock of what "here" has to offer in the way of support for human life and decide how he should go about remaining alive. Whether he survives or not will depend partly on what "here" really contains – whether it is too hot, too cold, too wet or too dry for him – and partly on his own desires and skills – whether he can utilize the resources available, adapt to what he can't change, and keep from going crazy. There may be other people "here" already, natives who are cooperative, indifferent or hostile. There may be animals, to be tamed, killed and eaten, or avoided. If, however, there is too large a gap between our hero's expectations and his environment he may develop culture shock or commit suicide.[2]

This cautious, untrusting, even suspicious approach to the environment, makes the settler wary when confronted with new possibilities. Thus white settlers, confronted with indigenous peoples, set about to eliminate a possible threat by force, instead of finding out whether those people might be co-operative, indifferent, or hostile. Given the evidence that they were considered "primitive," were non-white, and had less technologically sophisticated weaponry, the settler might ask, "Why not?" Yet this position is based on assumptions about what is "here" and not on warm-hearted attempts to determine the lay of the land. Take the horrendous example of Spain's annihilation of the Aztec empire, which was ruled by Montezuma (his name was really Moctezuma, but we have no more respect for his name than we had for his person) in Mexico, where the native people were robbed, raped, and killed in huge numbers. Or the hunting of the Beothuk people of Newfoundland for bounty, or the breaking of treaty after treaty in the United States and Canada by the more powerful whites, who broke their promises so often that the native Indians came to identify whites as having "forked tongues." In each case survival entailed eliminating the threat of danger, and not without a heavy dose of racism, by which the opposition is first denigrated as pagan, uncivilized, or even subhuman – as *other*.

A preoccupation with survival, which Atwood claims is the dominant theme in Canadian literature, is manifest in the overcoming of the "hostile" forces in nature, in the treatment of indigenous cultures, and even in the conflict between the two non-indigenous cultures, the English and the French. Life is a struggle, and Atwood does well to refer to this life-stance as "gloomy."[3] It is a gloomy diagnosis of an undesired situation. No doubt this is partly due to the attitudinal perspective or horizon of understanding that prepares us to read "here" with considerable caution, as though we were directly threatened, making us vigilantly self-protective and unwelcoming of those with a radically different perspective. Given this aperture of vision, it is little wonder that the environment came to be seen as a resource for human use and that the *extractive mentality* became the most common (although, of course, not the only) mode of interacting with the environment. Rather than being *related* to the environment, we saw ourselves as standing in opposition to it. Nature required subduing, needed to be cultured or civilized, needed pruning, for it was our birthright, bequeathed to us by God, to do with as we wished. And while there undoubtedly was a trace of stewardship implied in the bequeathing, our understanding of the transaction has generally been one of complete authority in our domination of nature. If we were to be God's stewards of nature, we tended to understand this to be a God-given right to make use of nature for our own benefit rather than a contractual obligation to care for and to nurture the animals, the trees and plants, the rivers and oceans, and the peoples of different colours and cultures. We thought of nature as a *resource* – note the strictly economic force of the word – and not as a friend, or a responsibility, or a divine expression, itself of intrinsic worth.

INSIGHT FROM THE EAST

There is a telling description, even though exaggerated, of the biblical account of the human relationship to nature, in an essay by the Japanese philosopher D.T. Suzuki:

The Nature-Man dichotomy issues, as I think, from the Biblical account in which the Creator is said to have given mankind the power to dominate all creation. It is fundamentally due to this story that Western people talk so much about conquering Nature. When they invent a flying machine they say that they have conquered the air; when they climb to the top of Mt. Everest they loudly announce that they have succeeded in conquering the mountain. This idea of conquest comes from the relationship between Nature and Man being regarded as that of power, and this relationship involves a state of mutual opposition and destruction.[4]

Adding Suzuki's insight to that of Atwood, we find that survival and the power-oriented need to conquer are two of the attitudinal characteristics of the Canadian, North American, and likely of the Western mind-set in general, ignoring the obvious differences in emphasis from region to region. For example, if you live near the Mediterranean Sea, you are less likely to emphasize the difficulties of climatic survival, although you may rightly stress the challenge of surviving the conflict, ever present in history, with neighbours who wish to conquer you. If we follow Suzuki's suggestion – that the opposition of human and nature is symbolized as the struggle between the mind (soul) as divine and the "flesh" as the base animalistic nature-in-us that needs to be subdued – then mind and body are symbolically estranged, as is the human from the rest of nature. The "between-ness" between them is more like a gulf that forever threatens to overcome us. Is there a Zen Buddhist/Japanese/Eastern account of "Where is here?" that might serve as a comparative contrast to the "survive and conquer" motif thus far sketched?

Suzuki says there is, and his contrastive account begins with a problem of translation. The Japanese word usually translated "environment" is *kyogai*. Suzuki contends that there is no word in English that exactly corresponds to this Japanese word, borrowed (along with Buddhism itself) from Chinese and further from Sanskrit; however, the English rendering, "a 'realm' or 'field' where any action may take place," comes close.[5] The Sanskrit source word means "the pasture" where domesticated animals graze:

As the cattle have their grazing field, man has a field or realm for his inner life. The wise man has his *Weltanschauung* whereby he views the whole world, and this enters into the content of his *kyogai*. The *kyogai* is his mode or frame or tone of consciousness from which all his reactions come and wherein all outside stimulations are absorbed. We generally imagine that we all live in the same objective world and behave in the same way. But the truth is that none of us has the same *kyogai*. For each of us lives in his inner sanctum, which is his subjectivity and which cannot be shared by any other individual. This strictly individual inner structure or frame of consciousness, utterly unique, is one's *kyogai*.[6]

Your outlook on the world is an individual one, and the attitudes you take towards things are, of course, personal. Still, just as it is possible to speak of the Western *kyogai*, allowing for the same individual differences, so it is possible to describe the broad outlines of a Zen Buddhist *kyogai*, again allowing for individual differences. Rather than attempting to tame nature, or to escape from its tyranny, Zen "shows no desire to escape from its tossing waves. It does not antagonize Nature; it does not treat Nature as if it were an enemy to be conquered, nor does it stand away from Nature. It is indeed Nature itself."[7]

Perhaps it is best to let Suzuki describe the Zen master's *kyogai*:

There is nothing, after all, in the Zen master's *kyogai* ... which differentiates itself as something wondrous or extraordinary. It consists, as in all other cases, in scenting the fragrance of the laurel in bloom and in listening to a bird singing on a spring day to its heart's content. What, however, makes a difference in the case of a Zen master is that he sees the flowers as they really are and not in a dreamy sort of way in which the flowers are not real flowers and the rivers are not really flowing rivers ... The whole universe which means Nature ceases to be "hostile" to us as we had hitherto regarded it from our selfish point of view. Nature, indeed, is no more something to be conquered and subdued. It is the bosom whence we come and whither we go.[8]

Do not misunderstand. The friendly and nurturing images of nature are not in any way meant to deny the horror of an earthquake, a monsoon wind, or a hurricane, the agony of starvation caused by drought in Ethiopia, or the diseases of life that must also be said to be "natural." These are all real, but for many they are not the major feature of our associations with nature. They are not dominant themes but subsidiary realities to contend with, and certainly not to be minimized by overlooking them.

FROM ZEN BUDDHISM TO SHINTŌISM

Rather than interacting in a confrontational manner with their environment, Zen practioners aim to "live in the love of nature, and always [to] see themselves as a part of all."[9] David Edward Shaner makes this point in the context of the Japanese outlook in general when he explores the Shintō term *kami*. *Kami* is sometimes translated as "God" or "gods," but it refers to whatever is worthy of awe, or reverence, as a divine presence. Shintō is the indigenous religion of the Japanese, and its influence on the Japanese people is evident throughout Japan. Shintō shrines, marked with the gateway symbol, may be found nearly everywhere in Japan. There are an estimated eighty thousand registered Shintō shrines throughout the Japanese islands, and each of them serves to call our attention to the existence of the wondrous, the awesome (or *awe-full*). As an American Japanologist explains, the stance of early Shintōism "was pantheistic or animistic, wherein all things were believed to participate equally in a 'seamless' web." Under the spell of this outlook, he concludes, "the natural world was thus considered to be intrinsically valuable. To adulterate the primordial condition of nature was to interfere with the dynamic processes that sustain the nature of nature."[10]

Here we have come to a great irony. The very sort of animistic stance that we have more recently come to attribute to the North and South American Indians is here lauded as instrumental in the creation of the nature-loving Japanese outlook. Animism, so often termed "primitive" by Christian missionaries, settlers, anthropologists, and scholars of all stripes, is here termed foundational in allowing the Japanese to appreciate nature and their own place – "here" – in it. Animism sees the entire world of nature as filled with gods, as places where divinities arise, as expressions of divine creativity to be cherished, nurtured, and benefited from. Is it primitive to treat the seasons as miraculous sources of joy and wonder, in spite of some difficulties encountered? Is it irrational to want to learn to "become intimate" with the tree that you are painting, or the rock that you are lying back on, or with the cat that stretches out on your book?

Does the very labelling of animism as "primitive" augur an unwillingness within monotheism to look on nature as anything more than created-for-use? Perhaps this needs to be explored in more detail.

INTIMACY WITH NATURE

The thirteenth-century Zen master Dōgen wrote that in order to be able to study and learn about the self, the first requirement or precondition is to *forget* that very self: "To study the buddha way is to study the self. To study the self is to forget the self. To forget the self is to be actualized by myriad things."[11] Then and only then do we possess the required "transparency" of ego that affords us a glimpse of whatever it is that we are attending to, in its "here-ness." We need not claim to have glimpsed things as they are in themselves (although Zen literature often appears to make this assertion) through forgetting our noisy egos; rather what this forgetting allows us is a flooding of our sensuality with concentrated awareness of whatever our focused attention has singled out. We are more "here" than we have ever been before, and this "being here" fills us with joy. "Zen is right in the midst of the ocean of becoming."[12]

It is when we have begun to forget ourselves and to achieve a transparency of ego-ness such that we can begin to look through ourselves, rather than at ourselves even while looking at the other, that we can begin to become enlightened or actualized by all things. We are enlightened by them because we are no longer an obstacle to their apprehension. No longer do we compare, contrast, classify, organize, sift out the economic implications, assess the technological benefits of this "resource," or seek out the long-term socio-political benefits of what is immediately before us. We become one with the flower, not by picking it –

Don't pick it up,
Just leave it there:
A clover in the field.[13]

– but by identifying with it emotionally, spiritually, physically. As Suzuki writes, "the real flower is enjoyed only when the poet-artist lives with it, in it; and when even a sense of identity is no longer here, much less the 'eternal tranquillity.'"[14] There is now only the flower, not the flower in *my* consciousness, for my ego has become temporarily transparent enough for me to "lose" myself in the flower, or in my lover, or in a child. The flower is "here," and here is everywhere, for there is nowhere else for the moment, nor is there anyone else or anything else. Everything is "here," and it is crammed full of the ecstasy of living fully in the moment, in an environment that you see, think, and feel yourself an inextricable part of.

Robert S. Hartman, not himself a Zen Buddhist but a German Jew who was among the first to speak out against Hitler and Nazism, makes an almost identical point in the following passage:

[Intrinsic valuation] is the capacity of complete concentration on a thing or person, the personal involvement of the artist, the inventor, the teacher: the capacity of empathy and sympathy. It is the kind of knowledge possessed in the highest degree by the creative genius. It is possible only in a person who is himself fully integrated and has all his powers available for outgoing and meeting persons or things ... It is the projecting of the whole person into others ... This kind of knowledge is direct, immediate, "intuitional"; it is that of the complete person encompassing the world.[15]

The capacity of the Japanese to attend to the immediately experienced in the *here and now* has often been characterized as a result of a primitive outlook, as has been noted already. Yet it is this capacity, this attitude that "provides the basis for becoming sensitive to the *detail* of nature's presence as evidenced by subtle variations of light, shadows, wind, seasonal change, and so on." It is an "emotional attachment to nature," an intimacy with things such that you can become "enlightened" by them, a "sensitivity to things,"[16] which Motoori Norinaga (1730–1801) wrote about in depth. Sensitivity to things (*mono no aware*) is, as Stuart Picken interprets it, an apt description of the "uniquely Japanese way of seeing the world and its beauty." It is an "aesthetic sensitivity," or a "sense of the beautiful" that is much more than the simple seeing of beauty and is more a "seeing with the heart into the natural beauty and goodness of all things."[17] Rather than seeing nature or humankind as *fallen*, the Far East generally thinks of the "ten thousand things" of this world, including human beings, as intrinsically good and intrinsically beautiful.

THE IMPORTANCE OF ANIMISM

The Shintō "horizon" insists that the world be viewed as filled with *kami*, with the divine, mysterious, awesome, mysterious flow of events that are worthy of reverence. It was Heidegger, we may recall, who insisted that we must *dwell* in the world in full consciousness of the "fourfold": earth, sky, humankind, and gods (the divine).[18] We now are in a position to remark that the fourfold is well in place in Shintō tradition, for the kami "are divine, yet close to the world of daily life."[19] Picken recognizes that kami are not just out there, distant from us, but that even *we* have kami-nature: "When something or someone is said to possess *kami*-nature, it or he has a power to awaken within us a sense of beauty, joy, love of nature, or fascination with the universe. This is not primitive nature worship, but rather nature awakening in man a sense of the divine at the heart of the universe."[20]

This seems to me an outlook that could be included in every theological tradition in the world. Indeed, if something like it does not emerge throughout the world, it may well be that the now often-predicted ecological disaster will overtake us. What will protect the environment in the short run will include laws, prohibitions, and sanctions, of course. But only when consciousness-raising has reached the level where the majority of us care about the natural world more deeply than we now do will the environment be both safe and cherished. Only when we cease to think of it as a resource only, or as an alien to conquer, or as a vast reservoir for our garbage, will real environmental progress be possible. To wait for an alteration in world-consciousness before undertaking legal and political reform is, of course, a bad mistake. But to imagine that a handful of laws and political structures will protect the environment seems equally preposterous. It is always relatively easy, for one who wants to, to get around any law or prohibition. There are never enough police, never enough courts, to protect the elephants of Africa or the rivers of the world or the ozone layer. Laws and institutions can only work well when those to whom they apply are more often than not already predisposed to obey them.

Picken sees the capacity to be sensitive to the things in one's environment as alive and well in modern Japan, although dulled by the industrial, economic, and technological requirements of Westernization:

Japan remains one of the few countries of the world where people can be found, in any significant numbers, who can write and illustrate their own poetry as a hobby, but who at other times are intensely preoccupied with the practical and often dull affairs of business and commerce. Such is the manner in which the sense of *mono no aware* imparted by Shintō comes as a source of renewal to the life of a modern civilization.

Visitors to Japan are frequently fascinated by the attention to detail exercised by the Japanese in the expression of the beautiful in the things of daily life. Trays of fish are garnished with tiny chrysanthemums, sandwiches by parsley, and *sushi* by seaweed. Toilets are decorated with potted plants, kitchens with fruit, and everywhere with flowers, sometimes even the dashboards

of taxis. These are not empty gestures. They are expressions of the unconscious desire to create an environment in which the spirit of the beautiful is
fostered to enrich life.[21]

THE ELDER AS HERO: I VISIT HAMADA

I was sitting in the dining-room of the head priest of a major
Buddhist sect who, together with his wife and family, was
entertaining me Japanese-style. The table was low to the floor,
and beneath it was a well into which Westerners could drop
their feet, while Japanese people were comfortably sitting in
the traditional cross-legged position. It meant a meal during
which I could concentrate on the people and the discussion,
and the wonderful visual and gastronomic delights of home-
cooked Japanese food, rather than on the aches and pains in
my folded legs and feet.

I was asked what I most wanted to do in Japan, and at the
top of my list was the dim hope of actually meeting the legendary potter Hamada Shōji. Hamada was often called the
premier potter of this century, in the world. Without a doubt
he was one of a handful of true greats world-wide. In Japan,
he was one of the seventy "Living National Treasures," whose
accomplishments carry such respect that the Japanese government makes of them heroes and heroines, amply supported
financially in their work, on the one condition that they
undertake the responsibility of bringing young apprentices
along the path of excellence so that the craft or art is not forgotten. Potters, paper-makers, actors, singers, musicians, pain-
ters, puppeteers, bell-makers, and fabric designers are
included in the ranks, and it is they who become the house-
hold names that baseball, football, basketball, and hockey
players become in North America.

My hostess reached behind her, picked up the telephone,
and dialled the number of Hamada's daughter, who happened
to be her close friend. Two days later I was up at dawn,
threading my way to Hamada's studio complex in Mashiko, a
one- to three-hour journey away, depending on the mode of
transportation you took. I took the local railway route, and
three hours later I asked a cab driver to take me to Hamada's
place. "Aaahhhhhhhhh, Hamada," he exclaimed, bowing his
head in reverence, and we were off.

The ten-minute drive took me past rice paddies and many other pottery studios. Hamada had established his own studio here after meticulously searching throughout Japan for the ideal potting clay. Other potters were drawn to this place, and now the entire town consisted mainly of potters working to create both commercial ware and art in community.

A woman greeted me at the gate of the compound and took me to the master. He was an old man, sitting cross-legged at his wheel when I arrived. The studio was plain. The floor was dirt. An old wood stove was the only source of heat, and on it stood an old aluminum tea kettle, able to hold enough water for twenty or thirty cups of tea. The windows were sliding *shōji* screens, covered with translucent rice paper. A dim, diffused light gave the studio a homespun and cosy feel.

There were several wheels in operation, and pottery in varying stages of completion was arranged in a more or less orderly way throughout. I was led to Hamada's wheel, invited to sit down and watch, and offered a cup of tea. Hamada greeted me warmly but quickly, explaining that he was in the midst of creating a piece. He spun the wheel, re-wetted his hands, and effortlessly pulled the clay upwards, pressing inwards as he neared the top, and then quickly outwards again. It was done, I thought, and beautiful too, although thicker than I had expected. He picked up a small knife and began to cut into the clay, making the lower portion of the vase hexagonal. He did this free handed, and with a gentleness and purposefulness that surprised me. He seemed to be as spontaneous as you would be when peeling an apple. Yet the finished product was perfectly spaced, perfectly even in thickness, and as smooth as it would have been had it come from a mould. He smiled, put the vase down, and handed me the knife. "Feel it," he encouraged, in fluent English. "I have had this one for over ten years, and it is the best I have ever used. Feel how it fits your hand."

We admired several of the pots and then left to visit the museum or showroom where his creations may be viewed. It had not yet opened to the public, so we had the place to ourselves. Hamada told me about his work, about his huge kilns, one of which held ten thousand pieces at one firing. It was an Okinawan-style kiln, made of mud clay and fired by wood – again, his choice, for his government stipend would have

allowed him to build or buy whatever he needed in the way
of equipment. The work was magnificent, *kami*-filled with
awe-inspiring beauty. It consisted of a variety of shapes and
styles, with glaze and brushwork that seemed haphazard in
its spontaneity, except that the finished result seemed so right
that I could not imagine it any other way. His most recent
work included red and green brushwork on pale glazes. They
were dazzling, and contrasted sharply with the subdued
browns, greys, yellows, and blues that were more common.
They all made me want to touch them, and to spend considerable time admiring them. We left as the doors of the
museum opened to the public. As we passed by the first
group of visitors to his museum, they prostrated themselves
on the ground before this gentle old man, indicating the reverence in which they held this treasure. He greeted them, and
we disappeared into the first of the traditional-styled thatched
houses that contain examples of fine crafts from around the
world.

Hamada had toured extensively the world over, teaching,
demonstrating, lecturing. He had spent much of his extra
time on such tours browsing through antique shops, second-
hand shops, art shops, looking for examples of craft objects of
unusual worth. He lamented the fact that they were often
simply sold off, or disappeared into the homes of the rich,
never again to emerge, or were lost altogether. As he was
curator of the folk-craft museum in Tokyo, he asked the Japanese government to allow him to purchase choice examples of
fine craft as he encountered it. They agreed enthusiastically,
and he set off with a virtually unlimited budget from that
time on.

On the upper level of one of the houses was a sort of mez-
zanine crammed with wooden chairs from all over the world.
Some were hand-carved, some skilfully put together, some
shaped unusually, some made of choice wood polished well
enough to reflect back one's face. We looked at trunks from
Spain, dressers from Europe and North America, armoires
from Quebec, huge clay pots from Okinawa, tables from Germany. I had never seen so much beauty in one place. Back on
the main floor we squatted before the open fireplace sunk
into the floor of the building we were in. The handyman had
recently built a fire in it, and we talked about spontaneity and
beauty as the smoke curled upwards to the partly covered
hole in the roof that served as a chimney.

We walked along a beautiful garden path to his home, and there we sat, on his screened-in porch, eating a simple meal together and discussing the nature of craft and its relation to art. Then he took me to a tall chest of small drawers, and he carefully cleared the table so that he might begin to take out the items stored within. We began with jade, each piece wrapped in soft cloth. He described each piece in detail: this one was very old, made of deep-coloured green jade, no longer available, and skilfully shaped and polished into a precious box for a ring, or a gemstone. He stroked it, estimated its age, admired the care taken in fashioning it to this perfection, and then carefully re-wrapped the piece. We spent two or three hours together at this, and I was impressed not only by his sensitivity to the beauty and craft of each piece but by the care he took in unwrapping and re-wrapping each piece. He might have left it for someone else to straighten things out, for it would have been quicker and easier. But the care taken in re-wrapping was an evident part of the ceremony that we were sharing. Re-wrapping is a chore only if it is made to be. Otherwise, it is a natural part of the showing and viewing of beautiful things. He cared individually for each piece of jade and knew about each in the greatest detail. Fondly he placed each on its wrap, and with delicate strokes placed the cloth-encased treasure back in its tray.

Then he skipped a drawer or two and began describing the exquisite craftsmanship of each pocket-watch brought from England and Europe. This one had an intricately engraved case, this one a complex alarm and day/night indicator. Another was beautiful, with its case open, for its jewelled gears and overall design. It had clearly been made with loving care. Again he re-wrapped each piece with gentle care. But attention to beauty and detail had tired him, and he pulled his own book on Okinawan pottery from its shelf – a large, coffee-table-sized book with full-colour pictures – and gave it to me, to keep, and to read while he rested. I asked him to sign it for me, and he pulled out his brush and ink and demonstrated his great skill at calligraphy. I read it then, and occasionally dozed, filled with awe at this man who looked so ordinary and yet whose life was surrounded by beautiful things placed in a picture-perfect setting, and whose focus was ever on appreciating beauty and creating it. I actually felt as though I had been dropped into an ideal world, a book world where beauty was the driving force and from which all ugliness, haste, bad manners, and bad temper had been expunged. I felt warmed and nourished by the sense of beauty that was everywhere.

Hamada was awake, and he led me to his kiln. It was being fired, and the excitement was apparent. People laughed, and anticipation was in the air. Black smoke billowed from the chimney. All the pieces inside were unsigned. As Hamada saw things, "I will make things to be used without the question of who has made them."[22] Yanagi reports that Hamada was once asked why he needed such a large kiln, and Hamada answered:

If a kiln is small, I might be able to control it completely, that is to say, my own self can become a controller, a master of the kiln. But man's own self is but a small thing after all. When I work at the large kiln, the power of my own self becomes so feeble that it cannot control it adequately. It means that for the large kiln, the power that is beyond me is necessary. Without the mercy of such invisible power I cannot get good pieces. One of the reasons why I wanted to have a large kiln is because I want to be a potter, if I may, who works more in grace than in his own power. You know nearly all the best old pots were done in huge kilns.[23]

I didn't ever get to see the finished results of this firing, for my stay was but one full day long. But I was ushered into his storeroom and told to take whatever I wanted of his priceless pottery. I was stunned. I asked whether I should limit myself to one and was told again to take what I wanted. I selected four Hamada treasures, and they were immediately packaged for travel. I thanked Hamada Shōji for one of the most exquisite days of my life. He had already phoned a taxi, and he asked me which way I had come. I told him I had come the long way but did not tell him that it was in part because it was about ten times cheaper. I was on a strict budget, and simply could not afford the quicker express route. He intervened, however, and told me that the ease of the shorter route more than made up for the added expense of the more expensive train ticket and the considerably longer taxi ride to the express station. I could say nothing, and waving to the entire compound staff who were seeing me off, waving back to me at the gate, we sped down the laneway. I settled in for a longer taxi ride and accepted the added expense that would have me eating noodles for days. The meter, in yen, totalled about $45.00 U.S. I had made the entire trip to Mashiko, including taxi, for about $15.00. And there was still the express train fare to come. The driver pulled up at the station and opened the door for me. He held the packed pottery with a gentleness that contrasted with the brusqueness of taxi drivers I have known the world over, and when I offered to pay him he waved me off, saying "Hamada already pay. Hamada already pay."

Back at International House in Tokyo I asked the official packer at this institute for visiting scholars of things Japanese to ship the pottery back to Canada for me. This meant repacking the pots and making them ready for a lengthy and less than ideal journey by ship back home. He surprised me by declining, saying that these were Hamada pots and that he did not have the courage to package anything as precious as this. He apologized over and over again, saying that he was very sorry to disappoint me and suggesting that I contact a professional packer somewhere in sprawling Tokyo.

I slept on the problem for the night and then went to visit a famous Zen scholar the next day. I returned to International House that evening and my packer-friend rushed up to me, bowed, and said that he had contemplated the packing of the Hamada pots all night and practised a bit during the day. The result was that he was now willing to undertake this great responsibility if I would trust him to do it. He felt certain that he would now be able to do the appropriate job for such precious articles. I was astonished and impressed by his meticulous concern and disarming honesty. Enthusiastically I agreed. Two months later the pottery arrived, in perfect condition. Three of them sit on a special shelf in my living room; the fourth I gave to a potter-philosopher who had long admired the creations of Hamada Shōji. Hamada is, for me, the simple man who most represents the life of divine beauty in this world.

FROM KAMI-NATURE TO BUDDHA-NATURE

If *satori* or enlightenment means the seeing of the nature of all things, including your own nature, then it is but a small walk from the Shinto appreciation of the *kami*-nature in all things, including yourself, to the *Buddha*-nature in all things. Iino Norimoto writes that the Buddhist idea of interdependence, that everything is connected with, related to every other thing, reaches its fullness when the entire cosmos is seen as one "Crimson Heart of Cosmic Compassion."[24] Interdependence points in the opposite direction from the narrowness of individual, self-centred egoism. The Buddhist sense of interconnectedness, writes Iino of Dōgen's teaching, includes intense attention to "the murmuring of the brook and the cry of the monkey," for these represent the "perpetual teaching of the reality of cosmic compassion to one whose spiritual eyes have been opened." Indeed, "the fragrance of the chrysanthemum, the water boiling in the teakettle, and the twinkling of the star are signs of the same compassion."[25] All things possess Buddha-nature because all things are expressions of the Buddha, of the interconnectedness of all things, of the great Cosmic Compassion. Nakamura Hajime states this in more philosophical terms when he writes that "even a flower itself has no separate existence in the metaphysical sense. It cannot sever itself from the past ... The tiny violet droops its head just so much, and no more, because it is balanced by the universe. It is a violet, not an oak, because it is the outcome of the interrelational existence of certain members of a beginningless series."[26]

Whether Buddhist or Shintōist, the background to Japanese thought and culture encourages people to cultivate the capacity to engage in emotional intimacy with nature and with whatever aspect of the cosmos they encounter. Relatedness, Shaner holds, is dependent on "caring and compassion [which] emanate from individuals who are capable of entering into intimate relations."[27] The capacity to interpenetrate, to lose yourself in the other, is the message of Japanese aesthetics, ethics, and the love of nature that is ubiquitous among the people who live there. The medical scientist Hirai Tomio sums up this sentiment well when he defines the Buddha-nature in the following sentence: "In my opinion the best English word to use to describe that nature is *compassion*."[28]

WESTERN COUNTERPARTS

The West is not without its nature-minded, ecologically sensitive thinkers and traditions. St Francis has long been hailed as a model of sensitivity to nature, and Albert Schweitzer in this century articulated the principle of "reverence for life" that has influenced many. Henry David Thoreau and Ralph Waldo Emerson were among the early representatives of environmental sensitivity in New England, and Wordsworth and the nature poets of England have had their considerable effect, not to mention Aldo Leopold and the many who have followed his lead in our own century. I will say more about the contemporary scene shortly. But any account of nature-minded traditions in the West must begin with some mention of the "ways" of North America's aboriginal peoples. It has been recognized that the "ecological Indian" is a stereotype and that this image may well be the favoured one culled from the many other genuine strands of aboriginal practice and ideology.[29] Nevertheless, it *is* the stereotype that has been recovered by native and non-native traditions alike as worth attending to and learning from in the present age of ecological gloom and anticipated disaster.

NORTH AMERICAN NATIVE TRADITIONS

While it is impossible to do anything more than highlight a few of the areas of common agreement among the many distinctive Indian cultures of North America that have relevance to the several themes of this book, it is none the less clear that these traditions are profound examples of dwelling in a world that is considered to be of inherent worth and towards which considerable care is shown. The interrelatedness of human beings with all other things of the world is taken as the starting-point of understanding. In the following passage Doug Boyd interprets the teachings of the *savant* or elder called Rolling Thunder:

Understanding begins with love and respect. It begins with respect for the Great Spirit, and the Great Spirit is the life that is in all things – all the creatures and the plants and even the rocks and the minerals. All things – and I mean *all* things – have their own will and their own way and their own purpose; this is what is to be respected.

Such respect is not a feeling or an attitude only. It's a way of life. Such respect means that we never stop realizing and never neglect to carry out our obligation to ourselves and our environment.[30]

Such ways are known through the oral teachings and ceremonial practices that are practised whole in some areas, while in others they are being revived and reconstructed from ethnographic accounts that capture fragments of a world-view. The teachings of elders who have received, sought out, and preserved traditional knowledge must be distinguished from interpretations and applications of these teachings to present-day issues. Thus, in interpreting Boyd's identification of a common thread linking certain traditional native perspectives (itself an interpretation of oral teachings), there seems to be clear recognition of an energy linking all things in the natural world with the greater source of that energy itself. This results in a sense that all things are connected, and "that *all things in the universe are dependent on one another*."[31] Indeed, the particular sense of interdependence and interconnectedness that results includes a heightened awareness of the equality of all existence. As Vine Deloria describes this,

All species, all forms of life, have equal status before the presence of the universal power to which all are subject. The religious requirement for all life-forms is thus harmony, and this requirement holds for every species, ours included. The natural world has a great bond that brings together all living entities, each species gaining an identity and meaning as it forms a part of the complex whole ...

Primitive peoples somehow maintain this attitude toward the world and toward other life-forms. As long as the bond of life is respected, all species have value and meaning.[32]

Rolling Thunder makes a similar point when he states that "Nature is to be respected. All life and every single living being is to be respected. That's the only answer."[33]

It is evident that native traditions demonstrate a caring respect for nature that results from the belief that all is related and that the loss of an awareness of our connectedness with things will result in the impoverishment of ourselves as well as of our environment. In fact, such impoverishment represents an imbalance to be contended with, for it is a contributor to "illness or disease."[34] Human disease is often thought to be the result of a breakdown in one's systemic harmony, and the natural extension – or is it ground? – of this is that the world too is an organism that manifests various symptoms of disease or well-being. Boyd concludes that

he [Rolling Thunder] had called the earth an organism. I had never heard it just like that. After my return from years spent in Asia, I had begun to see the oneness of the world. I could think of the world as a single mind, in a sense, by thinking of all the nations and races and problems collectively ... Rolling Thunder had somehow gone from streams to veins of flowing blood. Somehow the sand, soil, plants, rivers, streams and air were a body ... this earth a body, a gigantic body of a conscious, struggling living being. The body belongs to a being, an individual with an identity and a purpose. That being exists here now. We have to be within it – like cells.[35]

The native ways of life display a continuing attempt to remain in touch with other living things. Rather than viewing the world as alien, or as mere material-at-hand for exploitation, native traditions speak of closeness to the earth. Furthermore, this closeness is often personalized, not only in so far as the Great Spirit of the universe is thought and felt to be a person but in that the earth too is typically referred to as "Holy Mother Earth, the trees and all nature," and the soil of the earth actually symbolizes this "mothering power":

The Lakota was a true naturist – a lover of nature. He loved the earth and all things of the earth, the attachment growing with age. The old people came literally to love the soil and they sat or reclined on the ground with a feeling of being close to a mothering power. It was good for the skin to touch the earth and the old people like to remove their moccasins and walk with bare feet on the sacred earth ... That is why the old Indian still sits upon the earth instead of propping himself up and away from its life-giving forces. For him, to sit or lie upon the ground is to be able to think more deeply and to feel more keenly; he can see more clearly into the mysteries of life and come closer in kinship to other lives about him ... The old Lakota was wise. He knows that man's heart away from nature becomes hard; he knew that lack of respect for growing, living things soon led to lack of respect for humans too. So he kept his youth close to its softening influence.[36]

The softening effect of the more feminine earth on men and women alike suggests that there is considerable awareness of the importance of the caring and nurturing aspects of the human personality. Indeed, in words reminiscent of Far Eastern thought, native people often speak of the female *and* the male aspects of the human being as coexisting within each person, to varying degrees, of course. Professor Marlene Castellano, herself a native person, recapitulated for me a conversation with Jake Thomas, hereditary chief of the Cayuga nation (one of the Six Nations of the Iroquois Confederacy), that amplifies this well.[37] Even the slightest details of character, and the psychological and physical state of both patient and healder are important to the medicinal power of the herbs gathered for healing. The healer must know that what is being asked for is appropriate, else the Medicine Spirit will not support it. The name of the ill person must be told, for the remedy must be a specific one. The healer must have no alcohol, and must be in the proper mental and emotional state, spiritually prepared and balanced, or the medicine will hide and the Medicine Spirit will not assist. He or she must be in balance, and this balance includes the proper integration of male and female characteristics, which we all possess. Medicinal plants grow in families, and the male and the female must be collected together. The baby plants are left to mature, as they represent the future, unless the remedy sought is one for a human baby in need of healing. It is imperative that both male and female plants be used together, or the medicine will have no power.

When we apply this teaching about medicine to everyday life, it would appear to relate to each of us as individuals. It would seem that we must maintain within ourselves the proper balance between the male and the female aspects in whatever we do, or we will lose our power, and possibly our health as well. The entire universe may be thought of as composed of male and female aspects, and in so far as we are manifestations of the whole and as such continue to be more or less whole ourselves, the balance of male and female characteristics will be maintained.

A final word needs to be added to complete Chief Thomas's story. When we prepare the medicine, the water in which it is to be boiled must come from a flowing stream. We are directed to "dip our bucket with the flow of the stream; otherwise our medicine will have no power." It is essential to appeal to the Spirit of the Water to assist in the healing as well.

The interrelatedness of each ingredient and specified action required to make powerful medicine, including the attitudes of the participants, makes it abundantly clear that no detail of living is unimportant to the quality of the results obtained. We dwell within a cosmic web of interconnected significance, no strand of which should be neglected. The health of the whole is itself dependent on the health of the part. The part is of the utmost importance to the well-being of the whole, just as the whole is of the utmost importance to the well-being of the part. Wholeness lies in the harmony of whole and part, part and whole, male and female, human and non-human, animate and inanimate, for all are inextricably interconnected, and the health of one depends, at least to some extent, on the health of all the others.

Being in a personal relationship with Mother Earth and with all other living things demands that you show respect towards them in all your actions. The taking of life, as when you hunt an animal or gather food, demands that you be respectfully mindful of what it is that you have done, and you must give back something in return. The life taken is a gift, and not a right to be thoughtlessly cashed in: "If all life is considered equal, then we are no more or less than anything else. Therefore, all life must be respected. Whether it is a tree, a deer, a fish, or a bird, it must be respected because it is equal."[38]

This respect for life appears to extend beyond the living to what Western culture terms the inanimate. Hyemeyohsts Storm, using the Plains Indian people's "medicine wheel" image to represent the universe, writes that "all of the things of the Universe Wheel have spirit and life, including the rivers, rocks, earth, sky, plants and animals."[39] We must learn to adapt to this whole that is the entire universe such that we are in harmony with it. Western European science, in seeking to achieve an objectivity by means of separating the knower from the known, the intellect from feeling, and even this world from the sacred "next world," establishes a series of exclusive oppositions that impoverish our understanding of nature's connected wholeness. As Deloria describes this dichotomization, "this point of departure separates primitive people from the rest of the human species; it distinguishes civilized from primitive, and unleashes the energies of our species on a path of conquest of the rest of nature, which has now been reduced to the status of an object."[40] The sense of the equality of things is lost in the very act that renders the other an object. The other is depersonalized, and the scientific knower becomes the centre and most valued part of the world due to his or her intellectual and manipulative power. When we consider nature to be a source of potential power to be forcibly harnessed, rather than a nourishing parent to be respectfully cherished, we lose our sense of connectedness. The result is an atomistic unrelatedness and sense of alienation from the earth as well as from each other, and from the other creatures with whom we dwell.

Not that killing is alien to the native world-view: native traditions have a long history of hunting, fishing, and trapping. Yet killing ought not to be taken lightly or for granted, but as part of a wider vision of the great chain of existence that includes the notions of *offering* and *sacrifice*. Professor Castellano illustrates this way of understanding with a story from her own experience.

While on a spiritual quest in the rolling grasslands of Wyoming, Professor Castellano emerged from her tent one morning to find countless points of dew on the grass glistening in the morning sunshine. She was both moved and transfixed by a reorientation of perspective that allowed her to see the dewdrops as apparently willing offerings of nourishment to the grass. The grass too appeared to her as graciously willing to sacrifice itself as nourishment for an old swaybacked horse, who had so willingly and patiently offered its services for hours on end the previous afternoon to the children who wished to ride her.[41] Professor Castellano suggested to me that this sense of precious offering and willing sacrifice provides a partial glimpse of the spirit in which hunting and trapping ought to be carried out within native cultures.

What may allow us to regain our sense of connection with the world is a fact of which we are by and large unaware, that we are always already identical with the whole of which we necessarily are

an organic part. We are microcosmic mirror images of the macrocosm, writes Doug Boyd, summing up Rolling Thunder's teachings:

Man's inner nature is identical with the nature of the universe, and thus man
learns about his own nature from nature herself. The technological and mate-
rialistic path of contemporary Western society is the most unnatural way of
life man has ever tried. The people of this society are farthest removed from
the trees, the birds, the insects, the animals, the growing plants and the
weather. They are therefore the least in touch with their own inner nature.[42]

Our sense of relationship to the earth gives rise to our custodial
responsibilities for the earth. We are not custodians because we were
instructed to be but because we empathetically and spontaneously
identify with the macrocosm of which we are an exact mirror image,
and an inextricable part. The native peoples still think of themselves
as keepers of the land. They do not accept the view that officially
parcels out the land and bestows legal ownership of it: "We don't
claim that we own the land, and nobody else does either ... We are
the keepers of the land ... We are supposed to work together to
make life good for all of us, all who live upon this Mother Earth,"
concludes Rolling Thunder.[43]

   The native sense of identification, nurture, respect, and kinship
arises out of a "whole story" metaphysics that provides an understanding of the universe as an integrated entity, at least to the extent
that any metaphysical account is able to convey it. Indeed, each of
us is a powerful medicine wheel within the whole medicine-wheel
universe.[44] The same is true of all other living things, again reminiscent of the jewel net of Indra in the Buddhist tradition, wherein every
mirror or jewelled facet reflects every other mirror or facet:

In many ways this Circle, the Medicine Wheel, can best be understood if
you think of it as a mirror in which everything is reflected. "The Universe
is the Mirror of the People," the old Teachers tell us, "and each person is a
Mirror to every other person."
   Any idea, person or object can be a Medicine Wheel, a Mirror, for man.
The tiniest flower can be such a Mirror, as can a wolf, a story, a touch, a
religion or a mountain top.[45]

   This sense of interrelatedness demands that you think not merely
about yourself, or your family, or even of your own short-term interests, but rather about life-long interests. The point is powerfully
made, as Lyons relates in his account of the Iroquois decision-making
maxim that requires that the well-being of future generations be

included in any ethical calculation of the effects of an action envisaged, by asking what effects this action will have on the welfare of the next seven generations! "The common interest should be ... the welfare of the seventh generation to come. Every decision should be made in reference to how that decision will affect the seventh generation in the future."[46] And the reason that such identification with generations yet unborn can become so strong is that "it's more useful to think of every other person as another *you* – to think of every individual as a representative of the universe."[47] For "every person is plugged into the whole works," and even "the worst criminal in life imprisonment sitting in his cell – the center of him is the same seed, the seed of the whole creation."[48] Such a view provides a rich sense of meaning and of community "as long as we treat our apprehension of the great mystery with respect."[49] The bond with nature and the sense of belonging to the still-mysterious cosmos are essential aspects of the native American understanding of spirituality.

At the beginning of this chapter the white settlers were described as struggling to survive in an environment that was perceived as threatening. The aim was survival against hostile forces, and life was a gloomy affair, obsessed with keeping the wilderness at bay. How striking it is by contrast to read the words of Chief Luther Standing Bear, who said in his autobiography, of himself and his people:

We did not think of the great open plains, the beautiful rolling hills, and winding streams with tangled growth as "wild." Only to the white men was nature a "wilderness" and only to him was the land "infested" with "wild" animals and "savage" people. To us it was tame. Earth was bountiful and we were surrounded with the blessings of the Great Mystery. Not until the hairy man from the east came and with brutal frenzy heaped injustices upon us and the families that we loved was it "wild" for us. When the very animals of the forest began fleeing from his approach, then it was that for us the "Wild West" began.[50]

The native Indians understood themselves to be in a friendly and bountiful environment that had religious significance to them. Within that perspective everything had a worthy function that human beings had to try to comprehend, and even to learn from. Wise native spiritual people sought to discover and to preserve in their teachings the proper relationships between the people and the other living and non-living things. The recognition of the equality of things was grounded in the accepted fact that all that existed was the creation of a higher power, and thus its perceived worth was not simply a human attribution.[51] The ordinary was the offspring of the divine.

CONTEMPORARY NON-NATIVE WESTERN ECOLOGICAL THEORIES

Currently, J.E. Lovelock's Gaia hypothesis and the deep ecology of Arne Naess and others are perhaps the dominant theories within the ecological thinking of the West. The Gaia hypothesis contends that "the Earth's living matter, air, oceans, and land surface form a complex system which can be seen as a single organism and which has the capacity to keep our planet a fit place for life."[52] I do not wish to rehearse that hypothesis in detail here except to note that it is holistic, or interconnected, in its emphasis on the atmospheric or environmental adaptation and adjustment to the requirements of the living organisms in that environment. The entire earth is an interconnected whole whose inanimate portions adjust to maintain a habitable environment for the animate portions of itself. In Lovelock's words, Gaia (Greek for Earth, but with the sense of something more like "Mother Earth," although it is well to remember that Gaia was one of the goddesses whom Zeus *subdued*) is "a complex entity involving the Earth's biosphere, atmosphere, oceans, and soil; the totality constituting a feedback or cybernetic system which seeks an optimal physical and chemical environment for life on this planet. The maintenance of relatively constant conditions by active control may be conveniently described by the term 'homeostasis.'"[53]

It is worth observing that Lovelock himself sees the Gaia hypothesis as an antidote to the more traditional conquer-to-survive approach to our relationship with nature. He says, "The Gaia hypothesis is for those who like to walk or simply to stand and stare, to wonder about the Earth and the life it bears, and to speculate about the consequences of our own presence here." Then he describes it as "an alternative to that pessimistic view which sees nature as a primitive force to be subdued and conquered."[54] While thoroughly grounded in science, the Gaia hypothesis fits well with the Japanese sensitivity I have described, and it critiques the same simplistic view of nature as an alien and non-living resource to be plundered and conquered. It requires us to live with Gaia, as friends and interconnected collaborators, if we are to survive and to flourish.

Lovelock's vision of this "living" earth includes a conception of specific parts of the organism called Gaia as "vital organs" that are as important to this large organism as our vital organs are to us. To pollute the forest-lungs, or to poison the cleansing and nurturing river-blood, is tantamount to suicide, except that in so far as it affects all other living things, it reaches even beyond homicide. The Gaia hypothesis is a view that reduces us to our real size as coexistents in a broad world and a vast cosmos who must learn to dwell in harmonious integration, or perish. Gaia is the centre of an enveloping hypothesis that enhances our earthly perspective by conceiving of "our planet and its creatures" as constituting "a single self-regulating system that is in fact a great living being, or organism."[55]

Sahtouris contrasts the contemporary world's "aggressive and destructive motives of domination, conquest, control, and profit, [which] have been presented to us as human nature by historians as well as by sociologists," with new evidence for an older view of things that "strongly suggests that human societies were for the greater part of civilized history based on cooperation and reverence for life and nature, not on competition and obsession with death and technology." The earlier or "primitive" view was guided by "images of a near and nurturing Mother Goddess before a cruel and distant Father God replaced her in influence."[56] Sahtouris compares the relation of nature to humankind to that of a near, tender, caring mother to a child currently in a period of rebellion. She traces humankind's development from infant-like dependency, and expresses hope for a greater maturity that will make possible successful relationships with other human beings. We learn from mother how to relate, as Noddings makes amply clear:

It should be clear that my description of an ethic of caring as a feminine ethic does not imply a claim to speak for all women nor to exclude men ... [But] there is reason to believe that women are somewhat better equipped for caring than men are. This is partly a result of the construction of psychological deep structures in the mother-child relationship. A girl can identify with the one caring for her and thus maintain relation while establishing identity. A boy must, however, find his identity with the absent one – the father – and thus disengage himself from the intimate relation of caring.[57]

Not only have we conceived of the deity as male, but his authority and distance have tended to cause us increasingly to disengage from the intimate relation of caring in our environmental relationships. Estranged from the mother, at a distance from and cautious of God the father, we have tended to express this same estrangement with respect to the earth. It, too, is distant, "other", and exploitable, and we are "objective," practical, and by necessity too rushed for intimacy. No doubt precisely to the extent that the modern and contemporary world-view became increasingly *male* in orientation, so did the possibility of intimacy with the world and its riches recede as well. We are now in a sort of "adolescent crisis," a turning-point in our development that could lead to our own destruction, or we can humbly seek help instead from the nature that spawned us and thereby discover our intimate links as solutions to a vision of ourselves as a part of nature and not an alien enemy of it. Seeing ourselves as individual and nature as other, we could come to identify ourselves with the world and thereby adopt the alternative conception of the individual *as* nature.[58]

DEEP ECOLOGY

Deep ecology is even more compatible with Eastern thought. In a lyrical mode, Michael Tobias describes the sweep of the deep ecology movement:

Deep Ecology concerns those personal moods, values, aesthetic and philosophical convictions which serve no necessarily utilitarian, nor rational end. By definition their sole justification rests upon the goodness, balance, truth and beauty of the natural world, and of a human being's biological and psychological need to be fully integrated within it. This is a premise easily ignored in our world, where the possessive case – our – increases unchecked with each new bit of legislation, industrial outreach and scientific hubris. This technological and conceptual tendency of civilization has served to isolate our species from all others, save perhaps for certain rodents, insect scavengers, French poodles, Siamese cats, horses, spider plants, and marigolds.[59]

The "deep" in deep ecology refers to the depth of questions asked, indicating that these questions are fundamental inquiries into the "presuppositions of valuation as well as of facts and hypotheses."[60] Thus, "the deep ecological movement tries to clarify the fundamental presuppositions underlying our economic approach in terms of value priorities, philosophy, and religion."[61] Deep ecologists write of the "love of nature," the "beauty of the world," of the "intrinsic value" of species and the environment as a whole. These expressions imply a wider-than-usual *context* of attention and understanding, one that extends all the way to the edges of the known cosmos.

Devall and Sessions describe this extended vision as one that "goes beyond a limited piecemeal shallow approach to environmental problems and attempts to articulate a comprehensive religious and philosophical world view."[62] Paul Shepard writes that "ecological thinking ... requires a kind of vision across boundaries." He adds that "the epidermis of the skin is ecologically like a pond surface or a forest soil, not a shell so much as delicate permeable membranes. It reveals the self ennobled and extended rather than threatened as part of the landscape and ecosystem, because the beauty and complexity of nature are continuous with ourselves."[63] Arne Naess makes a related point when he calls our attention to the Kantian dictum "Never use a person solely as a means, but only as an end," or rather, never as a means *alone*, but always as an end as well. In so far as every living being has a value in itself (i.e. *values* itself), "this opposes the notion that one may be justified in treating any living being as just a means to an end ... Identification tells me: if I have a right to live, *you* have the same right."[64] This might well be expanded to include the inanimate, as suggested in chapter 1, as a "respect for things" generally.

Naess himself emphasizes this as one of the two *ultimate norms* or intuitions that serve as the foundations of deep ecology: the principle of "biocentric equality" is the "basic intuition ... that all organisms and entities in the ecosphere, as parts of the interrelated whole, are equal in intrinsic worth."[65] You respect another human being to the extent that you recognize that person as a centre or source of worth: as an intrinsically valuable *existent*; as a real or conceivable object with which you have, or can imagine yourself having, a relationship of caring, and/or feeling intimacy. Naess summarizes the broad range of implications resulting from a "deeper" and "softer" deep-ecological position:

- Animals have value in themselves, not only as resources for humans [we have no *right* to use them].
- Animals have a right to live even if of no use to humans [we have no *right* to kill them].
- We have no right to destroy the natural features of this planet.
- Nature does not belong to man [we have no *right* to use *it*].
- Nature is worth defending, whatever the fate of humans [we *should* defend it].
- A wilderness area has a value independent of whether humans have access to it [we *should* protect and preserve it].[66]

Deep ecology is a different mode of questioning and attempts to investigate all assumptions, whether philosophical, religious, cultural, political, or economic. It is termed "deeper" not because it claims to have found and established deeper answers but because of its relentlessness in asking more probing and discomforting questions about our value assumptions and unacknowledged priorities, both personal and political.

INTRINSIC VALUE AND
ECOLOGY

To claim that nature or any part of it is of *intrinsic value* is, at least in part, to argue that a merely *instrumental* view of nature is unacceptable. An instrumental view allows us to comprehend the natural world as material-at-hand for our use rather than as worthwhile "in itself" or "for its own sake." Such phrases as valuable "in itself," or "for its own sake" are regularly associated with claims of intrinsic worth, which in turn is usually associated with "objective" value. As will perhaps be remembered from chapter 1, while such shorthand and colloquial labels are often helpful in making the instrumental versus non-instrumental distinction, there is much more that needs to be said if you wish to present a consistent and thoroughly thought-through pattern of value analysis.

The claim that intrinsic value is objective is, to my mind, an altogether wrong path to take.[67] In fact, I think the cut has to be made quite differently. C.I. Lewis, it will be recalled, is the theorist who best articulates this position, arguing that *"the goodness of good objects consists in the possibility of their leading to some realization of directly experienced goodness."*[68] It follows from this that even human beings do not *have* intrinsic value, for it is the experiences they may have, and they alone, that can be valued in themselves, or for their own sakes. At the same time, *I do wish to maintain that **anything whatever** may be intrinsically valued and that the leading candidates for such intrinsic valuation are human beings and other sentient creatures, many of whom are capable of having experiences of (apparent) intrinsic value themselves.* To *have* an intrinsic-value experience is not the same, however, as *being* of intrinsic value.

To say that nature is "intrinsically valuable" is merely to express the sentiment that it is a foundational part of our human "valuescape." It is also to warn against a merely instrumentalist perspective that takes nature lightly, as usable and disposable at our pleasure. According to this sentiment, we value forms of nature not only because of their economic and societal benefits but because of their "rock-bottom" worthwhileness in themselves. In the broadest of senses, we warm to them and are warmed by them. We are enhanced in our own sense of meaningfulness by their existence, and our lives are enriched by their presence. The world of nature is a constant source of experiences of intrinsic immediate value.

Yet in the very process of being warmed by the things that we derive immediate worth from, we are also aware that we care about them, and such caring and prizing imply *nurture* and the protection of that which we value. We *transcend* the more restrictive concern with our own pleasure and *identify* with the sources of our delight and meaning. We reach out through this identification, embracing that which we value, recognizing that such *objects of value* are *inherently valuable*. They are inherently valuable, then, because most people, or sensitive caring people would, if presented with a magnificent mountain vista, or the soaring of an eagle, find enormous pleasure or joy in such experiences. The eagle is inherently valuable because, in accordance with this extension of human caring, it affords us countless experiences of intrinsic value. Still, this is a radically homocentric or anthropocentric position. If something is valuable only because it gives pleasure to at least one human being, then presumably, should no human being take any pleasure in it, it would seem to be worthless and expendable.

The way beyond this human-centred outlook is afforded by our human capacity to *identify* or *empathize* with another human or non-human being. We would protect a child even at risk to our own lives, if need be, and not only because we could not live with ourselves if we did not. Rather, we extend our sense of *self*-preservation to include the child, and such extension is, both in principle and in actual practice, quite unlimited. A Saint Francis, an Albert Schweitzer, or a Buddha are capable of manifesting compassion of a sort that extends their empathetic and identificatory embrace to all humans, all life-forms, and even to the totality of process that is the entire cosmic ebb and flow. And when this loving and compassionate embrace is described in the abstract, it will take the form of an intensity of caring that seeks to identify that which is prized or treasured as being of "intrinsic value," "unconditional worth," "absolute value," or as "sacred," in order to *protect* it from mere economic and other exploitative use and abuse. As the public-works people come to a neighbourhood to put in new sidewalks by chopping at the roots of hundred-year-old maples, I have to resist them, and even to threaten, just as I would were they to attempt to harm my own body, or that of my child. Otherwise, the implications of the sense of identification with the trees, which I feel but the workers appear not to, would not be comprehended. A sensitivity to trees must be expressed as a willingness to resist, even at considerable cost to self, in the same way that a mother "digs in" in order to protect her child from harm at the hands of a hardened one who thinks of children as commodities for use or abuse or sale.

Trees and animals, and even human beings may be claimed to be of intrinsic value, and the claim is understandable. Technically, they are, however, *inherently* valuable, but the term "inherent value" carries with it little of the historic force of claims of "intrinsic," "absolute," or "objective" value. Now when we attempt to unpack the claim that a tree is intrinsically valuable, we need to speak first of our sense of the worth of self, of the joy we find in being in the midst of a healthy and richly varied natural environment, of our sense of identification with the worth of the tree, and of our sense of its being as worthy of existence (in the same sense, but not necessarily to the same degree, under all conceivable circumstances) as I am. The worth of the tree might also carry something of the "sacredness" of existence, as Heidegger suggested when he included in his "fourfold" the gods, or the divine, along with mortals, earth, and sky. To the extent that we envisage ourselves as part of the workings of the universe, and given the sense of the whole that I have laboured to describe, then the world itself is wondrous, divine in some sense, and we and everything else in it are worthy of existence, all other things being equal.

"Value" is a human creation, therefore, and while many other things no doubt elect, choose, select, and prize to varying degrees, it is likely that humans alone have axiology, the science of systematic valuation, which begins by positing that there is a classification of awarenesses named "values." Intrinsic values are immediately given in experience, and no doubt many conscious creatures have such positive experiences of immediate worth. My argument suggests that things, objects, insects are not intrinsically valuable, but they *are* inherently valuable for us by virtue of the intrinsic-value experiences they afford. By extension they are centres of fundamental value, for they themselves are capable of experiences of positive immediacy.

INTRINSIC VALUATION

Trees may not be of intrinsic value, nor may they be capable of having intrinsic-value experiences themselves, but *they are capable of being valued intrinsically*. One who is sensitive to the incredible worth of the world of nature and is able to identify with it, who is capable of valuing it deeply as an end and not just as a means, values intrinsically that with which he or she is identified. The psychology of intrinsic valuation has been explored by Robert S. Hartman, who, while offering yet another meaning of "intrinsic value," nevertheless provides an account of *intrinsic valuation* that is in accord with what I have argued here. In the act of intrinsically valuing something, you apprehend that thing in its full concreteness, not seeing it merely as a log or as lumber or pulp (in the case of a tree) but as an infinitely rich source of properties, such as habitat for birds, insects, and squirrels, as a source of shade and cool dampness, fall colour, spring brightness, and so on. For Hartman the essence of intrinsic valuation is identification, or compenetration, such that "thing and observer are one continuous entity,"[69] as though you were that very thing being apprehended for the moment. You have become that tree, have reached out to it, embraced it, and in so doing have forgotten yourself. There is only the experience of treeness, in wonderful richness.

Valuing is a *human* act, and it is we who, by extension, find the tree to be a significant source of value, and worthwhile in itself in the same sense that a child is worthwhile, although for most of us to a considerably lesser degree. A child is not worthwhile or valuable "in itself" simply because it has conscious experience, although that might well be a good reason for thinking it *more* valuable, but because we *identify* with the life of the child and seek to preserve it. It is because we are capable of transcending our sense of self and the limits of our skins that we are able to embrace more and more of that which is around us as worthy of preservation and protection. We are capable of feeling and conceiving of ourselves as related to and even identified with a greater, transpersonal whole that may extend to the edges of our conception of the cosmos. Whatever needlessly harms, diminishes, or destroys it, or significant portions of it, will prove immediately disvaluable to us.

The issue in question is not so much the "objectivity" or "subjectivity" of such value responses but rather that some people do not respond to very much beyond the confines of their own egos and skins. It has been an ongoing concern of this book to show that enhanced meaning and value satisfaction arises from taking a wider rather than a narrower view of our place in the world and cosmos; that we are in relation to other people from the beginning of our lives, and that this sense of relatedness needs to be encouraged and widened; that caring is a nurturing and protective act that both recognizes our connectedness and cherishes and preserves what we are connected with; and that our connectedness can extend all the way to intense mystical experiences of identification with the greater whole.

TRANSPERSONAL ECOLOGY

Quite recently deep ecology has come to recognize that some of its theorists have moved to a position called "transpersonal ecology," a term coined by Warwick Fox in his book *Toward a Transpersonal Ecology*.[70] Fox develops Abraham Maslow's and Anthony J. Sutich's transpersonal psychology along ecological pathways. Maslow and Sutich were foundational figures in the humanistic psychology movement in the 1960s and 1970s.[71] Central to Maslow's view was the concept of "self-actualization," the actualizing or realizing of a person's potential for personal growth and creative achievement. Maslow studied self-actualizers, both living and dead (through their writings, achievements, and biographies), in an attempt to *profile* their value preferences, outlooks on life, and character. As the humanistic school flourished, Maslow, Sutich, and others began to reflect upon their *human*istic emphasis on the single and virtually isolated conception of *self*. The *I* or *ego* was thought of as separate, or "as particle-like rather than field-like."[72] Yet Maslow's and Sutich's research into the "peak experiences" of self-actualizers, and their frequent encounters with mystical experiences they encountered, led them to suggest that these were "transpersonal." They extended the narrow limits of the self, actually bursting the conceptual and experiential apparent boundaries of the self, revealing its connections with a considerably greater whole.

Sutich, in his personal account of the gradual transition from humanistic to transpersonal psychology, remarks that humanistic psychology did not "give sufficient attention to the place of man in the universe or cosmos."[73] As Fox chronicles the formative events, Maslow had come to hold that there was a developmental level *beyond* self-actualization, comprised of those individuals who had transcended self-actualization. Quite in line with the overall thesis of the present book, Fox's apt summary of Maslow's revised position is very much to the point:

Maslow repeatedly describes transcendence and transcenders in terms of both the Spinozist ideal of living "under the aspect of eternity" and the Taoist ideal of living in harmony with the nature of things by allowing them to develop or unfold in their own way. Transcenders live in a Kingdom of Ends (i.e., they see people and other entities in the world as ends in themselves rather than in terms of their use value), and they identify their own good with the good of greater wholes (humankind, the cosmos).[74]

The new "fourth psychology" (humanistic psychology having been the "third-force psychology") was to be cosmic- rather than human-centred, transpersonal rather than personal, embracive rather than isolationist. Fox quotes Roger Walsh in pointing out that the transpersonal perspective is more readily evident in Eastern thought, although it is to be found in Spinoza's writings and in the legacy of Christian mysticism:

Western psychologists usually assume that our normal, natural, and optimal identity is egoic. However, Eastern and transpersonal psychologies suggest that our sense of self potentially may be considerably more plastic than we usually recognize.

They suggest that our sense of self can expand to include aspects of both the mind and the world that we usually regard as "other" or "not me." ... [They suggest that] the individual can also identify with aspects of the world and humanity beyond the body, transcending the condition of separateness and isolation in recognition of the interrelated unity of existence.[75]

Applying transpersonal psychology to transpersonal ecology, Fox singles out the deep ecologist Arne Naess as one who holds a "cosmologically based" sense of identification with things.[76] You identify with the universe, feel a kinship with it, thrill to its wonder and beauty, and against this background focus on individuals and parts in understanding its detail. By contrast, a more *personally* based vision of the whole *can* emphasize that each of the parts is related to *me*, to *my* family, *my* community, *my* country, and so on. Cosmically oriented identification is likely to be more impartial, therefore, although no less personal in its dealings with individuals and smaller parts of the whole. Transpersonal ecology, of the cosmologically based sort, is not anthropocentric but is centred in the cosmos, and such a view has the power to give renewed meaning to our lives and new hope to our world. In Maslow's words, "without the transcendent and the transpersonal, we get sick, violent, and nihilistic, or else hopeless and apathetic. We need something 'bigger than we are' to be awed by and to commit ourselves to in a new, naturalistic, empirical, non-churchly sense, perhaps as Thoreau and Whitman did."[77]

BEYOND MORALITY

Fox argues at some length that ordinary *objective* intrinsic-value theorists, and theorists who argue that ecological thinking is a clear "demand of morality," tend to do so from a confined and limited sense of self:

It is important to note that even if the moral demands of the normative-judgmental self are of the (unusual) kind that one *ought* to abandon exclusive identification with a narrow, atomistic, or particle-like sense of self and develop a wide, expansive, or field-like sense of self, the self that is being addressed – the self that "ought" to do this – is still this particular self as distinct from other particular selves. Moral demands, in other words, *proceed* from the assumption of a narrow conception of self even when the *end* they aim for is the realization of an expansive sense of self. There is no way around this; it is inherent in the nature of moral demands. Moral demands necessarily emphasize a self that is capable of choice, a self that is a centre of volitional activity, yet our sense of self can be far more expansive than that of being a centre of volitional activity.[78]

By contrast, "the transpersonal ecology conception of self is a wide, expansive, or field-like conception from the outset."[79] Thus, while the route to an expanded sense of self *may* take you through increasingly widening circles of embracive moral concern and identification, through the "stages" of moral awareness for some, then for all of mankind, and so on, ultimately you must move *beyond* ethics, as ordinarily understood:

This has the highly interesting, even startling, consequence that ethics (conceived as being concerned with moral "oughts") is rendered superfluous! The reason for this is that if one has a wide, expansive, or field-like sense of self then (assuming that one is not self-destructive) one will naturally (i.e. spontaneously) protect the natural (spontaneous) unfolding of this expansive self (the ecosphere, the cosmos) in all its aspects.[80]

The Zen Buddhist and Taoist have similarly argued that one who is enlightened – that is, one who has seen into his or her own ego-empty depths and has come to see the interconnectedness of the cosmic process – will have no reason or desire whatsoever to do harm to anything or anyone. Naess's position seems remarkably similar:

Care flows naturally if the "self" is widened and deepened so that protection of free Nature is felt and conceived as protection of ourselves ... Just as we need not morals to make us breathe ... [so] if your "self" in the wide sense embraces another being, you need no moral exhortation to show care ... You care for yourself without feeling any moral pressure to do it – provided you have not succumbed to a neurosis of some kind, developing self-destructive tendencies, or hating yourself.[81]

In Zen Buddhist thought, enlightenment is a non-dual state in which the self, as emptied, is simply that which it apprehends or is aware of. At the deepest level, you identify with others and with everything as clearly as you identify with your own body and mind. If you identify with the whole world, then you care about all of it, just as you once cared only for yourself. The great delusion is that of selfishness, of self-centred action. But to avoid selfish behaviour, you must eliminate all distinctions that divide one person or one group from another, and this includes moral distinctions. Only selfless thinking, willing, and feeling will take us beyond the ego focus of moral codes. The ultimate in selfless thinking is awareness that eliminates the self altogether, that empties it and allows us to mirror the whole of existence. Delusion is the failure to see that you are a manifestation of the whole and, as such, actually represent the macrocosm in your own microcosm.

The absence of this kind of selfless thinking, says the Buddhist, is delusion: the failure to see that you are a manifestation of the whole and that as such you actually represent the macrocosm in your microcosm. Ignorance, and the resulting delusion of individualization or separation, come to be the source of suffering, which to the Buddhist is evil. When there is not a trace of a sense of the whole, the result is alienation from the cosmos, the world, and eventually even from yourself. Evil is separation, wilful aggression, selfish separation, painful isolation. "Someone who manipulates the world merely for his own advantage increasingly dualizes himself from it. Those who live in this way cannot help expecting the same from others, leading to a life based on fear and the need to control situations."[82] It is not that you cannot pick out the good and evil paths or ways when you apply your analytic mind to the subject-matter, rather that you can learn to live and act in accordance with things, respecting them as being of the same worth as your own self, and your beloved, and your family. It might never arise, therefore, that you would wish to harm another. It is no longer a matter of refraining from harming others, for there is no reason not to be inclined to maintain the whole.

Compassionate identification is the natural way for this perspective. For one who has glimpsed the interconnectedness of things, it is inevitable. As Hajime Nakamura writes, if "we allow the virtue of compassion to grow in us, it will not occur to us to harm anyone else, any more than we would willingly harm ourselves." Nakamura encourages us to think that *meditation* is a chief way of cultivating this expanded sense of self: "[The effects of meditation are] to abolish our deep-rooted egoism in our own existence: it aims at cherishing compassion and love towards others. By dissolving our human existence into component parts, we can get rid of the notion of ego, and through that meditation we are led to a limitless expansion of the self in a practical sense, because one identifies oneself with more and more living beings."[83]

Rather than a rule-, act-, or consequences-oriented moral stance, Zen Buddhism is *agent* oriented, with emphasis on the *transformation* of self or character rather than on moral precepts. One who is compassionate and able to identify with my needs is unlikely to do me any harm, except unwittingly. One who follows the rules may be unable to do more than the minimum required, and at that, only when someone is looking. Still, a good person is one who acts generally as morality requires. The compassionate person acts morally spontaneously, and without first thinking about either his or her own skin or about the complexities of overall moral requirements, and often goes well beyond what the minimalistic rules of morality prescribe.

A LAST LOOK AT INTRINSIC VALUE

While Naess rejects the technical uses of "intrinsic value" as helpful chartings along the way to ecological consciousness, he continues to use the term in a non-technical sense, as most people use it, in referring to things that are worthwhile "for their own sakes." He writes, "among people who are not heavily influenced by certain philosophical or juridical terminology, it is common to be concerned about animals regardless of sentience, and for flowers, patches of landscapes, ecosystems, *for their own sake*."[84] In summarizing Naess's position, Fox concludes:

Now what most distinguishes the other main writers on deep ecology (and those considered to be closely associated with them) from the mainstream of writers on ecophilosophy (i.e., from philosophical intrinsic value theorists) is that they agree not only with Naess's rejection of formal intrinsic value theory approaches but also with the transpersonal, realization-of-as-expansive-a-sense-of-self-as-possible approach that Naess advocates in preference to these approaches.[85]

I have no quarrel with this abandoning of formal intrinsic value theory, although I see no reason why Lewis's clarification of the *immediacy* of intrinsic value *as* experience cannot serve as a formal foundation for expansive, transpersonal ecology. What you need to argue, however, is that the widening of your sense of self is worthwhile both in terms of joy, happiness, meaningful living, and improved interpersonal relationships, *and* as a rationally and emotionally compelling form of understanding of who and where you are. But it is not the only worthy vision, nor the only "whole story" in town. You choose your story on the basis of its overall explanatory strength, its comprehensiveness, its capacity to satisfy your intuitive sense about yourself, others, and the world, its valuational sensitivity and richness, and of its capacity to make you feel at home in the world.

Finally, those who wish to "check out" Warwick Fox's interpretation of Naess and other like-minded deep ecologists would benefit from his "mini-reader" collection of passages taken from their works, in his *Towards a Transpersonal Ecology*.[86] As a sample of that collection, and as a final word towards understanding the distinctiveness of *deep ecology*, Freya Mathews remarks that, "from the point of view of deep ecology, what is wrong with our culture is that it offers us an inaccurate conception of the self. It depicts the personal self as existing in competition with and in opposition to nature ... [We thereby fail to realize that] if we destroy our environment, we are destroying what is in fact our larger self."[87]

FINAL COMMENTS

In summary, deep ecology generally, and transpersonal ecology in particular, recommend the acceptance of a horizon of understanding, a "story" of considerably wider inclusion than the usual, and a "whole story" involving feelings of identification, relational intimacy, and caring. They herald "an ecologically harmonious social paradigm shift [that] is going to require a *total* reorientation of the thrust of Western culture."[88] No doubt the new paradigm will include a great deal of the older layers of paradigms of the history of the world, but selectively appropriated by the new "whole story" that serves as the wide-angle lenses through which we will look at ourselves, our actions and institutions, and at the world in which we live. Indeed, Naess employs language that links well with the language of the wider horizon, the most comprehensive whole story that you are capable of articulating, and the stage-seven thinking that I have been using in this book: "Spiritual growth ... begins when we cease to understand or see ourselves as isolated and narrow competing egos and begin to identify with other humans from our family and friends to, eventually, other species."[89] Then, the ecological sense itself is exceeded, and the cosmic vision, as I have called it, is affirmed by Naess: "But the deep ecology sense of self requires a further maturity and growth, an identification which goes beyond humanity to include the nonhuman world."[90]

You can see that I have been unable to provide anything more than a brief description of this new paradigm, or of the Gaia hypothesis. What I have tried to sketch is a view of the world as integrated, rich with meaning for us if we but take the time to look with open receptivity, to dwell in it rather than to use it, and which is possibly even *responsive* to us, as the Gaia theory propounds. This is not to say that the earth or the cosmos is conscious, that it is yet another God-figure to contend with. It "has no conscious mind with which to think about its great complexity or plan its future," and yet as a system it "functions intelligently and wisely on its billions of years of experience without conscious thought."[91] It is we who are conscious, and it may well be that we are "the newest Gaian experiment."[92]

Up to now there has been little to suggest that conscious intelligence has advanced even one small step in the evolution of Gaia, and indeed it may turn out to be an unworkable blind alley of exploration. Neither you nor I will accept that position quite yet, however, and hence the urgency with which we must explore our relationships with nature in all its forms if the occasionally glimpsed promise of conscious intelligence is to be realized, even to a small degree. In a powerful account of the sense of the oneness of things, where boundaries between the ego and everything else have been taken down to reveal the intimate spread of existence, Ken Wilbur compares the individuals of existence to waves, and the whole to the ocean: "Unity consciousness, however, is not so much a particular wave as it is the *water* itself. And there is no boundary, no difference, no separation between water and any of the waves. That is, the water is equally present in *all* waves, in the sense that no wave is wetter than another."[93]

Identification with the wetness of the water as an expression of the great ocean of existence is what Wilbur articulates. And yet, in the paradoxical manner of the East, identification with the whole does not eliminate you as an individual but enhances your own self-awareness. You study the self by forgetting your self, and only then can you truly make intimate contact with the people and things of this world as the transparent lenses of caring attention. The result is that by losing yourself you find yourself – a truth that appears in many cultures of the world, including the Christian cultural heritage. What you find is a non-alienated, intimately related, *caring* aperture tuned to receiving others from the vantage point of a position "here and now." That position includes recognizing that the less self-oriented a horizon/perspective/vision is defined by the nurturing whole of which it is a part, and which is only ever partially glimpsed in the apertures of perception available to us.

We may see more and more, but the emptiness of the unknown forever stretches beyond us, like a receding universe, ever tempting us to try again to arrive at a whole story, a paradigm, a horizon of understanding that will include more than the last. If we try, we find meaning by means of this very quest, a meaning that arises ever renewed; all this happens as we enrich our perspective while growing in capacity, in sensitivity, and in humility. Just as life is defined as biological change and death as its lack, so *meaning in life* is characterized by the application of stable patterns to changing circumstances and the replacing of old patterns of understanding by new

and exploratory ones. Meaning is found in the losing of it, the searching after it, and in the finding of it again. The meaning in your life
is in flux and is to be found in the flux (the flow) of meaning, which
is therefore itself a source of meaning in your life. All this does
require, however, the developing of a tolerance for ambiguity, of a
willingness to accept the inevitability of change and the precarious-
ness of your present vision, and of an openness to the unending
richness in your experience of the world in its manifold variety and
diversity.

CHERRY BLOSSOMS: SYMBOLS OF THE CHANGEABILITY OF LIFE

It was cherry-blossom time in Japan. The parks were swarm-
ing with people who wanted to take in the pink air above
and around them. The trees formed a close-up second "sky"
overhead, for they were planted in such a way that the
branches from one overhung the branches of those around it.
It was an accidental metaphor for the interconnectedness of
all things and for the sense of community that is such a vital
part of Japanese thinking. I was filled with delight at the
totally pink environment, so dense that even the air around
and beneath the trees took on something of the pink hue
above. People picnicked, frolicked, drank beer, played games
with their children, and laughed heartily with office colleagues. It was a working day, and yet because the day was so
perfect, lunch hours in many businesses and industries were
lengthened, schools were let out early, and along the sidewalks near the emperor's palace in Tokyo, hospital patients
and the elderly were being wheeled along to view the blossoms.

   The cherry blossoms are a symbol for the Japanese of the
fragility and the changeability of life. In cities across Japan
dozens and dozens of gardeners spend incredible amounts of
time taking care of the cherry trees and the surrounding gardens in order to ensure that the blossoms will be at their best
in late April or May. Special lanterns are hung from the trees,
and even hand-painted and inscribed strips of paper are
attached to the branches, with poetry on them. The strips are
reachable and more or less at eye level, so you can read and
enjoy the poetry as you view the blossoms, all the while
attending to the piped-in music in the background. The *blos-*

som event is so significant a part of Japanese life that there is even a special name given to cherry-blossom viewing *at night*; *yosakura*, with the *yo* added to *sakura*, which means "cherry blossoms." Families with young children bring them to see the night blossoms, for the viewing is so different then, and the smells too are different in the cooler night dampness. There is such an air of happiness and delight that it is difficult not to share in the occasion.

Like much in Japan, the moods of the people are common, shared moods, and the shared aspect only enhances the mood and receptivity of the individual. And yet, however carefully the trees are tended, and however much is planned and ready to enhance the viewing of the blossoms, they may be there to enjoy for but a few hours or a few days. One storm, one windy day, and the months of anticipation and preparation will have been blown aside, and the festival will be over almost before it has begun. The moral – the cultural metaphor – is that you must be sure to enjoy the blossoms deeply and fully while they are here, for they may last but a moment, and then be gone forever ... or gone at least until next year, when a new crop will emerge from the cycle of seasons.

Still, this *particular* festival will never happen again, and it is imperative that you enter into it fully *here and now*, for each moment is irreplaceable and irretrievable. So it is with such menial tasks as washing the dishes, sweeping the floor, preparing a meal, brushing your teeth, and, more obviously, being with your loved one *now*. This is the central emphasis of Zen Buddhist training. It is not uncommon for a new monk to be told almost nothing of Zen itself for months. He or she is included in the daily routines of living and nothing more, for part of the training involves the winding down from the mindlessness of ordinary ego-filled life and the opening to the *mind-full mindlessness of being there, and only there*, which is essential to Zen openness to things *just as they are*. The mind, the emotions, and the body must all *clear*, un-tense, de-stress, un-think and un-conceptualize, and "de-verbalize," in order for old habits and outlooks to fall away sufficiently for new ones to take root.

There is a powerful yet simple passage in Zen Master Dōgen's instructions to a monk whose task is to prepare food in the monastery: "When you wash rice and prepare vegetables, you must do it with your own hands, and with your own eyes, making sincere effort. Do not be idle even for a moment. Do not be careful about one thing and careless about another. Do not give away your opportunity even if it is merely a drop in the ocean of merit; do not fail to place even a single particle of earth at the summit of the mountain of wholesome deeds."[94] No act is too mundane, no motion unimportant, no idle thought too insignificant to matter. Awareness means to be focused, to attain transparency to the extent that you are remarkably aware of the scent of the breeze, the fluttering sound of the blossoms overhead, the staccato of the falling petals from each heavily laden tree, and the softness of the pink cover on the ground on which you are walking lightly, as if to protect even these from damage underfoot.

Then they are gone. A brief storm in the night, and the trees are nearly bare, except for the budding green leaves that are now visible. The pink surround is now back to normal, and the world is again coloured as you remember. There is a sadness that this intense beauty is past, and yet a determination to get on with things in a more normal way, refreshed by the moments of ecstasy that the astonishing array of blossoms occasioned. The streets are still lined with paper- and plastic-blossomed branches, and these will stay up for a while, a reminder of the natural magnificence that is past. Oddly now, those artificial branches look less out of place, tucked into windows, doorways, attached to street lights, traffic lights, mailboxes, telephone poles, traffic-sign poles, and trees that do not bloom. They look less out of place now, bright welcome reminders that the real blossoms are past. They extend the season for a bit and keep our focus on the change of season, on renewal, and on the details of spring coming alive everywhere. The breezes of spring now blow through each of us and not just around us, and we are cleansed, opened, and made newly receptive to the events of natural unfolding.

CHAPTER SIX

Deconstructing Meaning

Nikos Kazantzakis, whom I quoted in beginning the discussion about the sense of identification of self with the whole sweep of entities constituting the cosmos, ends *The Saviours of God* with a credal-poetic repetition of the key insights of his exploration. The eighth entry in the string of nine reads "Blessed be all those who free You and become united with You, Lord, and who say: You and I are one." It is a comforting way to end, because it brings the reader back to what appears to be a conventional rendering of religious understanding: however difficult it is to make sense of the spilling of blood and the suffering of the creatures of this earth, there is still a stable and purposeful higher reality on which you can pin your hopes: "and behind His ceaseless flux I discern an indestructible unity." Then, without hesitation or remorse, the ample table set with reassurances and hopes of a recognizable sort is upset. Like a magician Kazantzakis grasps the linen tablecloth of assurances and pulls briskly, taking away everything that had been given, upsetting the table as well: "And thrice blessed be those who bear on their shoulders and do not buckle under this great, sublime, and terrifying secret: THAT EVEN THIS ONE DOES NOT EXIST!"[1] There is no divine Oneness – or if there is, it is beyond our comprehension – and there is no God, no "indestructible unity," only the ceaseless struggle to understand, to cope, to find meaning in life, and to invent new meanings and new models of understanding whenever the old cease to function.

Not only is there no meaning to life that can be "verified" as the correct or better one generally; there is no guarantee that traditional sources of meaning will continue to apply. When Nietzsche announced that "God was dead," he meant to announce with the same cry that absolute value and preordained meaning-in-life was dead as well. *If there is no God, no stable value-structure that is pre-given, no meaning to be counted on, then perhaps there is no "stage seven" either. Perhaps there is no "whole story" that can claim to be anything more than a "story."* Some of the most contrived of childrens' stories provide comfort where there really is none. They achieve this by hiding the uncertainties of life and establishing the "good ending" as the necessary prerequisite for the "suitable for children of all ages" label. Hollywood is the "grown-up" version of this kind of legacy, where the good guy is both identifiable and somehow protected against even overwhelming odds and ill will. For adults, however, it may be that part of what it means to mature is to discover that it is not always obvious who the good guys are, nor is there anything even close to a guarantee that things will end well. Indeed, it is now recognized that good things do, in fact, happen often to bad people, and that bad things do, in fact, happen often to good people.

This entire excursion into *meaning and valuation* that I have engaged you in, could be but another "story" that I have woven together in order to provide you with hope and purpose. Or if that is too presumptuous, then at least let it be known that the story told has provided *me* with hope and purpose. Yet this autobiographical fact is of no use to anyone else who has come along on this journey, for what I claimed to be doing was something more than telling stories about my own now-adult childhood. I have implied throughout that what I have been at pains to present was significant well beyond the limits of my own skin, and that it might shed light on various dimensions of the search for meaning in life, both mine and at least some others.

TEXTS AS ANALOGS

Were we to read a poem together, the chances are that we would not entirely agree about its meaning and significance. We might agree to a considerable degree, or we might not agree at all. It is the same with art. Two stark white canvases, hung one slightly below and beside the other, might strike you as a critique of traditional art, art critics, and the hanging of paintings in a gallery. They might occasion me to howl that the avant-garde is adept at ripping off the general public, of pulling the wool over our eyes. Yet we are generally more relaxed when it comes to poetry and art, for it is a commonplace that disagreement in interpretation abounds, and we are likely to be tolerant enough to announce that each person is entitled to her/his own opinions and tastes. Fiction, too, allows such variation of interpretation, but science, medicine, most "serious" prose, academic scholarship, news reports, the reading of religious texts, and *ethics* are kept in tight control for fear of unleashing a doubt so strong and so harmful that the so-called civilized world would cease to be a world in which we would want to live.

Meaning in life, too, is like this, for if we have been able to live happily and joyfully to this point, or even if we have only been able to hang on, at least we are functioning within the limits we have made our own. To shatter even these might bring about an encounter with the abyss of doubt, uncertainty, and despair. It was Dostoevsky who concluded that if God was dead, then everything was permitted, for without the assurance of some stability in ethical decision-making from on high, then we humans might well justify any decision as being as good as any other. The horror of relativism and the inevitability of a radical scepticism seemed to him the direct result of denying absolute guarantees for our moral codes and ethical norms. And given the Nazi experience of this century and the persistence of torture and violence at present, nearly the world over, we must wonder whether he might have been right.

Belief in God is not at its cultural height, nor do most of us find the ancient codes either adequate or clear enough to deal with the problems of the present age. It was John Ruskin who, at the age of three, upon hearing an intense discussion downstairs before falling to sleep, placed himself at the top of the stairs and pleaded, "People, be good!" It was the beginning of an ethical stance, to be sure, but not quite enough to decide how you ought to think and feel with respect to abortion, or how a politician ought to conduct her/himself while in office, or whether businesses ought to operate within the same codes of behaviour as the best ordinary citizens. Similarly, a recent advertisement depicts a modern woman, groomed and coiffed to the nines, addressing city hall with the profound insight that "If we just showed good manners, we wouldn't need laws."[2] We need considerably more to still the flux of possibilities, such that our choices appear to be well founded, standing firmly as the best of the alternatives available to us.

Yet how is this to be done? Is there general agreement across the diversity of cultures that a specific way of life is to be preferred? Obviously not, I would conclude, even though there may well be similarities, and in some very specific ways general agreement. Joseph Margolis has pointed out that we tend to find agreement in ethics at the level of extreme evil and not at the level where we fine-tune the details of ethical living or the principles on which it might be said to be based. Thus, we agree that torture is not morally acceptable, nor is causing undue suffering for the self-pleasure of it.[3] Yet torture is epidemic as a political weapon, and suffering of an unnecessary sort continues apace.

The issue is not whether we can decide how to act or how to find meaning in our lives but whether we should view such decisions as final, unchanging, guaranteed, and more or less unrevisable. In order to live we must decide on one course of action rather than another, moment by moment. We declare our values and take our stands in both small ways and large. Were we to admit that we are *never certain* that we have chosen correctly, are never reassured that this chosen course was the correct course of action, then we would be *open* to unending exploration and revision in our way of living. We would have learned to put our prejudices and assumptions, our convictions and beliefs *at risk*. Yet we would stand fast when a decision was required, on the recognition that given the information at hand and given our vision of the alternatives open to us, this was the *best* decision to make at this moment. We would not stand paralysed because there might be a better one, or because we couldn't be absolutely sure. We would abandon the possibility of absolute certainty and accept instead "tentative closure." We would "close" on the debate, on the decision, even though we couldn't be certain, because we would be as informed as we can be that, given our horizon of understanding, this is the course we ought to follow.

Humility reminds us that we might well be wrong and that experience may show this to be the case in the results that follow, in the light of reactions to our decision. *When you abandon the expectation that certainty is possible, you open yourself to the proliferation of possibilities, to the proliferation of alternative visions of the "best" that are available, and you reconcile yourself to the realization that this process is without end.* You never get it exactly right. Every answer, every act is but *provisional*. You "read" a poem or a painting provisionally, working out the range of possible interpretive meanings, and then you listen to other readings and interpretations, and you re-read again, and again, and again.

DECONSTRUCTION

The process is never completed, any more than the sweeping of the kitchen floor is ever completed. You simply keep on sweeping, day by day, in order to keep the rubble and dust below the level where you could no longer live successfully. Yet the assurance of comfort, of stilling the play of possibilities, never comes. As John Caputo describes this with respect to Jacques Derrida's strategy of deconstruction,

I favor the Socratic analogy when dealing with Derrida: the practitioner of disruptive strategies whose point – whose style/stylus – is to unmask pretension, to foil the claim to knowledge. And as Socrates did not avoid the semblance of sophism, neither does Derrida avoid the semblance of a wanton aestheticism and anarchism. Like Socrates, Derrida's daimon is not positive. We do not need encouragement to construct schemes, to lay things out in a political program, in a metaphysical panorama or a bureaucratic flow chart. Indeed, it is always in the name of these totalizing views that the police do their work. Blood is usually shed in the name of Being, God, or truth, even and especially when it is shed in the name of "country." Pro deo et patria. The constructions of metaphysics, like the poor, are always with us. But it is the Socratic role to keep us honest about these schemes, to remind us of their contingency and alterability, to make the police think twice, or perhaps think in the first place.

Furthermore, it will do no good to propose revolutionary schemes which are then formulated in the terms of the ruling discourse. For they thereby are already assimilated and declawed. The task of deconstruction is to keep the ruling discourse in question, to expose its vulnerability and the tensions by which it is torn.[4]

On the one hand, all interpretation, all metaphysics, all science, all religion, and every whole story is a quest for order and intelligibility. As such, each of these "privileges" itself by holding that it is the best perspective, the authoritative interpretation, or the "rational" understanding of things. But no view is the master view because no interpretation has the master key that unlocks the unknown and reveals the mystery. There may be no ultimate unknown at all, only the succession of knowings. We have to remain in the flux of life, without final comfort, continually trying to understand what never quite fits our schema without remainder. We keep tucking it in here and it pops out there, revealing still more what we have not yet been able to account for.

The human situation is an unending *tension* between trying to figure out which point of view makes the most sense and the recognition that none of the alternatives makes perfect sense. No view is beyond question. You experience chaos or flux and you stretch a schema of understanding over it, to reveal selective and imposed patterns of repetition and continuity. To an extent this works effectively, but patterns are never quite the same from one instance to another or from one time to the next, nor do they last forever, for the flux of change and *difference* is ever present. What worked before will not necessarily work now, and what was rejected previously may now suit the new circumstances well. Rather than trying to reduce the world of experienced change to some kind of *stasis* that shields us from the flux, deconstruction wishes to restore the original difficulty of deciding, of making sense of that which is before us, of finding the interpretive stance that allows us to *defer* all claims that we have understanding. Deconstruction plunges us back into the flux and prohibits from now onwards any possibility of stemming the flow, of covering over the incessant flux of things.

Deconstruction *insinuates*[5] its doubting into a heretofore trusting and accepting mind. To insinuate is to cause doubt, to cause distrust by means of a change in outlook. The force of the strategy of deconstruction is that it renders us willing to face the possibility that what we have heretofore thought or practised might be open to serious question. Every critically minded person must test a trusted understanding by injecting into it a fair amount of doubt. The difference is that, for the most part, he/she expects to have reached the correct understanding, or to move closer to it by this sort of course correction. The deconstructionist abandons the hope and the belief that there is any correct view, or an unquestionably correct and decisive action. Nothing is beyond doubt, beyond correction, beyond revision, beyond the corruption of change and variation. You can never get it right, whatever position you hold.

The result is not scepticism, however, for the sceptic holds that no decision and no understanding is better or worse than any other. You might as well flip a coin or do as you please at this moment. The practitioner of deconstruction, by contrast, while admitting that one never retards or stops the flux, nevertheless questions in order to free her or himself from the power and rigidity of the dominant mode of understanding, the dominant institutions of power and authority, and the unquestioned "morality" of the status quo and those who speak for it. To free yourself is to know that all views are foundationless in that they can never remove all doubt, can never show conclusively that they are the justifiably favoured view. Nor can any view separate itself from the flux of change, from alterations of perspective or of information, from the awareness of alternative possibilities.

HERACLITUS REVISITED

The deconstruction and reconstruction of thought as the history of thought will doubtless continue without end. The only truth is that there is no truth.[6] It is of interest to note that Heraclitus, the pre-Socratic whom Plato criticized so fiercely because of Heraclitus' insistence that the world of experience is flux, may become one of the late-sung heroes of the postmodern world. Heraclitus is the odd man out in the history of philosophy in the West because of what his contemporaries found to be his enigmatic utterances. He continues to confound and perplex with the cryptic and inscrutable tone of the handful of fragments left to us from his writings. What is clearly focal in Heraclitus' philosophy is the affirmation that *paradox* is not an incomplete and premature understanding of things but a deep and profound intimation of the nature of our contact with so-called reality. Heraclitus is not the hopelessly confused relativist whose position a clever Socrates could easily expose as a vicious scepticism, with no epistemological ground to stand on. Heraclitus' stand was that to adopt a univocal and non-paradoxical viewpoint or understanding of things is to *distort* our experience. It is non-paradoxical utterance that wrests things from the flow of real experience, and places you in a conceptual realm of human forms where they are harmlessly pinned down like a collection of butterflies on a board. As Wheelwright states,

The most characteristic difficulty in Heraclitus' philosophy lies in the demand which it makes upon its hearers to transcend the "either-or" type of thinking and to recognize in each phase of experience that a relationship of "both-and" may be present in subtle ways that escape a dulled intelligence ... To him nothing is exclusively this or that; in various ways he affirms something to be *both* of two disparates or two contraries, leaving the reader to contemplate the paradox, the full semantic possibilities of which can never be exhausted by plain prose statements.[7]

Heraclitus himself wrote more cryptically, less obviously than Wheelwright, but the flow, which can best be grasped as opposites in tension, is as readily apparent:

(36) God is day and night, winter and summer, war and peace, surfeit and hunger; but he takes various shapes, just as fire, when it is mingled with spices, is named according to the savour of each.
   (45) Men do not know how what is at variance agrees with itself. It is an attunement of opposite tensions, like that of the bow and the lyre.[8]

The rigidity and the precision of either-or logic make it impossible to give expression to the flux of the everyday world, the shifting and paradoxically this-and-yet-not-this (or that) manifested in the flow of experience. The paradoxicality is not to be taken as a confusion, temporary or otherwise. Rather, the paradox is itself the only way that we, as rationally linguistic beings, can express the inherent complexity and ambiguity given in experience.

Yet even though the deconstructionist and Heraclitus would seem to have so much in common, Heraclitus makes a move upon which the deconstructer will pounce. Heraclitus does give flux its due, but then he appears to take it away again by invoking the notion of "the unity of opposites." This stands as a "truth whose primary application for human beings lies in a deeper understanding of their own experience of life and death, sleeping and waking, youth and old age."[9] Emphasis on "unity" is an attempt to stop the flow, even if only at the "deeper" level of understanding. But where is this deeper level to be encountered? Not in experience but more as a template of the mind, fitted over experience itself in order to make it intelligible and, likely, bearable.

If you were to limit yourself to experience-as-languaged, as expressed and thought, there would simply remain an ongoing account of the continually changing rivers or streams of consciousness. Nevertheless, what makes deconstruction possible as a critical reflection upon any and all claims to understanding is the existence of claims to order, to regularity, to repetitions of a pattern, to consensus in ethics, politics, or ways of living in the world. A great tension has arisen between the strategy of deconstruction and the necessity of there being something to deconstruct. You can't have one without the other, for the simple reason that deconstruction without anything to deconstruct would become the ruling discourse, the status quo, the established view. Deconstruction would then have to be deconstructed, making itself the source of order and the ruling discourse long enough to knock itself off its temporary pedestal.

Deconstruction takes it as a given that you will never get the better of the flux, for, as Heraclitus indicated, fresh water is always flowing in upon you. The flow of circumstances makes it necessary that we not grow rigid but keep all notions, all claims, all systems, all norms, and all smug satisfaction about having found the "secret" *in play*. However tempting it may be, you must keep *closure*, or the termination of searching and questioning, at bay. The issues must be kept in play, alive, open to revision and/or temporary rejection altogether. At the same time, we must live some way, decide somehow, and act in one way or another at all moments of our lives.

ALBERT CAMUS

A central insight into the nature and importance of *tension* as a characteristic of what it means to be open-minded, to be willing to place your own assumptions and principles at risk, is provided by Albert

Camus. Camus was not, of course, a practitioner of deconstructive techniques, and his works are more likely to be texts *for* deconstructive practice than instances of it. But his insights into the structure of tension, disorder (absurdity), and flux are as helpful today as they were when they first appeared. Camus contends that most human beings have a strong desire or "nostalgia" for unity (order, system, regularity, pattern, answers to live by), while at the same time he recognizes that experience itself provides us with ample evidence of disunity (disorder, pattern anomalies, the inadequacy of systems and theories in accounting for the complexity of things).[10] The tension within us is between our desire for order and our experience of disorder.

Whereas Camus thinks of order as mere nostalgia, a rational/intellectual superimposition on to the flux of experience, I am more inclined to add that there is an actual experience of unity in the world and not just a desire or a hope that there is. Otherwise, our empirical attempts at experimentation and confirmation in the natural and social sciences would be doomed from the start, however temporary and partial they may be. Similarly, at the level of values, unless there were wide similarities in value preference, we could hardly do each other any good or any harm. The issue is not whether all order is merely imposed, for that denies to experience any pattern whatsoever, but whether any pattern is a guarantee that things will continue to be so patterned and whether a further analysis will not place any alleged order into a radically different context of interpretation, resulting in a restructuring of immense significance. Thus, a helpful drug may be seen as harmful if we follow through on its long-term effects rather than concentrating on short-term effects alone. A breakthrough in technology such as the internal-combustion engine may turn out to be a major cause of the destruction of our livable environment, making the innovation a catastrophe. The assumption that "blacks" are inferior, merely sources of cheap labour, may be the result of the imposition of an ugly prejudice and the latent cause of racial hatred for centuries to come.

The world appears to be both ordered and disordered, lawful and lawless. We remember the disorder if we never assume that a finding is final, that a pattern is eternal, that an answer is definitive, and that a way of life is anything like the "best." What we have instead is some claim that given the evidence to this point, this decision seems the best available. However, new information or a change in perspective may cause us to rethink our position. The other side of deconstructive *arrogance* is deconstructive *humility*. In this it *is* quite Socratic.

RELATIVISM

A concern that one might have with deconstructive activity is that it opens the door to relativism. The charge of relativism is one that deconstruction will likely see as beside the point, however, for the *deferring* of the achievement of a final truth is not a failure but an opening to a gathering of perspectives rather than a strict focusing on a single one. Yet to give free play to all possible perspectives and voices is not itself an assurance that the results will be positive. Rather, some of the voices may attempt to seize power ruthlessly, or argue out of a strictly selfish hidden agenda, or disrupt the patient hearing of many voices because of their own contagious psychopathology. It seems to me that what is demanded is some set of value commitments, however tentatively grounded, by means of which each of us can decide what is valuable or "better" or right, both personally and collectively. There is no protection inherent in simply being a good listener: you must also learn from what you hear, accepting what is conducive (seemingly) to the general good (which includes the personal in the decision-making process) and rejecting what (seemingly) is not.

At its best deconstruction demands of us that we listen to what are habitually the undertones of a familiar melody, and reach out to experiment with the allegedly "non-melodious" in order to decide whether our musical ears are attuned or culturally *trained* to listen to the established and customary. Focus on what is rejected as unmusical and thereby open yourself to other musical possibilities, as well as to the modification or abandonment of the old sense of musical, *which demanded that no other forms be heard*. As Christopher Norris observes in his summary of Nietzsche's deconstructive analysis of philosophy and morality, "behind all the big guns of reason and morality is a fundamental will to persuade which craftily disguises its workings by imputing them always to the adversary camp. Truth is simply the honorific title assumed by an argument which has got the upper hand – and kept it – in this war of competing persuasions."[11]

At its worst, however, deconstruction leaves us in the position of rejecting any and all candidates as unmusical groups of notes, each attempting to dominate and control. Perpetual revisability does not imply the perpetual rejection of all possibilities of understanding, only the willingness to re-examine the value and worth of a possibility that has been enacted and has "sedimented" or solidified into the expected and approved in order to be in a position to decide afresh whether it still is the best available. Deconstruction is a *tool* and not an end in itself. It is a perpetual call to conscience, a demand that we remain awake and intensely aware of the implications of what we hold to be better, and of the alternatives that continue to swirl before us. It is a strategy for releasing "a multiplicity of meaning" where before only one could be discerned.[12]

The history of Western thought begins with the struggle between the relativists and sceptics on the one hand and, on the other, those who, with Plato and Socrates, search for some ground on which unchanging knowledge-claims might be based. It seemed as though relativism had to be shown to be wrong or else the very enterprise of philosophy, and even the possibility of civilization itself, was doomed. Yet in a way, "if anything, the sophist comes closer to wisdom by implicitly acknowledging what Socrates has to deny: that thinking is always and inseparably bound to the rhetorical devices that support it."[13] The feared relativism is the view that all opinions and claims are equally true and equally false. I shall call this position "epistemological relativism," and Lawrence Kohlberg is among the many who fear that "acceptance of the idea that *all* values are relative does, logically, lead to the conclusion that the teacher should not attempt to teach any particular moral values ... The students of a teacher who has been successful in communicating moral relativism will believe, like the teacher, that 'everyone has his own bag' and that 'everyone should keep doing his thing.'"[14] In ancient Greece the art of the Sophist was to make the (apparently) stronger argument appear to be weaker and the (apparently) weaker argument appear to be stronger. In fact, they were claiming that no argument is justifiably stronger or weaker than any other. All are equal, and therefore the issue is deciding which to choose on the non-rational grounds of personal preference, at the moment.

Of all the Sophists of Plato's time, there was one (Protagoras) whom he did not take lightly, nor did he ever pretend to dismiss him easily. Gregory Vlastos urges that this is so because Protagoras had "moral inhibitions" and refused to identify "a life of pleasure with the good life."[15] Protagoras somehow established *limits* to the sorts of actions that were acceptable. He was a chief deconstructer of the thought of his times, but he maintained the capacity to judge that some courses of action were better and others worse, that some viewpoints were better and others worse. If we are to take Protagoras' claims seriously, then he is not an "epistemological relativist." Whether Protagoras had worked out his own relativistic variation may be impossible to tell. In our own day relativistic positions have begun to appear in many places, and work is underway to sort out their varieties and successes.

Consider, for example, the view that maintains that one's most basic presuppositions, perspective, horizon, or framework are not themselves ultimately and finally justifiable. They are chosen or selected as those values or starting-points without which no other values or significant stances of any kind would or could arise. I shall call such a position "perspectivism."[16] A compelling account of such a relativism is provided by Jack W. Meiland, who identifies a position that "holds that one's beliefs are relative to one's perspective, presuppositions, or framework and freely chosen by the individual rather than forced on him by his historical-cultural situation."[17] Relativism of this type need not yield a complete or paralytic scepticism. To quote a recent statement of such a position, "it is not that all beliefs are equally true or equally false, but regardless of truth and falsity the fact of their credibility is to be seen as *equally problematic*."[18] In other words, while the choice of presuppositions, framework, or perspective may be subjective or personal, nevertheless, "once these presuppositions are chosen, the rest of one's intellectual activity can be quite objective. For, given these presuppositions, certain statements will be true. They will be true for *anyone* who adopts those presuppositions."[19]

The usual criticism of this position is that relativism is self-vitiating in that there would be no objective and rational grounds for adopting the initial presuppositions. As Meiland argues, however, "emphasis on this sort of rationality (or on any other sort, or on any sort of non-rationality either) is itself an ideology."[20] Rationality, like morality or religion, is a commitment to such values as logical consistency and generality, without which it would not matter what you did or thought. Such axioms are but starting-points, or, more candidly, assumptions from which the objectivity of the rest of the system follows. To assume that every part of every doctrine must rest on there being sufficient ground or conclusive grounds for its adoption is not only to deny the ongoing development of all human knowledge but to fly in the face of Gödel's great discovery in even as exact a science as mathematics – namely, that no system has the capacity for *self*-justification. No system can justify itself by means of its own axioms. Such justification is possible only by means of a metatheory, a theory that both embraces the original and serves to justify that system from a position beyond it. But in turn, the metatheory cannot justify itself, and so a meta-metatheory is required, and so on.

In this important sense, the axiomatic beginnings of a system are *taken*, not given or proved. What serves as a partial establishment of their validity is the fruitfulness of the system built on them and the degree to which its findings accord with the empirical evidence as understood. Hence, it may be quite accurate to observe, with Protagoras, that human beings are the measure of all things, and yet to conclude, as did Protagoras, that there is a better and a worse to moral theorizing. Perhaps this was why Protagoras maintained to the end that he had something worthwhile to teach, although none of it necessarily final or guaranteed by a source external to human understanding itself. The tension between the understanding gained from adopting the *limits* necessary for distinguishing anything from anything else, including the *limits* specified in ethics such that you can judge the morally better and worse, and the never-ending deconstructive critique of these posited limits is interminable. Nevertheless, while you can never be certain that the limits that you have established are the best ones, are adequate, or are not soon to be abandoned because of anomalies that threaten the very focus they were assigned to protect, these limits do appear to be better, for a time, than the alternatives. We do the best we can, and part of what it means to try for the best is *to be willing to revise your starting-points and assumptions in the light of new evidence, new circumstances, and an encounter with an alternative that appears to succeed better still.*

ON WALKING OUT INTO THE FLUX

Deconstruction insists that the uncertainty of the flux not be denied. All understanding strives to still the flux, to achieve some kind of *stasis* that shields us from the uncertainty of the inevitability of change, revision, and the rejection of previous "truths," which turn out not to be true after all. Deconstruction wishes to restore "life to its original difficulty,"[21] to plunge us back into the flux, and to prohibit from now onwards any possibility of stemming the flow by covering over the incessant novelty and uncertainty of experience. Rather than seeking out, as did Heidegger, a deeper outlook on reality by means of the meditative or receptive mode of experience, deconstruction simply lets the play continue at the surface of things, changing as it goes along. There is no deeper sense; there is only variety, difference, alterity. Still, even if we do not insist on the receptive mode of awareness as more true, it still is most useful as a deconstructive strategy to rescramble the perceptual and conceptual world of experience in order to be open to what had not heretofore been seen. The scrambling effect is what causes the old horizon to shudder and then to bend or stretch, if not to shatter altogether, as happens when an old world-view gives way to a new.

ZEN AND DECONSTRUCTION

I have tried to make this same point in a study of the notion of *nothingness* in Japanese philosophy, taking "pure experience" as the point of reference. So-called *pure experience* is a term that Nishida Kitarō adapted from the writings of the American pragmatist, William James:

Pure experience is the beginning of Zen. It is awareness stripped of all thought, all conceptualization, all categorization, and all distinctions between subject-as-having-an-experience, and as experience-as-having-been-had-by-a-subject. It is *prior* to all judgment. Pure experience is without all distinction; it is pure no-thingness, pure no-this-or-that. It is *empty* of any and all distinctions. It is absolutely nothing at all. Yet its emptiness and nothingness is a chock-a-block fullness, for it is all-experience-to-come. It is rose, child, river, anger, death, pain, rocks, and cicada sounds. We carve these discrete events and entities out of a richer-yet-non-distinct manifold of pure experience.[22]

Yet even though the *method* of scrambling previously held horizontal viewing is effective, neither Heidegger nor Zen Buddhists keep from *positing a positive way out of the flux in order finally to come to an understanding*. To posit a "richer-yet-non-distinct" deeper reality is to still the flux, unless you carefully and humbly admit that it is but an ideology, a theory, a tentative stage seven, and not a doctrine, a dogma, or a given.

Deconstruction may never take a position, may never rest, and certainly may never rest content, but must keep the flux in play. In a way, this may be the message of Zen Buddhism too, although this is not the place to try to prove it. As a step in the direction of showing why I have not given up on Zen as a form of deconstruction, however, I will quote from my study of Nishida once more, where I focus on the unending process that is called *emptying* in Zen thought:

Empty the self itself, lose the ego, and there is but pure experience. But how do we convey this point philosophically? The self is empty, or simply the self is the emptying insofar as it is the place where pure experience arises, and yet, to recognize it as pure experience is already to be separate from it, to be a subject aware of it as an object of consciousness, and to contrast it with something else, and hence to classify it in thought. Empty "pure experience" once more, and empty the "self" as well. Empty emptiness itself, and keep everything nonsubstantial and in the flow of movement in being-time. Empty being-time, too, so that it points to the going on of events, and then empty the event of any fixity or substance. Nothingness is the empty, or the emptying, or the filling and emptying, or the empty as full, or the emptied as filling, and the filled as emptying – for it is the *process* that one is to focus on and come to grasp.[23]

Nothingness isn't any-thing, for it is the process of peeling away the preconceptions and preconditions of seeing. It is the *process* of questioning everything, and of letting go of the assumptions of world-making, even the assumption that you know what "Buddha" means. Let even this go, and let a tentative filling occur again in order to "understand" and to act right now. Then let everything go empty again, then fill again as the flow requires. This seems to me to be a reasonable cousin of deconstruction, even though it is expressed in terms far different from those of Derrida and company.[24]

LEARNING TO PLAY

Letting the process go on, never attempting to arrest its flow except for purposes of *temporary closure*, tentative though it might be, is difficult to do. John Caputo notes that

the world places little confidence in the play of things, and a great deal of reliance on constraints, authority, and institutional structures, and that is why we are overrun with creeds and criteria, rules of life and rules of method. The fact is that the advocates of free play meet resistance at every step. They are suspected of anarchism, nihilism, of intellectual, social, and moral irresponsibility. Those who would dance and play before their God have constantly to dodge the theological bullets aimed their way by the defenders of the true faith.[25]

We are more likely to retain a sense of free-play in art, poetry, fiction, and possibly drama, but we tend to turn "real life" and ethics into deadly serious activities, with but occasional moments specifically set aside for *play*.

Play, especially unbounded play, is lighthearted, good-natured, exploratory, inventive, a form of creative self-expression, and it seems a shame that it is limited to but a very few of the situations of life. It seems to include, after all, many of the traits that make us worth knowing as people, and in this mode we are generally considerably less difficult to be with. It is when play turns serious that we run into stresses. Play makes us laugh, dance, skip, and caress. It can cause us to abandon our worries, our "serious" standing in the world, much as does the small door of the tea-room that renders us all the same height and prepares a fresh environment for our activities. Play need not make us frivolous, at least not always, for the objectives of the game inspire us to do what is required, and sometimes more. But we are more willing to change the rules that determine the goals we set for ourselves and the ways we play to attain them. Play renders us open, if we are truly at play, and this, too, renders us amenable to new sources of meaning in our existence.

Still, there are problems with thinking about life as play in a world where women are raped, children die of starvation, and people are shot for playing a slightly different game. I do not mean to make light of suffering, of injustice, and of the need for a moral code-of-the-time with bite in it. Ethics is the place where speculative ease usually must give way to compassion and rigour. However, ethics is easier to express and to maintain if you can envision yourself as being in the midst of a vast cosmos of which you know very little, the reasons given for the existence of which are as varied as the games of men and women throughout the entire course of history. Humility applies to ethics, to values, and to ways of life. We must exert ourselves to maintain our moral steadfastness while at the same time recognizing how inadequate our vision is of what it means to be moral. We must teach, and practice, even if we but dimly glimpse what a human being can become. We do the best we can, and we ought to do it playfully as often as we can, and humbly the rest of the time. Playfulness and humility are two of the requirements of deconstructive activity. Of course, if it is *your* game that is under attack, you will more likely think that it is arrogance and not humility that is important to the activity of deconstruction. It is then that a healthy dose of play would do both sides a considerable amount of good.

ON PLAY

Play is transformative. We let go of our stresses, our minds clear, and we focus on the game itself, which is now our whole world. You can play half-heartedly, but usually we are engaged immediately, and with considerable intensity. The playful mode is less likely to be deadly serious, although you can recall games that ceased to be "fun" because they became serious. On the whole, light-heartedness is the stance we take when playing a game, and cheerful good humour is the overriding mood. The warmth of happy interactions with others is the norm. Things can get out of hand, but then the game ceases to be fun and becomes something other than the game we sought to play.

The interpretation of texts ought to be more like play, contend the postmodernists. Indeed, it often is. We often read a novel in the same spirit that we play a game. We relax, slip into it, and play with the various possible interpretations as we go along, and when we have finished, try to drink dry the subtle vistas that keep opening up as we think about what we have read. Film viewing might serve as yet another example of the playful attitude, encouraging a wide variety of alternate interpretations, each contributing yet further to the enjoyment of the film itself. We can debate for hours afterwards over coffee about the implications of what we have just seen. As Derrida and the deconstructionists urge, the reading of a text ought to bring to light multiple meanings, a plurality of meanings, a polyphony of interpretive voices.[26]

The meaning of a novel is the reading of it, and the meaning is quite different for each person. The meaning of a film is the seeing of it, and the result is usually a considerable range of interpretive understandings, which continue to unfold the more you reflect upon what you have seen and the more times you return to view it again. *The meaning of life is to be found in the living of it, and even for the individual a considerable range of possibilities and an unending flow of reflections upon your life constitutes part of that meaning.* Play has no ultimate goal, no serious goal that will bring it to an end, but rather renews itself in constant repetition, with no repetition being an exact repeat of a prior instance. Living has a series of goals and is serious as well as playful, and yet the goals are always in transformation, or at least always in doubt. Circumstances are often similar, but it is not easy to specify exactness in your lived experience, even with someone with whom you have lived most of your life.

Part of what makes people interesting to each other is the transformation that is ongoing throughout life, however slight and imperceptible it is day by day. Even without perceptible change we learn more about the other, without end, as demanding events bring out aspects of the other by which we are surprised, perhaps delighted. People watch each other grow, mature, gain in skill and occasionally "wisdom," take on the responsibilities of parenthood, care for an aging mother, become a friend to a dying victim of AIDS. Gadamer remarks that viewing a work of art can provoke an experience "changing the person experiencing it."[27] The ups and downs of life, with its various interactions and demands, also change people. What is valuable to the child is not likely valuable to the adult, unless perhaps you return to it with a child of your own. The light-heartedness of youth gives way to the seriousness of the worker or professional trying to pay the mortgage and the medical bills. It is important not to bog down, to lose the lightness of being in a world of possibilities, some of them etched with suffering, but others riding on the joyful.

It is often out of fear that we close out our possibilities, not willing to risk again, staying close to the tried and true. It is, of course, wise to maintain this ingredient in the tension I am describing, for just as deconstruction depend on a stability, on a majority position to critique, so experiment and the risk of openness depend on the stability of counting on people you love, on an income, on the basic necessities of life, and on preparing the young in your charge for a future of meaningful living. Yet it is precisely these "serious" concerns that can make you draw back altogether, no longer able to risk questioning your lifestyle, your marriage, your vocation, your leisure time, rendering them nothing more than meaningless habits. The result is that we eventually die, never having deliberately lived. The tension must be maintained throughout life.

We do well to reflect steadfastly on our "majoritarian" activities and to engage seriously the various "minoritarian" options to are all to easy to push aside, or even to condemn. The task and the challenge are to reflect critically in order to bring richer and less exclusive perspectives to the fore. In this sense deconstruction will, to use James Risser's image, recognize that Socrates was both *gadfly* and *midwife*.[28] As critic, Socrates does not fall into the trap of *closure* and the maintainance of a self-satisfied and unreflective acceptance of a power-drenched status quo. As midwife, his "disruptive play is always mindful of the human community"[29] as he seeks new and better ways of understanding and living that will enrich and liberate.

Just as there is no uniquely correct interpretation of a text, a historical event, or another person, so there is no uniquely correct way of life. Instead, there are options, possible modifications, and transformative events, each of which might move us yet again to rethink just how meaningful and valuable our way of life is. Continued intellectual and emotional openness is not easy to maintain. In his *Doubt and Certainty in Science* the noted physiologist J.Z. Young suggests that by and large the rules by which the brain works are not inherent but have been learned in the process of growing up.[30] The rules for processing information gained from within and without and for turning it into a coherent system of recognition and understanding are slowly and progressively developed by each and every one of us. The rules themselves are not fixed but emerge as we grow, and can be encouraged or drawn out for examination.

Precisely because they are learned, they may also be altered or even eliminated. We may be "taught" to process materials according to new rules – that is, we may be led to see things in new ways. An encounter with a new "point of view," by means of which the learner may either gain new information that may force her/him to change the "rules" or come to see old information in a new light, is a source of new input or of a revised perspective. Suppleness of mind, the ability to rethink an issue or to revise your outlook, is not a common quality. It is possible to encourage such suppleness, argues Young, because some people seek out the novel, willingly placing some aspect of their way-of- being-in-the-world at significant risk. He notes that existing and habitual organization does reduce the number of alternative or fresh organizational patterns open to the brain: "The cortex of the new-born baby has perhaps few innate traits; it is in the main a blank sheet of possibilities. But the very fact that it becomes organized minute by minute, day by day, throughout the years, reduces progressively the number of possible alternative ways of action."[31]

What we must seek out, concludes Young, is a source of new ideas, new circumstances, fresh possibilities to consider. New circumstances may themselves come to our aid by reversing or altering brain patterns that seem inflexibly and unalterably present and operative: "We may forget, or learn new ways of speaking about the world. Some people manage to go on learning new ways much longer than others. Probably a part of their secret is that they constantly seek new circumstances. The temptation to go on relying only upon the rules already used year in and year out is very strong. A really useful and interesting brain is always starting off on new ways. But it is a common experience that this gets more difficult as we grow older."[32]

What is being encouraged is a willingness to place old habits at risk and to playfully engage in exploring other traditions, perspectives, and ways of living and seeing. The greatest deterrent to this sort of suppleness, this capacity for fresh insight, is the assumption that your ways are the true ways, or that an alternative is inevitably an attack on the "holy." There is no uniquely correct perspective. Just as feminist thought has called into question not only Kohlberg's stages of moral development but the entire modern tradition of ethics as justice reasoning, so the comfort and obviousness of many of our living ways will also be challenged in the years ahead. Feminist thought has offered a minoritarian way into ethics by emphasizing caring and de-emphasizing justice, fairness, and the controlling claims of rationality. But every answer always already gives rise to a new set of problems to be addressed and (tentatively and temporarily) resolved, and it is to be expected that caring and justice ought not to be thought of as forever antagonistic and utterly irreconcilable. Perhaps justice will come to be the shorthand, or outer cover of caring, and caring will serve as the inner critic and conscience of justice and law, as well as its humane tutor. It should not surprise us that here, too, a tension needs to be maintained in order for growth to take place and health to emerge. Feminist thought has made this tension possible once more, and let us hope that the lesson will not quickly be forgotten.

The political changes in Central Europe are even more startling and could not have been entertained, let alone predicted, but a few short months ago. The experience of change is ever present, and rather than letting the change wash over us while we cling to a safe limb, it is important to let go from time to time and to stay in the play where it is less safe. We are capable of finding unending meaning in a world of constant, shimmering, sometimes threatening change. The task is to keep the question of the meaning of life in question, and to find in it an unending source of joy and possibility, even in the darkest of times. It is *within* the constant overcoming of our own limitations and habits, and of the established views of our age, that passive happiness and unreflective contentment are lost, then to be replaced by joyful activity and a glimpse of a broader, more enriching, and more responsible awareness than we have been capable of before.

ON KILLING THE BUDDHA

Dōgen, the thirteenth-century Zen Master, is considered to be one of Japan's most outstanding philosophers, and possibly its most creative thinker. He argued that *impermanence* is reality and that reality is impermanence. Basing his conclusion, or insight, on the Buddhist doctrine of emptiness, he saw that objects of the world are non-substantial, as are subjects (egos), hence nothing more than nodules of temporary cohesive integration, for a time. Thus, it is in the moment, the *nikon* of "reality appearing fully right-here-now," that we should dwell, as participants rather than as observers. We too are a part of the flux, and the only wise outlook on the reality of change is to step into the flux and to flow with it.

It is little wonder that in Buddhism, Zen Buddhism in particular, we hear such aphorisms as "If you see the Buddha walking down the street, kill him" and "The Buddha is improving: when will he be finished?" The Buddha symbolizes the flow of things, which is itself ultimate. For it not to change would be for it not to be. Reality is change. Similarly, to see the Buddha "in the flesh," as it were, is to fix your conception of reality, to stop the flow. In so doing it is you who have killed the Buddha, for the Buddha is impermanence itself. To catch sight of him is to lose him, to succumb to idolatry. Every conception must change, just as the Buddha must be said to be changing every instant. To know reality is to know change, and to know change is to throw yourself into the flux – to swim with the change, observing what you can along the way. The markers we find will be our sources of meaning, but even they must not be clung to, turned into permanent markers. Reality is a process, and our understanding of it is an unending process.

This was brought home to me vividly in the midst of a dialogue with an internationally famous Zen Buddhist scholar in Kyoto. We sat in his living-room, a small room in his typically tiny but extremely inviting home, sipping green tea and discussing the Zen notion of "ultimate reality." I do not now recall how either of us came to talk the language of ultimate reality, but we were not only willing to talk about it; we had actually begun to diagram it! My friend spoke convincingly, but abstractly, for several minutes, and then resorted to drawing a diagram to make as clear as he could what it was that he thought about this incredible notion. I looked at his diagram, and quickly found an ambiguity in the drawing. I drew a second diagram, and handed it across the table to my colleague. He glanced at it and then quickly drew a third sketch to modify the obvious shortcomings of my vision.

All the while we talked, reaching for concepts to carry the weight of our mental probing, until there were nearly a dozen diagrams strewn about on the table. He finished the last diagram and then began to laugh, and his laughter increased steadily in intensity. I sensed what had happened, and laughter overcame me as well. The laughter continued until tears rolled down our cheeks in shared delight at our presumption, and my learned friend actually slapped his thigh beneath his dark Zen robe. He shook his head in merriment, and then blurted out, "Forgive me. I am sorry, but somehow this always happens to me when I try to talk about ultimate reality."

EPILOGUE

Deconstruction is an ever-present goad, an unending corrective to irrevocable commitment and closure, which would shut out rethinking, relearning, and re-experiencing ourselves, others, or the world. It is a powerful method for cutting through the assumed and all-too-rigidly set (i.e. sedimented) structures of perception, knowledge-gathering, acting, and understanding. It critically refocuses our sensibilities by breaking down the seemingly sacrosanct and habitual, thereby making way for a fluid and creatively shifting and growing comprehension and awareness.

At the same time, without a perspective on which and from which to make your selections and choices of action, either a paralysis will set in that precludes meaningful choice or else the choices made will have the flavour of the arbitrary, the expedient, or the hopelessly transient. Sometimes deconstruction does take on just this numbing and skeptical form, and while it is too easy to conclude here that such an approach is untenable, it has been my thesis throughout that there is always, and always must be a place to be found that is, while shifting and tentative, none the less a "better" place to stand and from which to think than the others available to you. And the "better" is not to be justified by any simple account, but rather requires the *whole story* in which it is embedded to be told and argued for.

It may be that those deconstructionists who maintain that the only "justifiable" outcome is the multiple existence of an unending diversity of positions, stories, and voices prefer that we not choose. Perhaps this proliferation of voices may turn out to be the only justification there is, and therefore we must learn to listen attentively to the many voices that speak. An evaluation of this position needs to be undertaken in detail to assess its merits and its eventual fallout.

In the meantime, it is enough to conclude here that the myth of final closure is, or so it seems to me, no more acceptable than the equally unacceptable myth that no closure or stance is any better than any other, and hence that any one of them is as correct or worthy as any other. It is over the tricky terrain between these two extremes that I have attempted to chart a course, a course that I have urged you to consider as a potentially fruitful approach to the development of a whole story that is less restrictive and more open to multiple influences, including those from quite foreign and relatively uncharted sources. I have suggested as well that all stances are at best tentative but that the "better" among them is to be held no less firmly, passionately, and whole-heartedly for that. The fine line between commitment, without which there can be no decision, and for that matter no values or facts, and absolute commitment to a position about which there can be no change or fruitful debate is very narrow indeed. Commitment is necessary if we are to avoid paralysis of action and utter indecisiveness in our thinking and our living. Irrevocable commitment, however, is to be avoided, if only because we do not yet know nearly enough about this surprising cosmos of which we are a part, let alone about ourselves. The great and learned answers of the centuries, from East and West, to questions of ultimate concern relating to the living of our lives are still as hotly and profitably debated as when first entertained.

Yet it is through the taking of cross-cultural perspectives that fresh insight may be gained concerning the assumptions, habits, expectations, and values of your own tradition or set of traditions. It is also through cross-cultural inquiry that a renewed suppleness of mind is often achieved. This study has been an attempt to create something of a bridge between East and West, and as such is comparativist in approach. And it is not insignificant that it was Martin Heidegger, whose example of the *bridge* formed a major part of the first chapter, who also investigated what might be required in order to build a bridge of understanding and communication between himself as a Western thinker and a Japanese colleague.[33] He sought to discover just how many of our assumptions must be jettisoned if genuine dialogue with someone from a radically different cultural perspective was to be made genuinely possible and productive. Indeed, how can you know whether you have in fact sufficiently set aside your own presuppositions, such that you are actually able to hear what another is saying, rather than overriding what is being conveyed by rendering it non-threatening and customary? It is necessary to put as many of your assumptions "at risk" as you can, and the great surprise and benefit of the comparative approach is that it regularly causes heretofore unrecognized and unconscious assumptions to float free, up to the surface of everyday awareness. Even a relatively superficial encounter with a culture that is significantly unlike your own can unsettle the customary enough to bring unexpected insights about your habits and your patterns of perception and thought to the fore.

The comparativist approach achieves an openness of both mind and method by (ideally) identifying blindly with either of the contrasting perspectives under consideration. The comparativist increasingly realizes that the work of philosophy, and the goal of understanding and decision-making in general, is both an Eastern and a Western activity and takes as its material the overlapping as well as the contrasting insights of people anywhere in the world, producing from that material a totality of thought that transcends any particular cultural perspective. Each of us, if we are good at building our own philosophical world-view or story, must glean her or his insights from several distinctively different cultural directions. In this sense, to be postmodern means to have moved from the orthodoxy and domination of any one cultural perspective to the liberation – and sometimes towards the confusion – of a multicultural and ongoing (i.e. open-ended) creation of a perspective that is truly your own.

Quality philosophizing is increasingly and inevitably world-philosophy by nature. Surely one of the continuing aims of comparative thought is that it allows traditions to become less "foreign," less inscrutable, less incomprehensibly "other," and therefore more likely to be seen as possessing at least more of the qualities of "neighbourhood" and familiarity than might otherwise be expected to be the case. This is not to say that other voices should become *like* your own, or yours exactly like theirs, for either way that would be to confront yet another brand of intellectual imperialism. Instead, it is the *strangeness* and *irrelevance* that ought to vanish, allowing us to "hear" the distinctive voice or voices of other cultures, other individuals, and even to respond sensitively to animals, oceans, and bamboo trees.

The results of a ventured comparative approach will likely include the enhancement of the capacity to perceive and to appreciate the differences in other persons, cultural traditions, and objects, as well as assisting us in the letting go of some of our intellectual and emotional rigidity and arrogance. The ability to become bamboo is a metaphor for reaching beyond the perceptual, intellectual, and feeling habits, expectations, and assumptions of your own psyche and traditions in order to allow the embracing and the understanding of those of another. In actually becoming bamboo it is essential to listen to another with an open mind and heart, and thereby to embrace what you were previously unwilling or unable genuinely to encounter. Whether or not you decide to emulate that which you have come to understand through empathetic identification, you will never be quite the same again. In learning to think and to feel, to understand and to value more like another, you will have grown in your own self-understanding and in your capacity to speak and interact with others. You, and that which you are now able to embrace, may well find in one another nurture, respect, protection, and enrichment. It is in such qualities of living that true meaning will be encountered, however tentative and fluctuating that meaning may be. It is in the very midst of the flux of the meaningful that its perpetuation and its renewal is to be found.

Notes

INTRODUCTION

1 Laird, *The Idea of Value*, 302, 304.
2 Ibid., 305.
3 Shigematsu, *A Zen Harvest: Japanese Folk Zen Sayings*, xxv.

CHAPTER ONE: VALUES AND VALUATION

1 Stace, "Man Against Darkness," in Sanders and Cheney, eds., *The Meaning of Life*, 37. The essay originally appeared in the Atlantic Monthly, Sept. 1948.
2 Ibid.
3 I will say more about "intrinsic value" below. I have given a considerably more detailed account of the various meanings of the term in chapter 5 of my book *Dimensions of Moral Education*.
4 Bennett, "The Meaning of Life", 582, 583. Italics mine.
5 Ibid., 587, 590.
6 Lewis, *An Analysis of Knowledge and Valuation* 387. Hereafter referred to as *AKV*.
7 Ibid.
8 Ibid., 405.
9 Ibid., 395.
10 Ibid., 407.
11 Lewis, *Our Social Inheritance*, 79–80.
12 Lewis, *AKV*, 400.
13 Ibid., viii.
14 Ibid., 190.
15 Ibid., 179.
16 Ibid.

17 Ibid., 179.

18 Ibid., 203.

19 Ibid., 389.

20 Ibid., 383.

21 Ibid., 385.

22 Ibid., 486–510.

23 Stace, *The Nature of the World*, 194.

24 Ibid, 41.

25 Ibid., 42.

26 Peters, *Reason and Compassion*, 73.

27 Ibid., 76.

28 Macmurray, *Reason and Emotion*, 15, 16.

29 See Plato's *Phaedo*, especially 66a–68c. Plato has Socrates remark that "serious philosophers" must understand that "the body provides us with innumerable distractions in the pursuit of our necessary sustenance, and any diseases which attack us hinder our quest for reality. Besides, the body fills us with loves and desires and fears and all sorts of fancies and a great deal of nonsense, with the result that we literally never get an opportunity to think at all about anything" (trans. Hugh Tredennick).

30 Macmurray, *Reason and Emotion*, 26.

31 Ibid., 30.

32 Ibid.

33 Ibid., 31.

34 Ibid., 36.

35 Ibid., 37.

36 Ibid., 38.

37 Ibid., 40, 41.

38 Macmurray, "Developing Emotions," an unpublished manuscript of three pages in length, and available from the John Macmurray Society, Toronto. The reference is to page 2, which continues: "Our attitude to the world may be 'contemplative.' In that case we seek not to use but to enjoy the world. We live in our senses instead of using them to provide useful information. We see for the sake of seeing and listen for the joy of hearing, as when we watch a brilliant sunset or listen to the singing of birds. Now this way of using our senses does not lead to intellectual activity, to abstracting and classifying and drawing inferences. It leads instead to an emotional activity of discrimination and valuation."

39 Heidegger, *Discourse on Thinking*, "Memorial Address," 43–57.

40 Macmurray, *Reason and Emotion*, 49.

41 Ibid., 43.

42 Ibid., 44.

43 Ibid., 76.
44 Stace, *The Nature of the World*, 196.
45 See the powerful recent book by Farías, *Heidegger and Nazism*. Farías argues in detail that Heidegger's links with Nazism cannot be dismissed as naïveté, or relatively innocent opportunism, for Heidegger's own views betray numerous areas of sympathy with aspects of Nazi thinking.
46 See "The Question Concerning Technology," in Martin Heidegger, *Basic Writings*, 287–317.
47 Heidegger, "Building Dwelling Thinking," in *Poetry, Language, Thought*, 145, 146.
48 Ibid., 146–7.
49 Ibid., 149.
50 Ibid., 150.
51 Ibid., 151.
52 Ibid., 152.
53 Heidegger, "Memorial Address," in *Discourse on Thinking*, 46.
54 Ibid., 54.
55 Ibid., 53–4.
56 Camus, *The Myth of Sisyphus and Other Essays*. See espec. 88–91.
57 Camus works out his "notion of the absurd" in *The Rebel*. A discussion of his position may be found in my *Dimensions of Moral Education*, chap. 3.
58 Nietzsche, *Thus Spoke Zarathustra*, 220–1 (pt 3, sec. 13). Also to be found in Nietzsche's *The Gay Science* (sec. 341), and in the short concluding section of his *The Will to Power*, which was edited (and scraped "clean") by Nietzsche's sister.
59 Nietzsche "transvalues," or revalues values such that the highest are made the lowest, and any that are to be thought of as "better" will have to be human-made, for God, and any other external authority, is dead and buried. In spite of this situation, indeed *because* of it, human beings are now free to take their destiny into their own hands and to *overcome* whatever needs to be overcome in deciding how life is to be lived joyfully. See his *Beyond Good and Evil* and the various themes of "overcoming" in *Thus Spake Zarathustra*.
60 Lewis, AKV, 423–4. Lewis continues: "If there is any hope that we can, by our reasonably directed efforts, effect any improvement in the quality of living, for ourselves or for anybody else, then there must be a solid core of what is both veridical and common, underlying the personal and the inter-personal variabilities of our value-findings in the presence of external things."
61 Stace, *The Nature of the World*, 198.

CHAPTER TWO: KOHLBERG'S STAGE SEVEN

1 There are several critiques of Kohlberg's stage theory, including Gilligan's *In a Different Voice* Gibbs's essay, "Kohlberg's Stages of Moral Judgment: A Constructive Critique" and my own "What is Lawrence Kohlberg Doing?" and *Dimensions of Moral Education*, chap. 2, also discuss problems related to the evidence for and the theory of the stages.

2 Gilligan, *In a Different Voice*, 18.

3 Ibid.

4 Ibid., 43.

5 Peters, *Reason and Compassion*, 24.

6 There are many accounts of the stages in Kohlberg, and the reader who wishes more detail might begin by consulting the appendix ("The Six Stages of Moral Judgment") in Kohlberg, *The Philosophy of Moral Development*.

7 Kohlberg, "Indoctrination Versus Relativity in Value Education," 295.

8 Scharf, ed., *Readings in Moral Education*, 37.

9 Hare, *The Language of Morals*, 69.

10 Kohlberg, *Philosophy of Moral Development*, 345, 368.

11 Carter, *Dimensions*, 101–5.

12 Fowler, "Stages in Faith" in Hennessey, *Values and Moral Development*, 209.

13 Fowler, *Stages of Faith:*, 4, 24, 28, 29, italics mine.

14 Mill, *Autobiography*, 113.

15 Fowler, *Stages of Faith*, 101.

16 Mill, *Autobiography*, 116, 117–18, 122.

17 Happold, *Mysticism*, 46.

18 Kohlberg, *The Philosophy of Moral Development*, 371, 345.

19 Happold, *Mysticism*, 43–50.

20 Friedländer, *Plato:* 80. Underhill, in *The Essentials of Mysticism and Other Essays*, 6, observes that "the one essential of mysticism" is "union between God and the soul." For a fuller discussion of this theme with particular reference to Plato, see my "Plato and Mysticism," *Idealistic Studies* 5, no. 3 (September 1975): 255–68.

21 Kohlberg, *The Philosophy of Moral Development*, 366.

22 Ibid., 343, 345, 362.

23 Baier, *The Moral Point of View*, chap. 12.

24 Stace, *The Concept of Morals*, 262–74.

25 Kohlberg, *The Philosophy of Moral Development*, 343.

26 Ibid., 337.

27 Fowler, *Stages of Faith*, 200–01.

28 Kohlberg, *The Philosophy of Moral Development*, 348.

29 Underhill, *Mysticism*, 416.

30 Kohlberg, *The Philosophy of Moral Development*, 348.
31 Underhill, *Mysticism*, 93.
32 Kohlberg, *The Philosophy of Moral Development*, 352.
33 Ibid., 205.
34 Gilligan, *In a Different Voice*, especially chap. 1. Gilligan's work will be discussed in chap. 4 below.
35 Kohlberg, *The Psychology of Moral Development*, 224–38.
36 Kohlberg, *The Philosophy of Moral Development*, 322.
37 Carter, *Dimensions*, 154–5. All of chap. 4 is an analysis of the meaning of "intrinsic value."
38 Søren Kierkegaard discusses the first, or *aesthetic* stage, in the first volume of *Either/Or*, the second, or *ethical* stage, in *Fear and Trembling*, and the third, or *religious* stage, in *The Sickness unto Death*, among other places. Don Juan is the stereotypical aesthete, Socrates the typifier of the ethical stage, and Abraham the knight of religious faith.
39 Kohlberg and Lickona, *The Stages of Ethical Development*, 435.
40 Horne, *The Moral Mystic*, 113.
41 Fowler, *Stages of Faith*, 203–04.
42 Frankl, *Man's Search for Meaning*.

CHAPTER THREE:
VIKTOR FRANKL AND LOGOTHERAPY

1 Frankl, *Man's Search for Meaning:*, 78.
2 Frankl, *Psychotherapy and Existentialism*, 57.
3 Ibid., 17.
4 Frankl, *The Unheard Cry for Meaning*, 29. Frankl gives credit to Abraham Maslow for the phrase "man's primary concern"; Maslow used it in his comments on a paper by Frankl in *Readings in Humanistic Psychology*.
5 Frankl, *Psychotherapy and Existentialism*, 20.
6 Ibid., 104–05.
7 Frankl, *Unheard Cry*, 41.
8 Pascal, *Pensées*, 39–43 (sec. II, #139), is an example of Pascal's insight into various entertainments and games as an escape from boredom in order to deflect the burning truth of reflection on one's empty and unsatisfying life.
9 Frankl, *Psychotherapy and Existentialism*, 125.
10 In evidence for this claim I mention works by such contemporaries as Gadamer, *Truth and Method*, the French postmodernists and deconstructionists Roland Barthes, Jacques Derrida, Félix Guattari, and Jean François Lyotard, Rorty's *The Consequences of Pragmatism*, Watson's *The Architectonics of Meaning*, Bohm's *Wholeness and the Implicate Order*, Hollis and Lukes' *Rationality and Relativism*, Caputo's *Radical Hermeneutics*, etc.

11 May, *Existential Psychology*. Quoted in Frankl, *The Unconscious God*, 121.
12 Kisch and Kroll, "Meaningfulness versus Effectiveness", 407, 407–8.
13 Frankl, *The Unconscious God*, 120, 121.
14 Frankl, *Psychotherapy and Existentialism*, 57.
15 Frankl, *The Unconscious God*, 123–4.
16 Frankl, *The Will to Meaning*, 51.
17 Frankl, *Psychotherapy and Existentialism*, 97.
18 Frankl, *The Doctor and the Soul*, 14–15.
19 Frankl, *Man's Search for Meaning*, 110.
20 Skinner, *Beyond Freedom and Dignity*.
21 Fabry, *The Pursuit of Meaning*, 23.
22 Frankl, *The Unheard Cry*, 47, 54, 55.
23 Frankl, *Man's Search for Meaning*, 159–60.
24 Frankl, *The Unheard Cry*, 35, 52–3.
25 Nietzsche, see n 59, chap. 1, above. A commentator on Nietzsche, Arthur Danto, in *Nietzsche as Philosopher*, 211–12, writes: "Without a goal, there is no meaning to life. And, by parity, there is no meaning to the universe if it has no end. So man must give it one. The doctrine of Eternal Recurrence entails the meaninglessness of things, and the doctrine of the *Ubermensch* is a response to that significance which man is obliged to will."
26 Danto, *Nietzsche as Philosopher*, 212.
27 Nietzsche, *Ecce Homo* (various editions), sec. #10, "Why Am I So Clever?"
28 Sartre, *Being and Nothingness*, 56: "Nothingness lies coiled in the heart of being – like a worm." Being more optimistic, I prefer the image of the snake, which, when understood, is a powerful creature living in harmony with its environment. And unlike the biblical story of the Garden of Eden, the snake is not evil but something one must learn to live with. It is powerful, like sexuality itself, for which it is often a metaphor, but it is not evil and may even become a powerful force for goodness, and a rich and major source of meaning and value. Usually, only when it is hidden or denied is it to be feared. For then it may strike unseen, or control through fear alone.
29 Frankl, *The Doctor and the Soul*, 268.
30 Ibid., 269.
31 See Macmurray, *The Self as Agent*, 134: "To possess free-will is simply to be able to determine the indeterminate, that is, the future. We can now see that this is implied in the very conception of action. The Agent is the determiner. To deny free-will is to deny the possibility of action." Furthermore, "the falsity of determinism lies simply in the dogma that the future is already determinate. But if this were so there would be no future; the future would be already past."

32 Carter, *Dimensions of Moral Education*, chap. 1, where the theme of "intellectual myopia" is further developed: "Another name for myopia is near-sightedness, and this results from the imperfect curve of the eye, causing parallel rays to come to focus in front of the retina rather than on or at it. One's vision is, in such cases, better for near objects than for far or, put another way, defective with respect to objects at any distance. The Greek root *myein* means 'to narrow (the eye) or squint' and so myopic intellect is one narrowed to new ideas and able to focus only on that which is at hand, recognizing only the familiar and habitual" (3).

33 Frankl, *The Will to Meaning*, 64.

34 Fabry, *The Pursuit of Meaning*, 105. Taken from a videotaped interview for the California College Association, "Value Dimensions in Teaching," in *Values Colloquium 1, A Person's Need and Search for Values* (The Religious Education Foundation, 343 South Madison Avenue, Pasadena, Calif., mimeo, Feb. 1964).

35 Frankl, *The Will to Meaning*, 85.

36 Ibid., 52.

37 Bulka, *The Quest for Ultimate Meaning*, 36, 56. From Arnold and Gasson, "Logotherapy and Existential Analysis", 486.

38 Bulka, *The Quest*, 10.

39 Frankl, *The Doctor and the Soul*, 270.

40 Frankl, *The Will to Meaning*, 54–6.

41 Frankl, *Man's Search for Meaning*, 106.

42 Frankl, *The Unconscious God*, 65, 67, 70.

43 Bulka, *The Quest*, 43.

44 Saint-Exupéry, *The Little Prince*, 62–71. Seeing five thousand wild roses, the little prince remarks that his lone rose on his mini-planet "has told him that she was the only one of her kind in the entire universe" (62). His friend the fox urges him to look beneath and beyond the obvious, for "you will understand now that yours is unique in all the world" (69–70). The insight comes to him when he realizes that "it is the time you have wasted for your rose that makes your rose so important" (71).

CHAPTER FOUR: RELATEDNESS

1 Kazantzakis, *The Saviors of God*, 124.

2 Williams, *Morality*, 23–4.

3 Ibid., 24.

4 Ibid., 25.

5 Ibid., 26. Italics mine.

6 Noddings, *Caring*, 134, 194.

7 Ibid., 132, 136.

8 Watsuji, "The Significance of Ethics as the Study of Man," 396.
9 See my book *The Nothingness Beyond God*, espec. chap. 4.
10 Watsuji, "The Significance of Ethics," 401.
11 Yuasa, *The Body*, 47.
12 Noddings, *Caring*, 43, 104, 134, 137–8.
13 Yuasa, *The Body*, 46. Yuasa indicates that this quotation is from an early work of Watsuji's, translated as *Ancient Japanese Culture*, from his collected works, *Zenshū*, vol. 3, pp 242, 257.
14 Noddings, *Caring*, 138.
15 Ibid., 96.
16 Gilligan, *In a Different Voice*, 17.
17 Noddings, *Caring*, 96. See Gilligan, *In a Different Voice*, chap. 1, for her detailed analysis of Kohlberg's assumptions.
18 Gilligan, *In a Different Voice*, 8, quoting Chodorow, *The Reproduction of Mothering*, 167.
19 Ibid., 11.
20 Gilligan and Attanucci, "Two Moral Orientations," in *Mapping the Moral Domain*, ed. Gilligan, Ward, and Taylor, 84–5.
21 Ibid., 21–2.
22 Belenky, Clinchy, Goldberger, and Tarule, eds., *Women's Ways of Knowing*, 8.
23 Ibid., 113.
24 Ibid., 141.
25 Noddings, *Caring*, 148.
26 Noddings, *Caring*, 149.
27 Burch, "Respect for Things," 1.
28 Bugbee, *The Inward Morning*, 155.
29 Ibid., 218, 219.
30 Macmurray, *Reason and Emotion*, 42.
31 Kishimoto, "The Immediacy of Zen Experience and Its Cultural Background," 30–1.
32 Izutsu, *Towards a Philosophy of Zen Buddhism*, 80.
33 Frankl, *The Unheard Cry for Meaning*, 72.
34 Odin, "An Explanation of Beauty. *Muga* is discussed on p 212.
35 Yanagi, *The Unknown Craftsman*, 127–8.
36 Ibid., 128.
37 Hisamatsu, *Zen and the Fine Arts*, 46.
38 Yanagi, *The Unknown Craftsman*, 137.
39 Hisamatsu, *Zen and the Fine Arts*, 53.
40 Nishida, *Art and Morality*, 100–1.
41 Hisamatsu, *Zen and the Fine Arts*, 52.
42 Ibid.
43 Nishida, *Intelligibility and the Philosophy of Nothingness*, 137.

44 Yanagi, *The Unknown Craftsman*, 150.
45 Hisamatsu, *Zen and the Fine Arts*, 59.
46 Sen; *Tea Life, Tea Mind*, 14.
47 Schinzinger, in Nishida, *Intelligibility and the Philosophy of Nothingness*, in the introduction, 41.
48 Ibid.
49 Sen, *Tea Life, Tea Mind*, 11.
50 Ibid., 13.
51 Ibid., 13–14.
52 Ibid., 77.
53 Ibid., 81.
54 Noddings, *Caring*, 125.
55 Burch, "Respect for Things," 4.
56 Makoto, *Matsuo Bashō*, 53.
57 Nobuyuki, *Bashō*, 9.

CHAPTER FIVE: "WHERE IS HERE?"

1 Atwood, *Survival*, 32–42, 17. The phrase is taken from Frye, *The Bush Garden*, 220.
2 Ibid, 17–18.
3 Ibid., 32, 41.
4 Suzuki, *Zen Buddhism*, 230.
5 Ibid., 249.
6 Ibid.
7 Ibid., 255.
8 Ibid., 255–6.
9 Shigematsu, *A Zen Harvest*, xxv.
10 Shaner, "The Japanese Experience of Nature," in *Nature in Asian Traditions of Thought* ed. Callicott and Ames, 165.
11 Dōgen, *Moon in a Dewdrop*, from the *Shōbōgenzō* (*Treasury of the Dharma Eye*) 70. Section 4 continues: "When actualized by myriad things, your body and mind as well as the bodies and minds of others drop away. No trace of realization remains, and this no-trace continues endlessly."
12 Suzuki, *Zen Buddhism*, 255.
13 Shigematsu, *A Zen Harvest*, xxvi.
14 Suzuki, *Zen and Japanese Culture*, 355.
15 Hartman, "The Nature of Valuation," 20. See his *The Structure of Value*.
16 Shaner and Duval, "Conservation Ethics and the Japanese Intellectual Tradition," 205, 212, 213.
17 Picken, *Shintō*, 57.
18 See chap. 1, above.
19 Picken, *Shintō*, 10.

20 Ibid., 10.
21 Ibid., 64.
22 Yanagi, *The Unknown Craftsman*, 224.
23 Ibid.
24 Iino, "Dōgen's Zen View of Interdependence," 52.
25 Ibid., 54.
26 Nakamura, "Interrelational Existence," 107.
27 Shaner, "The Japanese Experience," 175.
28 Hirai, *Zen and the Mind*, 28.
29 Cf. Beckhofer, *The White Man's Indian*.
30 Boyd, *Rolling Thunder*, 51–2.
31 Beck and Walters, *The Sacred*, 11.
32 Deloria, *The Metaphysics of Modern Existence*, 153–4.
33 Boyd, *Rolling Thunder*, 40.
34 Beck and Walters, *The Sacred*, 106.
35 Boyd, *Rolling Thunder*, 49–50.
36 McLuhan, *Touch the Earth*, 5, 6.
37 Professor Marlene Brant Castellano is a member of the Department of Native Studies, Trent University, Peterborough, Ont., and former chairperson of that department. Chief Jake Thomas is an artist as well as a native leader, a carver of wooden masks that have an international reputation for their aesthetic worth as well as for their authentic power.
38 Lyons, "Spirituality, Equality, and Natural Law," in *Pathways to Self-Determination*, ed. Little Bear, Boldt, and Long, 6.
39 Storm, *Seven Arrows*, 5.
40 Deloria, *The Metaphysics of Modern Existence*, 154.
41 As told to me by Professor Marlene Brant Castellano at my home in Peterborough, Ont., 12 March 1991.
42 Boyd, *Rolling Thunder*, 81.
43 Ibid., 260.
44 Ibid., 7.
45 Storm, 4–5.
46 Lyons, in Little Bear, Boldt, and Long, *Pathways to Self-Determination*, 8.
47 Boyd, *Rolling Thunder*, 244.
48 Ibid., 244–5.
49 Deloria, *The Metaphysics of Modern Existence*, 156.
50 Standing Bear, *Land of the Spotted Eagle*, xix.
51 Deloria, *God Is Red*, 102–6.
52 Lovelock, *Gaia*, x.
53 Ibid., 11.
54 Ibid., 12.
55 Sahtouris, *Gaia*, 9.
56 Ibid., 27–8.

57 Noddings, *Caring*, 97.
58 Gosney, "Survival or Transcendence – A Dialogue with Paolo Soleri," in *Deep Ecology* ed. Tobias, 288.
59 Tobias, *Deep Ecology*, vii.
60 Naess, "Identification as a Source of Deep Ecological Attitudes," in *Deep Ecology*, ed. Tobias, 256.
61 Naess, "The Deep Ecological Movement, 21.
62 Devall and Sessions, *Deep Ecology*, 65.
63 Shepard, "Ecology and Man," in *The Subversive Science*, ed. Shepard and McKinley, 2.
64 Naess, "Identification as a Source of Deep Ecological Attitudes," in Tobias, *Deep Ecology*, 266. The reference is to Immanuel Kant, *Foundations of the Metaphysics of Morals*, chap. 2: "*Act in such a way that you always treat humanity, whether in your own person or in the person of any other, never simply as a means, but always at the same time as an end.*"
65 Devall and Sessions, *Deep Ecology*, 67.
66 Naess, "Identification as a Source," in Tobias, *Deep Ecology*, 268.
67 See my *Dimensions of Moral Education*, chap. 4, for a sustained discussion of *nine* meanings of "intrinsic value." As well, my rejoinder to Beardsley's (see n 68 below) rejection of intrinsic value is found in my article "The Importance of Intrinsic Value." A discussion of Lewis's position is found in my "C.I. Lewis and the Immediacy of Intrinsic Value."
68 Lewis, *An Analysis of Knowledge and Valuation*, 387.
69 Hartman, "The Logic of Value," ms, 32.
70 Fox, *Toward a Transpersonal Ecology*.
71 Several important works by Abraham Maslow are *Toward a Psychology of Being, Religions, Values, and Peak-Experiences*, and *The Farther Reaches of Human Nature*. Various articles by both Maslow and Sutich may be found in the *Journal of Humanistic Psychology* and the *Journal of Transpersonal Psychology*.
72 Fox, *Transpersonal Ecology*, 292.
73 Sutich, "The Emergence of the Transpersonal Orientation: A Personal Account," 7, and quoted in Fox, *Transpersonal Ecology*, 293.
74 Fox, *Transpersonal Ecology*, 294, 295.
75 Walsh, "Transpersonal Psychology II" and "Asian Psychologies."
76 Fox, *Transpersonal Ecology*, 257.
77 Maslow, *Toward a Psychology of Being*. Quoted in Fox, *Transpersonal Ecology*, 201.
78 Fox, *Transpersonal Ecology*, 216–17.
79 Ibid., 217.
80 Ibid.
81 Naess, "Self-realization," 39–40. Quoted in Fox, *Transpersonal Ecology*, 217.

82 Loy, *Nonduality*, 298.
83 Nakamura, "The Basic Teachings of Buddhism," in *Buddhism in the Modern World*, ed. Dumoulin and Maraldo, 29.
84 Arne Naess, "Environmental Ethics and International Justice," 1987, ms, 8. Quoted in Fox, *Transpersonal Ecology*, 222.
85 Fox, *Transpersonal Ecology*, 224.
86 Ibid., 225–40.
87 Mathews, "Conservation and Self-Realization, 354. Quoted in Fox, *Transpersonal Ecology*, 237.
88 George Sessions, "Ecological Consciousness and Paradigm Change," in Tobias, *Deep Ecology*, 30.
89 Devall and Sessions, *Deep Ecology*, 67.
90 Ibid.
91 Sahtouris, *Gaia: The Human Journey*, 222.
92 Ibid.
93 Wilbur, *No Boundary*, 142.
94 Dōgen, *Moon in a Dewdrop*, 54.

CHAPTER SIX:
DECONSTRUCTING MEANING

1 Kazantzakis, *The Saviors of God*, 131.
2 *Flare*, Nov. 1989, advertisement, 41.
3 Margolis, "Radical Metaphysics," a lecture delivered at Trent University, 6 Feb. 1990.
4 Caputo, *Radical Hermeneutics*, 195.
5 Professor Joseph Margolis of Temple University suggested this term in a conversation with me at Trent University, Feb. 1990.
6 Caputo, *Radical Hermeneutics*, 156.
7 Wheelwright, *Heraclitus*, 92.
8 Burnet, *Early Greek Philosophy*, 136.
9 Kahn, *The Art and Thought of Heraclitus*, 21.
10 See pp 175–6 above. A detailed discussion of Camus' emphasis on the importance of maintaining the tension between the nostalgia for unity and the experience of absurdity can be found in chap. 3 of my *Dimensions of Moral Education*.
11 Norris, *Deconstruction*, 61.
12 Ibid., 70.
13 Ibid., 61.
14 Kohlberg, *The Philosophy of Moral Development*, 11.
15 Vlastos, *Plato's Protagoras*, xiii.
16 Danto, *Nietzsche as Philosopher*, 77.
17 Meiland, "On the Paradox of Cognitive Relativism," 122.

18 Barnes and Bloor, "Relativism, Rationalism, and the Sociology of Knowledge," in *Rationality and Relativism*, ed. Hollis and Lukes, 23.

19 Meiland, "On the Paradox," 123.

20 Ibid.

21 Caputo, *Radical Hermeneutics*, 1–9.

22 Carter, *The Nothingness beyond God*, 145–6.

23 Ibid., 146.

24 Magliola, *Derrida on the Mend*, has written an interesting comparison of Derrida with Chinese Taoist thought, the work of the Indian philosopher Nāgārjuna, and Zen.

25 Caputo, *Radical Hermeneutics*, 211.

26 Belsey, *Critical Practice*, 29, 104.

27 Gadamer, *Truth and Method*, 92.

28 James Risser, "The Two Faces of Socrates: Gadamer/Derrida," in *Dialogue and Deconstruction*, ed. Michelfelder and Palmer, 184.

29 Ibid.

30 Young, *Doubt and Certainty in Science*. I deal briefly with Young's work in my *Dimensions of Moral Education*, 32–8.

31 Ibid., 70.

32 Ibid., 106.

33 Heidegger, "Dialogue with a Japanese," in *On the Way to Language*.

Bibliography

Abe Masao. *Zen and Western Thought*. Ed. William R. LaFleur. Honolulu: University of Hawaii Press 1985.

Agera, Cassian R. "Vital Hermeneutics: The Problem of the Meaning of Life and Its Relation to Religion." *Journal of Dharma* 1 (Oct.—Dec. 1986): 379–96.

Arnold, Magda B. and John A. Gasson. "Logotherapy and Existential Analysis." In *The Human Person*, ed. Magda Blondin Arnold. New York: Ronald Press 1954.

Atwood, Margaret. *Survival: A Thematic Guide to Canadian Literature*. Toronto: House of Anansi Press 1972.

Ayer, A.J. *The Meaning of Life*. London: St Peters Press 1988.

Baier, Kurt. *The Moral Point of View: A Rational Basis for Ethics*. New York: Random House 1965.

Beck, Peggy V., & Anna L. Walters, eds. *The Sacred: Ways of Knowledge, Sources of Life*. Tsaile (Navaho Nation), Ariz.: Navaho Community College Press 1974.

Belenky, Mary Field, Blythe McVicker Clinchy, Nancy Rule and Goldberger, Jill Mattuck Tarule, eds. *Women's Ways of Knowing: The Development of Self, Voice, and Mind*. NewYork: Basic Books 1986.

Belgum, David R., ed. *Religion and Medicine: Essays on Meaning Values, and Health*. Ames, Iowa: Iowa State University Press 1967.

Belsey, Catherine. *Critical Practice*. London: Methuen & Co. 1980.

Bennett, James O. "'The Meaning of Life': A Qualitative Perspective." *Canadian Journal of Philosophy* 14, no. 4 (Dec. 1984): 582–92.

Berkhofer, Robert, Jr. *The White Man's Indian: Images of the American Indian from Columbus to the Present*. New York: Random House 1979.

Bernasconi, Robert. *The Question of Language in Heidegger's History of Being*. Atlantic Highlands, NJ: Humanities Press 1985.

Bernstein, Richard. *Beyond Objectivism and Relativism*: *Science, Hermeneutics, Praxis*. Philadelphia: University of Pennsylvania Press 1983.

Biehl, Janet. *Finding Our Way*: *Rethinking Ecofeminist Politics*. Montreal: Black Rose Books 1991.

Blum, Lawrence A. "Gilligan and Kohlberg: Implications for Moral Theory." *Ethics* (Apr. 1988): 472–91.

Bohm, David. *Wholeness and the Implicate Order*. London: Routledge & Kegan Paul 1980.

– *Unfolding Meaning*: *A Weekend of Dialogue with David Bohm*. London: Routledge & Kegan Paul, ARK Editions 1987.

Bookchin, Murray. *Toward an Ecological Society*. Montreal: Black Rose Books 1980.

Boyd, Doug. *Rolling Thunder*: *A Personal Exploration into the Secret Healing Powers of an American Indian Medicine Man*. New York: Dell Publishing, Delta Books 1974.

Brear, A.D. "The Nature and Status of Moral Behavior in Zen Buddhist Tradition." *Philosophy East and West* 24, no. 4 (Oct. 1974): 429–41.

Bugbee, Henry G., Jr. *The Inward Morning*: *A Philosophical Exploration in Journal Form*. State College, Penn.: Bald Eagle Press 1958.

Bulka, Reuven P. *The Quest for Ultimate Meaning*: *Principles and Applications of Logotherapy*. New York: Philosophical Library 1979.

Burch, George Bosworth. "Respect for Things." *Aryan Path* 31, no. 2 (Nov. 1960): 484–7.

Burnet, John. *Early Greek Philosophy*. New York: Meridian Books 1957.

Callicott, J. Baird. "Intrinsic Value, Quantum Theory, and Environmental Ethics." *Environmental Ethics* 7 (1985): 257–75.

– "On the Intrinsic Value of Nonhuman Species." In *The Preservation of Species*, ed. Bryan G. Norton. Princeton: Princeton University Press 1986. 138–71.

– "The Metaphysical Implications of Ecology." *Environmental Ethics* 8 (1986): 301–16. Repr. in *Nature in Asian Traditions of Thought*: *Essays in Environmental Philosophy*, ed. J. Baird Callicott and Roger T. Ames. Albany: State University of New York Press 1989.

Camus, Albert. *The Myth of Sisyphus and Other Essays*. New York: Vintage Books 1955.

– *The Rebel*: *An Essay on Man in Revolt*. New York: Vintage Books 1956.

Caputo, John D. *The Mystical Element in Heidegger's Thought*. New York: Fordham University Press 1986.

– *Radical Hermeneutics*: *Repetition, Deconstruction, and the Hermeneutic Project*. Bloomington: Indiana University Press 1987.

Carter, Robert E. "The Importance of Intrinsic Value." *Philosophy and Phenomenological Research* 28, no. 4 (June 1968): 567–77.

– "Intrinsic Value and the Intrinsic Valuer." *Philosophy and Phenomenological Research* 34, no. 4 (June 1974): 504–14.

- "C.I. Lewis and the Immediacy of Intrinsic Value." *Journal of Value Inquiry* 9, no. 3 (Summer 1975): 204–09.
- "What is Lawrence Kohlberg Doing?" *Journal of Moral Education* 9, no. 2 (Jan. 1980): 88–102.
- *Dimensions of Moral Education*. Toronto: University of Toronto Press 1984.
- "Beyond Justice." *Journal of Moral Education* 16, no. 2 (May 1987): 83–98.
- *The Nothingness beyond God: An Introduction to the Philosophy of Nishida Kitarō*. New York: Paragon House 1989.

Chodorow, Nancy. *The Reproduction of Mothering*. Berkeley: University of California Press 1978.

Colorado, Pam. "Bridging Native and Western Science." *Convergence* 21, no. 2/3 (1988): 49–66.

Czezowski, Tadeusz. "The Meaning and Value of Life." *Dialectic and Humanism* 7 (Summer 1980): 67–72.

Dahl, Norman. "Morality and the Meaning of Life: Some First Thoughts." *Canadian Journal of Philosophy* 17, no. 1 (Mar. 1987): 1–22.

Danto, Arthur C. *Nietzsche as Philosopher*. New York: Macmillan 1965.
- *Mysticism and Morality: Oriental Thought and Moral Philosophy*. New York: Harper & Row 1972.

Davis, William H. "The Creation of Meaning." *Philosophy Today* 30 (Summer 1986): 151–67.

Deikman, Arthur J. *The Observing Self: Mysticism and Psychotherapy*. Boston: Beacon Press 1982.

Deloria, Vine, Jr. *God Is Red*. New York: Dell Publishing, Delta Books 1973.
- *The Metaphysics of Modern Existence*. San Francisco: Harper & Row 1979.

Derrida, Jacques. *Speech and Phenomena, and Other Essays on Husserl's Theory of Signs*. Evanston, Ill.: Northwestern University Press 1973.
- *Of Grammatology*. trans. Gayatri Spivak. Baltimore: Johns Hopkins University Press 1976.
- *Writing and Difference*. Chicago: University of Chicago Press 1978.

Devall, Bill. "The Deep Ecology Movement." *Natural Resources Journal* 20 (1980): 299–322.
- *Simple in Means, Rich in Ends: Practicing Deep Ecology*. Salt Lake City: Gibbs Smith, Peregrine Smith Books 1988.
- and George Sessions. *Deep Ecology*. Salt Lake City: Gibbs M. Smith, Peregrine Smith Books 1985.

Diamond, Irene, and Gloria Orenstein, eds. *Reweaving the World: The Emergence of Ecofeminism*. San Francisco: Sierra Club Books 1990.

Dōgen. Moon in a Dewdrop: Writings of Zen Master Dōgen. Ed. Kazuaki Tanahaski, San Francisco: North Point Press 1985.

Dumoulin, Heinrich, and John C. Maraldo, eds. *Buddhism in the Modern World*. New York: Collier Books 1976.

Durant, Will. *On the Meaning of Life*. New York: Ray Long and Richard R. Smith 1932.

Evernden, Neil. *The Natural Alien: Humankind and Environment*. Toronto: University of Toronto Press 1985.

Fabry, Joseph B. *The Pursuit of Meaning: Viktor Frankl, Logotherapy, and Life*. San Francisco: Harper & Row 1968.

Farías, Victor. *Heidegger and Nazism*. Philadelphia: Temple University Press 1989.

Fowler, James W., and Sam Keen. *Life-Maps: Conversations on the Journey of Faith*. Waco, Tex.: World Books 1978.

– and Antoine Vergote, eds. *Toward Moral and Religious Maturity*. Morristown, NJ: Silver Burdett Company 1980.

– *Stages of Faith: The Psychology of Human Development and the Quest for Meaning*. New York: Harper & Row 1981.

Fox, Douglas A. "Zen and Ethics: Dōgen's Synthesis." *Philosophy East and West* 21, no. 1 (Jan. 1971): 33–41.

Fox, Warwick. "The Deep Ecology-Ecofeminism Debate and Its Parallels." *Environmental Ethics* 11 (1989): 5–25.

– *Toward a Transpersonal Ecology: Developing New Foundations for Environmentalism*. Boston: Shambhala Publications 1990.

Frankl, Viktor E. *The Doctor and the Soul: An Introduction to Logotherapy*. New York: Alfred A. Knopf 1963.

– *Man's Search for Meaning: An Introduction to Logotherapy*. Boston: Beacon Press 1959. New York: Simon and Schuster, Pocket Books 1963. Trans. of *Ein Psychologerlebt das konzentrationslager*, 1946.

– "The Philosophical Foundations of Logotherapy" In *Phenomenology: Pure and Applied*, ed. Erwin Straus. Pittsburgh: Duquesne University 1964.

– *Psychotherapy and Existentialism: Selected Papers on Logotherapy*. New York: Simon & Schuster, Clarion Books 1967.

– *The Unheard Cry for Meaning: Psychotherapy and Humanism*. New York: World Publishing 1969.

– *The Will to Meaning: Foundations and Applications of Logotherapy*. New York: World Publishing Company 1969.

– *The Unconscious God: Psychotherapy and Theology*. New York: Simon and Schuster 1975.

Friedländer, Paul. *Plato: An Introduction*. New York: Pantheon Books 1958.

Frye, Northrop. *The Bush Garden: Essays on the Canadian Imagination*. Toronto: House of Anansi Press 1971.

Gadamer, Hans-Georg. *Truth and Method*. New York: Crossroad Publishing 1984.

Gibbs, John. "Kohlberg's Stages of Moral Judgment: A Constructive Critique." *Harvard Educational Review* 47 (1977): 43–61.

Gilligan, Carol. *In a Different Voice: Psychological Theory and Women's Development*. Cambridge: Harvard University Press 1982.

– Janie Victoria Ward, and Jill McLean Taylor, eds. *Mapping the Moral Domain*. Cambridge: Center for the Study of Gender, Education and Human Development, Harvard University Graduate School of Education, distr. Harvard University Press 1988.

Griffin, Susan. *Woman and Nature: The Roaring inside Her*. New York: Harper and Row 1978.

Happold, F.C. *Mysticism: A Study and an Anthology*. Harmondsworth: Penguin Books 1964.

Hare, R.M. *The Language of Morals*. Oxford: Oxford University Press 1952.

Hartman, Robert S. "The Nature of Valuation." Ms, n. d.

– *The Structure of Value*. Carbondale: Southern Illinois University Press 1967.

Heidegger, Martin. *Discourse on Thinking: A Translation of Gelassenheit*. Trans. John M. Anderson and E. Hans Freund. New York: Harper & Row, Harper Torchbooks 1966.

– *On the Way to Language*. Trans. Peter D. Hertz. San Francisco: Harper & Row 1971.

– *Poetry, Language, Thought*. Trans. Albert Hofstadter. New York: Harper & Row 1971.

– *Basic Writings*. Ed. David Farrell Krell. New York: Harper & Row 1977.

Heine, Steven. *Existential and Ontological Dimensions of Time in Heidegger and Dōgen*. Albany: State University of New York Press 1985.

Hennessey, T., ed. *Values and Moral Development*. New York: Paulist Press 1976.

Hepburn, Ronald W. "Optimism, Finitude and the Meaning of Life." In *Philosophical Frontiers of Christian Theology: Essays Presented to D.M. Mackinnon*, ed. Brian L. Hebblethwaite. Cambridge: Cambridge University Press 1982.

Hirai Tomio. *Zen Meditation Therapy*. Tokyo: Japan Publications 1975.

– *Zen and the Mind: Scientific Appproach to Zen Practice*. Tokyo: Japan Publications 1978.

Hisamatsu Shin'ichi. *Zen and the Fine Arts*. Tokyo: Kodansha International 1971.

Hocking, William Ernest. *The Meaning of God in Human Experience*. New Haven: Yale University Press 1912.

– *The Meaning of Immortality in Human Experience, including Thoughts on Death and Life*. New York: Harper & Brothers 1937.

Hollis, Martin, and Stephen Lukes, eds. *Rationality and Relativism*. Cambridge, Mass.: MIT Press 1982.

Hoover, Thomas. *Zen Culture*. New York: Random House, Vintage Books 1977.

Horne, James R. *The Moral Mystic*. Waterloo, Ont.: Wilfrid Laurier University Press 1983.

Hultkrantz, Ake. *The Study of American Indian Religions*. American Academy of Religion, Studies in Religion 29. New York: Crossroad Publishing Company & Scholars Press 1983.

Hurdy, John Major. *American Indian Religions*. Los Angeles: Sherbourne Press 1970.

Iino Norimoto. "Dōgen's Zen View of Interdependence." *Philosophy East and West* 12 (Apr. 1962): 51–7.

Izutsu Toshihiko. *Toward a Philosophy of Zen Buddhism*. Tehran: Imperial Iranian Academy of Philosophy 1977.

Jaffe, Aniela. *The Myth of Meaning in the Work of C.G. Jung*. Trans. R.F.C. Hull. London: Hodder and Stoughton 1970.

Jagger, Alison, and Susan R. Bordo, eds. *Gender – Body – Knowledge: Feminist Reconstruction of Being and Knowing*. New Brunswick, NJ: Rutgers University Press 1989.

Kahn, Charles H. *The Art and Thought of Heraclitus: An Edition of the Fragments with Translation and Commentary*. Cambridge: Cambridge University Press 1979.

Kasulis, Thomas P. *Zen Action/Zen Person*. Honolulu: University Press of Hawaii 1981.

Kaufman, Walter. *Nietzsche: Philosopher, Psychologist, Antichrist*. New York: Meridian Books 1956.

Kazantzakis, Nikos. *The Saviors of God: Spiritual Exercises*. Trans. Kimon Friar. New York: Simon & Schuster 1960.

Kisch, Jeremy, and Jerome Kroll. "Meaningfulness versus Effectiveness: Paradoxical Implications in the Evaluation of Psychotherapy." *Psychotherapy: Theory Research and Practice* 17, no. 4 (Winter 1980): 401–12.

Kishimoto Hideo. "The Immediacy of Zen Experience and Its Cultural Background." *Philosophical Studies of Japan* 3 (1961): 25–32.

Klemke, E.D. *The Meaning of Life*. Oxford: Oxford University Press 1981.

Klinger, Eric. *Meaning and Void: Inner Experience and the Incentives in People's Lives*. Minneapolis: University of Minnesota Press 1977.

Kohak, Erazim. *The Embers and the Stars: A Philosophical Inquiry into the Moral Sense of Nature*. Chicago: University of Chicago Press 1984.

Kohlberg, Lawrence. *The Philosophy of Moral Development: Moral Stages and the Idea of Justice*. Vol. 1, Essays on Moral Development. San Francisco: Harper & Row 1981.

– *The Psychology of Moral Development: The Nature and Validity of Moral Stages*. Vol. 2, Essays on Moral Development. San Francisco: Harper & Row 1984.

– and Thomas Lickona. *The Stages of Ethical Development: From Childhood through Old Age*. San Francisco: Harper & Row 1986.

Kurtz, Paul. *The Fullness of Life*. New York: Horizon Press 1974.

Laird, John. *The Idea of Value*. Cambridge: Cambridge University Press 1929.

Leopold, Aldo. *A Sand County Almanac.* Oxford: Oxford University Press 1949.

Levine, Michael P. "Camus, Hare, and the Meaning of Life." *Sophia* 27 (Oct. 1988): 13–30.

Lewis, Clarence I. *Mind and the World Order: A Theory of Knowledge.* New York: Dover Publications 1929.

– *Our Social Inheritance.* Bloomington: Indiana University Press 1957.

– *An Analysis of Knowledge and Valuation.* La Salle, Ill.: Open Court Publishing 1962.

Little Bear, Leroy Menno Boldt, and J. Anthony Long, eds. *Pathways to Self-Determination: Canadian Indians and the Canadian State.* Toronto: University of Toronto Press 1984.

Lovelock, J.E. *Gaia: A New Look at Life on Earth.* Oxford: Oxford University Press 1982.

– *The Ages of Gaia: A Biography of Our Living Earth.* New York: Bantam Books 1990.

Loy, David. *Nonduality: A Study in Comparative Philosophy.* New Haven: Yale University Press 1988.

Lukas, Elisabeth S. *Meaningful Living: Logotherapeutic Guide to Health.* Cambridge, Mass.: Schenkman Publishing Company 1984.

Lyotard, Jean Francois. *The Post-Modern Condition: A Report on Knowledge.* Trans. Geoff Bennington and Brian Massumi. Minneapolis: University of Minnesota Press 1984.

McGee, C. Douglas. *The Recovery of Meaning: An Essay on the Good Life.* New York: Random House 1966.

McLuhan, T.C., ed. *Touch the Earth: A Self-Portrait of Indian Existence.* Toronto: New Press 1971.

Macmurray, John. "Developing Emotions." Mimeo, John Macmurray Society, Toronto. 3 pp.

– *Reason and Emotion.* London: Faber and Faber Limited 1935.

– *The Self as Agent.* London: Faber and Faber Limited 1953.

Magliola, Robert. *Derrida on the Mend.* West Lafayette, Ind.: Purdue University Press 1984.

Manes, Christopher. *Green Rage: Radical Environmentalism and the Unmaking of Civilization.* Boston: Little, Brown 1990.

Maslow, Abraham H. *Religions, Values, and Peak-Experiences.* Columbus, Ohio: Ohio State University Press 1964; New York: Viking Press 1970.

– *Toward a Psychology of Being.* 2nd ed. Princeton: D. Van Nostrand 1968.

– *The Farther Reaches of Human Nature.* New York: Viking Press 1971.

– *Readings in Humanistic Psychology.* New York: Free Press 1969.

Mathews, Freya. "Concentration and Self-Realization: A Deep Ecological Perspective." *Environmental Ethics* 10 (1988).

May, Rollo. *Existential Psychology*. 2nd ed. New York: Random House 1969.

Mayeroff, Milton. *On Caring*. New York: Harper & Row, Perennial Library 1971.

Meiland, Jack W. "On the Paradox of Cognitive Relativism." *Metaphilosophy* 2, no. 2 (Apr. 1980): 115–26.

Merchant, Carolyn. *The Death of Nature: Women, Ecology, and the Scientific Revolution*. San Francisco: Harper and Row 1983.

Michelfelder, Diane P., and Richard E. Palmer, eds. *Dialogue & Deconstruction: The Gadamer-Derrida Encounter*. Albany: State University of New York Press 1989.

Mill, John Stuart. *Autobiography*. London: Oxford University Press 1958.

Modgil, Sohan, and Celia Modgil, eds. *Lawrence Kohlberg: Consensus and Controversy*. Philadelphia: Falmer Press 1985.

Naess, Arne. "The Shallow and the Deep, Long-Range Ecology Movement: A Summary." *Inquiry* 16 (1973): 95–100.

– *Freedom, Emotion and Self-Subsistence: The Structure of a Central Part of Spinoza's Ethics*. Oslo: University of Oslo Press 1975.

– "Through Spinoza to Mahayana Buddhism or Through Mahayana Buddhism to Spinoza?" In *Spinoza's Philosophy of Man: Proceedings of the Scandinavian Spinoza Symposium 1977*, ed. Jon Wetlesen. Oslo: University of Oslo Press 1978. 136–58.

– "The Deep Ecological Movement: Some Philosophical Aspects." *Philosophical Inquiry* 8 (1986): 10–31.

– "Self-realization: An Ecological Approach to Being in the World." *The Trumpeter* 4, no. 3 (1987): 35–42.

– *Ecology, Community and Lifestyle: Outline of an Ecosophy*. Trans. David Rothenberg. Cambridge: Cambridge University Press 1989.

Nakamura Hajime. *Ways of Thinking of Eastern Peoples: India-China-Tibet-Japan*. Honolulu: East-West Center Press 1964.

– "Interrelational Existence." *Philosophy East and West* 17, nos. 1–4 (1967): 107–12.

– "The Ideal of Compassion-Love." In *Sri Aurobindo: A Centenary Tribute*. Published in India, and presented at the International Seminar, New Delhi, Dec. 1972. 233–43.

Nietzsche, Friedrich. *Beyond Good and Evil: Prelude to a Philosophy of the Future*. Trans. Walter Kaufmann. New York: Random House, Vintage Books 1966.

– *Thus Spoke Zarathustra*. Trans. Walter Kaufmann. New York: Viking Press 1966.

– *The Portable Nietzsche*. Ed. Walter Kaufmann. New York: Viking Press 1954.

Nishida Kitarō. *Art and Morality*. Trans. David A. Dilworth and Valdo H. Viglielmo. Honolulu: University Press of Hawaii 1973.

– *Intelligibility and the Philosophy of Nothingness*. Trans. Robert Schinzinger. Westport, Conn.: Greenwood Press 1973.

- *An Inquiry into the Good*. Trans. Abe Masao and Christopher Ives. New Haven: Yale University Press 1990.

Nishitani Keiji, *Religion and Nothingness*. Trans. Jan Van Bragt. Berkeley: University of California Press 1982.

Noddings, Nel. *Caring: A Feminine Approach to Ethics & Moral Education*. Berkeley: University of California Press 1984.

- *Women and Evil*. Berkeley: University of California Press 1991.

Norris, Christopher. *Deconstruction: Theory & Practice*. London: Methuen 1982.

- *The Deconstructive Turn: Essays in the Rhetoric of Philosophy*. London: Methuen 1983.

Nye, Robert D. *What is B.F. Skinner Really Saying?* Englewood Cliffs, NJ: Prentice-Hall 1979.

Odin, Steve. "An Explanation of Beauty: Nishida Kitarō's *Bi no Setsumei*." *Monumenta Nipponica* 20, no. 2 (1987): 211–14.

Orenstein, Robert. *The Psychology of Consciousness*. New York: Viking Press 1972.

Parker, DeWitt H. "On the Notion of Value. " *Philosophical Review* 38, no. 4 (July 1929): 303–25.

Parkes, Graham, ed. *Heidegger and Asian Thought*. Honolulu: University of Hawaii Press 1987.

Pascal, Blaise. *Pensées*. New York: E.P. Dutton 1958.

Passmore, John. *Man's Responsibility for Nature: Ecological Problems and the Western Tradition*. London: Duckworth 1980.

Peters, Richard S. *Reason and Compassion*. London: Routledge & Kegan Paul 1973.

Picken, Stuart D.B. *Shintō: Japan's Spiritual Roots*. Tokyo: Kodansha International 1980.

Plant, Judith, ed. *Healing the Wounds: The Promise of Ecofeminism*. Philadephia: New Society Publishers 1989.

Reker, Gary T., and Paul T.P. Wong. "Aging as an Individual Process: Toward a Theory of Personal Meaning." In *Emergent Theories of Aging*, ed. J.E. Birren and V.L. Bengtson. New York: Springer Publishing 1988. 214–46.

Reynolds, David K. *The Quiet Therapies: Japanese Pathways to Personal Growth*. Honolulu: University of Hawaii Press 1980.

- *Naikan Psychotherapy: Meditation for Self-Development*. Chicago: University of Chicago Press 1983.

- *Playing Ball on Running Water: The Japanese Way To Building a Better Life*. New York: William Morrow and Company, Quill Paperbacks 1984.

- *Even in Summer the Ice Doesn't Melt*. New York: William Morrow and Company, Quill Paperbacks 1986.

- *Water Bears No Scars: Japanese Lifeways for Personal Growth*. New York: William Morrow and Company, Quill Paperbacks 1987.

Rorty, Richard. *Philosophy and the Mirror of Nature*. Princeton: Princeton University Press 1979.
- *The Consequences of Pragmatism*. Minneapolis: University of Minnesota Press 1982.
- *Contingency, Irony and Solidarity*. Cambridge: Cambridge University Press 1989.
Sahtouris, Elisabet. *Gaia: The Human Journey from Chaos to Cosmos*. New York: Simon & Schuster, Pocket Books 1989.
Saint-Exupéry, Marie-Antoine-Roger de. *The Little Prince*. Trans. Katherine Woods. New York: Harcourt, Brace & World 1943.
Sanders, Steven, and David R. Cheney, eds. *The Meaning of Life: Questions, Answers and Analysis*. Englewood Cliffs, NJ: Prentice-Hall 1980.
Sartre, Jean-Paul. *Being and Nothingness*. Trans. Hazel Barnes. New York: Washington Square Press, Pocket Books 1956.
Sato Koji. "Psychotherapeutic Implications of Zen." *Psychologia* no. 1 (1958): 213–18.
Scheffler, Israel. "In Praise of the Cognitive Emotions." *Teachers College Record* 79, no. 2 (December 1977): 171–86.
Sen Soshitsu, XV. *Tea Life, Tea Mind*. New York: Weatherhill, for the Urasenke Foundation, Kyoto, 1979.
Sessions, George. "Spinoza and Jeffers on Man in Nature." *Inquiry* 20 (1977): 481–528.
- "Shallow and Deep Ecology: A Review of the Philosophical Literature." In *Ecological Consciousness: Essays from the Earth-day X Colloquium*, ed. Robert C. Schultz and J. Donald Hughes. Washington, DC: University Press of America 1981. 391–462.
Shalom, Albert. "The Meaning of 'The Meaning of Life.'" *Dialectic and Humanism* 7 (Summer 1980): 95–8.
- "Meaning and Life." *Dialectic and Humanism* 9 (Winter 1982): 85–94.
Shaner, David Edward. *The Bodymind Experience in Japanese Buddhism: A Phenomenological Study of Kukai and Dogen*. Albany: State University of New York Press 1985.
- and R. Shannon Duval. "Conservation Ethics and the Japanese Intellectual Tradition." *Environmental Ethics* 11 (Fall 1989): 197–214.
Shepard, Paul, and David McKinley, eds. *The Subversive Science: Essays toward an Ecology of Man*. Boston: Houghton Mifflin 1969.
Shigematsu Sōiku. *A Zen Forest: Sayings of the Masters*. New York: Weatherhill 1981.
- *A Zen Harvest: Japanese Folk Zen Sayings*. San Francisco: North Point Press 1985.
Shiva, Vandana. *Staying Alive: Women, Ecology and Development*. London: Zed Books 1989.
Skinner, B.F. *Beyond Freedom and Dignity*. New York: Alfred A. Knopf 1971.

Smith, Barbara Herrnstein. *Contingencies of Value: Alternative Perspectives for Critical Theory.* Cambridge: Harvard University Press 1988.

Smith, Huston. *Condemned to Meaning.* New York: Harper & Row 1965.

Smith, Joseph Wayne. "Philosophy and the Meaning of Life." *Cogito* 2 (June 1984): 27–44.

Spretnak, Charlene. *The Politics of Women's Spirituality: Essays on the Rise of Spiritual Power within the Feminist Movement.* Garden City, NY: Anchor Books 1982.

Stace, Walter T. *The Concept of Morals.* New York: Macmillan 1962.

– *The Nature of the World: An Essay in Phenomenalist Metaphysics.* Princeton, IUS: Princeton University Press 1940; New York: Greenwood Press 1969.

Standing Bear, Luther. *Land of the Spotted Eagle.* Boston: Houghton Mifflin 1933.

Storm, Hyemeyohsts. *Seven Arrows.* New York: Ballantine Books 1972.

Suttich, Anthony J. "The Emergence of the Transpersonal Orientation: A Personal Account." Journal of Transpersonal Psychology 8 (1976).

Suzuki, Daisetz T. *Zen Buddhism: Selected Writings of D.T. Suzuki.* Ed. William Barrett. Garden City, NJ: Doubleday 1956.

– *Zen and Japanese Culture.* Princeton: Princeton University Press, Bollingen Series 64, 1959.

Sylvan, R.K., and N. Griffen. "Unravelling the Meanings of Life?" *Journal of the Indian Council on Philosophical Research* 4 (Autumn 1986): 23–71.

Takashima Hiroshi. *Psychosomatic Medicine and Logotherapy: Health Through Noö-Psychosomatic Medicine.* Oceanside, NY: Dabor Science Publications 1977.

Thompson, William Irwin. *Gaia: A Way of Knowing.* Great Barrington, Mass.: Lindisfarne 1987.

Tobias, Michael, ed. *Deep Ecology.* San Marcos, Calif.: Avant Books 1988.

Tonne, Herbert A. *The Human Dilemma: Finding Meaning in Life.* Buffalo: Prometheus Books 1980.

Ueda Makoto. *Matsuo Bāsho.* Tokyo: Kodansha International 1970.

Underhill, Evelyn. *Mysticism: A Study in the Nature of Man's Spiritual Consciousness.* New York: Meridian Books 1955.

– *The Essentials of Mysticism and Other Essays.* New York: E.P. Dutton 1960.

Vlastos, Gregory, ed. *Plato's Protagoras.* Indianapolis: Bobbs-Merrill, Library of Liberal Arts 1956.

Walsh, Roger. "Transpersonal Psychology II"; "Asian Psychologies." In *The Encyclopedia of Psychology.* Ed. Raymond J. Corsini. New York: John Wiley 1984.

Warnke, Georgia. *Gadamer: Hermeneutics, Tradition and Reason.* Stanford: Stanford University Press 1987.

Watanabe Masao. "The Conception of Nature in Japanese Culture." *Science* 183 (25 January 1974): 279–81.

Watson, Walter. *The Architectonics of Meaning: Foundations of the New Pluralism*. Albany: State University of New York Press 1985.

Watsuji Tetsurō. "The Significance of Ethics as the Study of Man." Trans. David A. Dilworth. *Monumenta Nipponica* 26, no. 3–4 (1971): 395–413.

Weinsheimer, Joel C. *Gadamer's Hermeneutics: A Reading of Truth and Method*. New Haven: Yale University Press 1985.

Wheelwright, Philip. *Heraclitus*. New York: Atheneum 1964.

Wiggins, David. "Truth, Invention, and the Meaning of Life." *Proceedings of the British Academy* 62 (1976): 331–78.

Wilber, Ken. *The Spectrum of Consciousness*. Wheaton, Ill.: Theosophical Publishing House, Quest Books 1977.

– *No Boundary: Eastern and Western Approaches to Personal Growth*. Los Angeles: Zen Center of Los Angeles and the Institute of Transcultural Studies 1979.

– *Eye to Eye: The Quest for the New Paradigm*. Garden City, NY: Anchor Books 1983.

Williams, Bernard. *Morality: An Introduction to Ethics*. Cambridge: Cambridge University Press 1972.

– *Ethics and the Limits of Philosophy*. London: Fontana Paperbacks and William Collins 1985.

Wilson, Edward O. *Biophilia*. Cambridge, Mass.: Harvard University Press 1984.

Yanagi Sōetsu. *The Unknown Craftsman: A Japanese Insight into Beauty*. Tokyo: Kodansha International 1972.

Young, J.Z. *Doubt and Certainty in Science: A Biologist's Reflections on the Brain*. Oxford: Oxford University Press, Galaxy Books 1960.

Yuasa Yasuo. *The Body: Toward an Eastern Mind-Body Theory*. Ed. T.P. Kasulis, trans. Nagatomo Shigenori and T.P. Kasulis. Albany: State University of New York Press 1987.

Index

SUBJECTS